"NINE ... TEN ... AND OUT !" explores more than just the ring battles of a legendary champion.It takes us from a roped-off arena to a far larger battleground, that of life itself.

Having fought 112 fights on five continents, the holder of six championship belts and appreciated as a warrior who took on all comers, Emile Griffith captivated the boxing world with his exciting style and a disarming personality. Enshrined in the International Boxing Hall of Fame as a charter inductee, Emile Griffith's place in boxing history as one of the greatest prizefighters ever to climb into a ring is assured.

However, Emile Griffith's toughest battle was waged without gloves and it was fought outside the ring. He battled ethereal demons and devils, and, at times, himself. It was an inner conflict, but a battle that he had to wage - a struggle to bring together two lives – both his.

Emile Griffith did not choose his career as a prizefighter. It just happened and it all came so naturally that he accepted that this was his world.

Nor did he choose his lifestyle, how he lived it or who he lived it with. It, too, came so naturally that he never questioned that this, also, was his world. However, there was always the apprehension that his two worlds were incompatible.

Emile Griffith, one of our greatest all time welterweight champions, was a joy to watch in the ring. His movements were fluid, he was fast of hand and foot, and he fought with a dancer's grace. And he could punch, as stalwarts like Benny Paret and Gaspar Ortega would testify. Emile's was a time of stellar welterweights, think Benny Biscoe, Benny Paret, Ernie Lopez, Joey Archer, Luis Rodriguez, Holly Mims, Ralph Dupas, Florentino Fernandez, and he beat all of them, including two with the appropriately named Dick Tiger. He fought three unforgettable, incredible contests with the Hall Of Famer Nino Benvenuti, he defeated the venerable contender Benny Biscoe, and nearing age forty in the rematch fought him to a draw. So Griffith's career is stuff of serious fistic history and the forthcoming biography, *"NINE...TEN...AND OUT! The Two Worlds of Emile Griffith"* by Ron Ross is a must-read for every true boxing aficionado.

- **Budd Schulberg**, *author of On the Waterfront, The Harder They Fall, What Makes Sammy Run and The Disenchanted*

Emile Griffith is complex, and I'm glad to see the former world champion's story is in the expert hands of Ron Ross, whose book on Bummy Davis is among the most cherished on my boxing bookshelf. Griffith has earned the care, honesty, and sensitivity that Ross brings to his subjects, and similarly, Ross deserves a subject as fascinating as Emile.

- **Steve Farhood**, *Showtime analyst and boxing historian, former editor-in-chief of "The Ring (magazine)" and "KO Magazine".*

Nine ... Ten ... And Out!

The Two Worlds of Emile Griffith

by
Ron Ross

DiBella Entertainment
350 Seventh Ave. Suite 800
New York, NY 10001

First published by DiBella Entertainment: 3/26/2008

ISBN: 978-0-9799-9471-5 (hc)
ISBN: 978-0-9799-9472-2 (sc)

Library of Congress Control Number: 2008901360

Printed in the United States of America
Bloomington, Indiana

This book is printed on acid-free paper.

Front cover design based on The Ring's May 1965 cover creation.
Back cover photos by George Kalinsky.

Dedication

Hank Kaplan was my very dear friend. His world was a squared circle, a world of blood and sweat, of stout hearts, of gallant men and heroic deeds and Hank made certain that the men of this world were cloaked with honor and dignity and that their great actions and accomplishments would be recorded for perpetuity. I find it hard to believe that I went through a large part of my life without knowing Hank Kaplan but that only made it easier to recognize and appreciate those special qualities that set him apart and forged a friendship that I will always cherish. As boxing's foremost historian and authority, Hank gave unstintingly of his time and resources. From cub reporter to publisher, from major Hollywood producer to film school student, the door to Hank Kaplan's home and archives was open to everyone. The help and input that he offered and gave on all of my undertakings were immeasurable and greatly appreciated, but to have had him as a dear friend – that is priceless. This one's for you, Hank.

Hank Kaplan
(April 15, 1919 - December 14, 2007)

Acknowledgement

O nce I began reconstructing the life, career and world of Emile Griffith, I needed much more than memory, personal scrapbooks and bio sketches from boxing programs could provide. Help was not lacking. Many of Emile Griffith's fans, friends and boxing buffs stepped forward with archival material, anecdotes and posters of his fights and I thank them all. However, a special vote of thanks goes to those who who loaded my dining room table, office desk and two file cabinets with the research material that made this work possible.

Over the years Hank Kaplan had become more than just a friend; he was like a member of my family. Still, this iconic Hall of Fame boxing historian never ceased to astound. When I told Hank that I would be working with Emile on his biography he puffed on his pipe, then asked me to join him in his Miami archive center, which has withstood huuricanes, floods and sit-ins from visiting boxing fanatics who would have moved in if given the option. Hank pulled about six file drawers marked "Emile Griffith" from their shelves and set them down before me, cutting my research to a fraction of what it would have been otherwise.

When Hank Kaplan passed away December 14, 2007, the boxing community lost one of its greatest stalwarts. I lost an irreplaceable friend.

Howie Albert's father, George, chronicled Emile's career in a series of fifteen artists-sketchbook-size scrapbooks that Howie graciously loaned to me at the outset of the project. To George and Howie, a heartfelt thank you.

A special vote of thanks to Luis Rodrigo for always making himself available in opening so many doors in Emile's life.

George Kalinsky's career as Madison Square Garden's photographer began with Emile Griffith as his first subject and it was his photo sessions with Griff that inspired George to revolutionize photographing prizefighters. His back cover photo of a lathered "Champ" in the shower is typical of George's creativity. We are extremely grateful for his generous contributions to Emile's biography.

The Ring, "the Bible of Boxing," graciously assisted in our compilation of facts and photographs. The front cover of "NINE ... TEN ... AND OUT!" is based on the cover created for Ring's May 1965 issue and several photos in the book from Emile Griffith's personal collection also appeared in The Ring. The cooperation and assistance of publisher Stuart Saks and his staff is greatly appreciated.

And to Gil Clancy – Thank You! You're the guy who really got the ball rolling.

Of course, the biggest vote of thanks goes to Emile Griffith. And that's for always being Emile – whoever you may be.

Author's Note

Emile Griffith's biography should simply be the story of a great prizefighter, a six-time world champion who fought more times at Madison Square Garden than any other fighter ever did – or undoubtedly ever will; about a legendary titleholder who fought the most championship rounds – 339 – of any fighter in the history of the sport. It should be the story of a true-to-life, flesh and blood champion whose deeds equaled or surpassed those of any Horatio Alger pen and ink hero.

It should be, it is, but there is more ...

Gil Clancy, Howie Albert and Emile Griffith are my friends and we go back a lot of years, to a time well before anyone stepped down and stirred up all the dust on the moon and Joe DiMaggio was still putting roses on the grave of Marilyn Monroe. It was also a time when a lot of my dinners got cold while I hung out, watching Emile go through his paces at the Solar Gym on 28th Street. He was special – special to look at in the ring and special to be with. He was also different.

So, when Gil and Howie, Emile's managers as well as surrogate fathers, spoke to me about writing Emile Griffith's biography I took it as an honor but "yes" was very slow in coming. Maybe I was bothered by delving into what made Emile Griffith different. Maybe I was bothered by breaking one of the commandments that comes after number ten – Thou shalt not mix business with friends. Or maybe I wanted to make absolutely sure that I would be doing the right thing.

Doing the right thing is sometimes very difficult to distinguish from doing the wrong thing. My main concern was whether I could be objective. If anything came up that could diminish Emile's image, or hurt him in any way, would I be able to tell it like it was or would I be looking to dodge the bullet? It's no secret that there were issues, innuendoes and suspicions in his life that were brought strongly into focus by a tragic benchmark event in boxing history.

Taking on the project with an open mind and an honest, dispassionate approach could very well have meant entering areas that would ordinarily be considered invasive and out of bounds. Realizing the possible negative reaction from certain conventional sectors, my intention and duty to render a detached, dispassionate portrait seemed mitigated. I found myself faced with a moral and emotional dilemma.

This changed suddenly and dramatically when Emile recently stepped forward and acknowledged that his love life and sex partners included both men and women. This came as no surprise within the gay community but, paradoxically, Emile, who made no attempt to hide his lifestyle as a regular at the gay scene in Times Square and Greenwich Village, still found it difficult to say the words, "I am gay." He did admit it, in print, on camera and in casual conversation, but as often as he admitted it, he denied it. The question of Emile Griffith's simultaneous acknowledgement and denial must be explored to be understood.

This was Emile Griffith's story – his life. It had to be viewed from his perspective. But his perspective was subjective reality and weighted truth which had to be balanced by all the available, pertinent facts. The details of his life needed to be laid bare so that objective truth could be measured and compared to the world perceived by Emile Griffith.

However, it must also be considered that the world remembered by Emile Griffith may not be the same world or may not have been seen by the same eyes as it once was. The thoughts and memories may be his but very often after being nurtured and influenced by family, friends and associates, those whom Emile had become dependent upon for his daily needs, those who cared for him as a person … and those who cared for him as a tool.

Writing a biography is not a very clean sport. There are no rules preventing you from hitting below the belt. In fact, it is sometimes expected. When you live in a world where, quite often, you need a scorecard to tell saints from sinners, where goodness and wickedness become confused and sensitivity is seen as being self-serving, you have to take a close look at a guy who has lived in a virtual glass house ever since a fateful day some forty-five years ago when he was taunted, when he had his manhood questioned and lifestyle mocked.

In today's more enlightened world there are many who may say, "What's the difference?" "Who cares?" Sadly, today's world is not Emile's world. Emile Griffith is of a time, a place and a world where who he was did make a difference. This is the world Emile remembers and this is the world he learned to cope with.

Like a diamond, there are many facets to Emile Griffith. The pity would be to be blinded by one facet that glares with an inexplicable overwhelming attraction.

Like a diamond, there is a toughness and a brilliance.

And like a diamond, to be truly appreciated, Emile Griffith must be examined in a proper setting.

It was only when I realized that I could neither diminish nor enhance Emile Griffith's image – this was something only he could do - that I said "yes" to Gil and Howie. So, I took a deep breath and jumped in head first knowing that it wasn't going to be easy to chronicle the complex life of one of the greatest prizefighters ever to climb into a ring.

Prologue

Emile Griffith
Born February 3, 1938 – Born Again April 13, 2005

Emile Griffith, at the age of sixty-seven, was free. He was now able to step forward from the shadows that had blanketed the person he truly was over the years.

The terrible guilt that he had lived with for more than four decades was finally lifted from his shoulders. When he left the Beekman Theater that April night in New York after viewing the premiere of RING OF FIRE he knew that a door had been opened. It was up to him to walk through it – and he did. Emile Griffith was again free. But he was reentering a world which, although he had been comfortable within its confines, was a world not quite comfortable with him. It was a world and a way of life whose rules would have to be relearned. There was anxiety, trepidation, and fear as he thought about what once was.

I killed a man but did not go to jail. I was angry at him – oh, yes, very angry - because he trashed me and insulted me in a very terrible way. He called me a maricon – a faggot. It wasn't just what he said, but the way he was ridiculing me, making a fool, a joke of me in front of a roomful of people who respected me. But even though I was angry, hurt and upset, I never wanted to kill him. That thought never even crossed my mind. But it happened. We are in a cruel business.

I keep thinking how strange it is, though. I kill a man and most people understand and forgive me. However, I love a man, and to so many people this is an unforgivable sin; this makes me an evil person. So even though I never went to jail, I have been in a prison almost all my life. I am a prizefighter. I won six world championships. My life could have and should have been like a wonderful dream. Some of it was but a good part of it was more like a nightmare ... .

CHAPTER ONE

I don't dream as much as I used to. Maybe that's normal as we get older because memories take the place of dreams. Kids' minds are always racing and their imaginations can control their thinking, which can be a very good thing. Sometimes you can be living in a nightmare but when you put your head on the pillow and dream about a better place than you are at, that becomes your real world.

When my dad left us, I didn't let him go because I'd keep seeing him coming back over the hill. He'd be small like a speck when I'd first see him way off but I knew it was him and as he got closer he'd get bigger and bigger and then there was no question it was him. We'd play catch and shoot a basketball at the hoop with both of us laughing away. And when Mommie had to go away to work in Puerto Rico she was with me all the time because I dreamed of her day and night. It was those dreams that made me forget or not realize some of the mean, unhappy things that happened to me. I got to know they were dreams but they were real also. I made them real. Like you have a big soap bubble and you're very careful with it so it doesn't burst.

Then there are the dreams that are not wish dreams, dreams you don't control at all and there are times when life, dreams and memories all become blended, mixed together and you don't know … you just don't know where these dreams will be taking you.

***

Telling the story of an Irishman, a Jew and a black kid winding up on an island together never gets very far because inevitably someone interrupts with the observation, "I think I heard that joke before."

Well, maybe it was heard before but it is absolutely not a joke. How Gil Clancy, Howard Albert and this kid with a calypso lilt, Emile Griffith, come together on the island of Manhattan could be called fate, it could be called an accident, a bizarre set of circumstances, a dream or even ... a fairy tale. It certainly begins as a fairy tale.

Once upon a time on an island paradise where summer was eternal and palm trees swayed to the beat of captivating calypso melodies, a land so desirable that legendary pirates of yore chose to plant their ill-gotten treasure chests upon its beaches and forego their lives on the bounding main for a more sedentary existence, such as drinking rum on a veranda overlooking tranquil harbors, there came a child whose exploits would someday make the storied deeds of these swashbuckling brigands pale by comparison ...

However, in this fairy tale we do not have a genie with a turban and harem pants popping out of a bottle or waving a wand and offering three wishes. Instead there is Howard Albert in a double-breasted suit popping out of the garment center. Howard cuts down a bit on quantity but substitutes quality, offering to grant Emile Griffith one huge "your dream-come-true" kind of wish. Since making a spontaneous on-the-spot wish can have a quite stupefying effect, he very considerately assists Emile in the molding and selection process. That this wish strongly resembles one that Howard the Genie has himself nurtured for years can undoubtedly be attributed to coincidence.

Being a garment center genie, Howard Albert is the possessor of a very good business head and recognizes the need to delegate specialized jobs. So he calls forth a truly Merlin-like magician, Gil Clancy, on whose broad shoulders he rests the task of making "wish" become "reality".

***

The problem with frying eggs on the sidewalk of 37th Street is – what are you going to do with them? Who's going to eat them? No matter, that's the kind of day it was, a day for frying eggs on the street. If the street is like a griddle, every building is like an oven.

Howard Albert Millinery was not a sweat shop – ordinarily. It was an establishment in the heart of New York City's garment center known to design and turn out a high-end line of ladies hats, but on this scorching summer day in 1956, perspiration flowed freely. The fans were all on high speed churning up the French fried air that spilled in from the open windows.

Mirages happen on such a day when layers of baked heat waves melt light rays and addle brains. Because they are not real, mirages cannot be touched and nobody tried to touch the mirage of a young man shaped like a vee from the waist up with muscles that rippled like the Mississippi River. Nobody touched but everybody looked and looked and looked. This mirage was real.

Howard Albert was not a Simon Legree. He had a ready smile and a kind word for all of his employees. Everything considered, he was an okay guy to have for a boss. He took a personal interest in the people who worked for him and thought he knew each of them pretty well until this steamy summer day.

"I'm walking through my plant on this very hot afternoon and I see nothing but protruding eyeballs, open mouths and motionless bodies. I begin discounting, one by one, it can't be a union job action – after all, I have one big happy family. What about a game of Simon Sez? – Nope. I may be a good boss, but I do not permit game-playing; also, the weather simply is not conducive to such an activity – and finally, maybe a curse placed by a competitor – a far-fetched possibility that I was just about to explore when I turn towards the stockroom door and, next thing I know, I am frozen like a statue, open-mouthed with protruding eyeballs."

It was less than a year ago when his stockroom man, Edigo Lambert, brought in his young cousin Emile to work under him in the stockroom. It wasn't that the youngster was unnoticed. His quick smile and always sunny disposition made him a company favorite. But what a difference a shirt makes! Rather, what a difference <u>no</u> shirt makes!

3

Whatever the women in the plant saw can only be assumed. It was certainly not what their employer saw. Howard Albert, who spent a good part of his teenage years dreaming of and trying to emulate the deeds of Benny Leonard, Gene Tunney and Max Baer, gave it his best shot but discovered he had the makings of a fine milliner. The dream never ended, though.

Howard did not have a one-track mind but the heat-distorted vision he saw of this youngster, Emile Griffith, had taken on the appearance of a combination of Sugar Ray Robinson and Joe Louis, fists slashing and stirring the oppressive stockroom air. He closed his eyes, squeezing hard. Robinson and Louis were gone but the original mirage was still there.

"Where did you get such a body?" Howard asked with a mixture of awe and wonder.

"From my father." The smile behind the answer was disarming and Howard Albert thought to himself – Some gifts are better than others. Immediately, a bond was forged between plant owner and stockroom boy.

"Emile, did you ever do any boxing?"

"Oh, yes."

"Okay. Where? Tell me about it."

"Right here, Mr. Albert and you should know; I've been doing it for almost one year now. Catherine and Mabel bring the hats in to me and I box them and place them on the proper shelves. Then Edigo comes in with the labels …"

Howard Albert felt it was time to squeeze his eyes shut once more. When he opened them again, Emile Griffith was still there. He was glad. He smiled and Emile smiled back.

Emile had never put on a pair of boxing gloves. As a youngster back in St. Thomas, his uncle, Murphy Griffith, had taught him a proper boxing stance and some of the basics that every school kid is taught. That was the extent of Emile Griffith's boxing background.

As he set out to teach the young Emile Griffith everything there was to know about The Manly Art of Self-Defense, Howard Albert did his best to convert his stockroom into an annex of Stillman's Gym.

Reaching back some two decades for skills he had hoped to master himself, Howard, at the age of thirty-six with a once well-defined torso, now slightly compromised by the tempting culinary delights of local eateries, thrilled at the prospect of developing this youngster with a body carved of granite into the fighting machine of his dreams.

At first, it began more as a lark than anything else. After all, no Mister America or any of those guys who flex their muscles on the back covers of comic books ever climbed into a ring and made a name as a boxer. But, then again, they never had a Howard Albert with a vision and a converted stockroom.

Sometimes enthusiasm can overwhelm common sense and it was a moment in Howard Albert's life when he was completely carried away on a wave of excitement. He took it upon himself to send in an application entering Emile in the Golden Gloves Tournament sponsored by the New York Daily News.

"I had no idea what a Golden Gloves Tournament was. One day Mommie tells me I have a letter," Emile recalls. *"It is from the Daily News telling me to report for a physical. I yell out, 'Mommie, I think I am being drafted.' It's not like we're not a patriotic family but no mother likes to see her son go off to war. And to tell the truth, I was not exactly thrilled at the thought of being a soldier but not one to turn my back on my country, I went for my physical. I was not quite sure what was going on but I did realize that I wasn't taking the physical to be a soldier, which made me feel pretty good. It was a physical to be a fighter. This did not make me feel pretty good.*

By the time I go back to work the next day I am already feeling that my boss, Mr. Howard Albert, knew a little bit about what was happening. When I walk in he hands me a gift – a pair of brand new boxing trunks and I understand that he knew a lot more than just a little bit about what was happening. I see then what I was getting into and I told him I don't want to be a fighter. He said – okay, but all the girls in the place were going to be very disappointed, that they were the ones who bought me the trunks and that they had boxing shoes for me also. Next thing I know the girls are saying things about how proud they were of me, but if I were afraid to fight, they would understand. After all ...

I don't know how tough Howard Albert would have been in the ring but he sure was tough outside of it. I did not want to be a fighter but I could not say 'no' now."

Howard Albert did not have much basis for comparison but after a couple of lessons in the back room he was certain that he was not dealing with any run-of-the-mill student. The kid moved like a cat, his reflexes were not to be believed and there wasn't a thing told to him that he didn't absorb immediately. It was when Howard was about to say, "Throw your left jab" and realized he was the only one around to throw it at that the thought of finding a real trainer came to mind.

He remembered reading a newspaper article about this Gil Clancy who was the boxing coach at the Parks Department gym on 28th Street. That afternoon, with a five-spot in his hand and a letter of introduction in his pocket, Emile Griffith, Jr. took his first ride in a New York City taxicab.

***

Gilbert T. Clancy did not know that he knew so much about "tough". That is because when you grow up in Irish Town – the Rockaways east of Beach 98th Street – "tough" is very natural and one simply does not think about it. Irish Town offered many advantages, one of which was that thirst-quenching was never a problem as there was not a street that did not have at least one watering-hole.

It was also a place where there was a lot of screaming and hollering. There were screams as the roller-coaster in Playland, which was the western boundary of Irish Town, came rumbling down a steep incline; there were screams of joy and frustration as guys showboating for their dates tossed baseballs at wooden milk bottles trying to win kewpie dolls for them; then there were the screams of the guys who came flying out of one or another of the local bars, propelled by a boot in the butt or a belt in the snoot, due to being on the short end of a difference of opinion, an occurrence no less commonplace than the rising and setting of the sun and on a good night the moon , also, could be included.

"Tough" was a way of life and it was evident from the way you played the game to the way you spoke. You did not have to stretch your vocabulary to make your point. A word as simple as "So" said it all.

"So whatcha gonna do about it?"

"So's yer old man!"

"So what?"

And for the really strong, silent type there was just plain *"So?"*

As for the way you played the game, there weren't very many things tougher than driving for the basket against the three McGuire brothers – Al, Dick and John – at the schoolyard court on Beach 108th Street. It was a time when the two hand set shot was king and basketball was a game of strategy, technique and hard play with plenty of body contact. There were no referees, so if anyone yelled "Foul" it was just assumed that his mother was shopping at the poultry market.

Gil Clancy was eighteen when the subway system from Rockaway to the city was completed. What it did for Gil was make it a lot easier for him to do the daily journey to NYU where he earned his B.A. and Master's in Physical Education. Not that he wouldn't have gotten those sheepskins without the train. They just might have wound up a bit soggy because he would have swum across Reynold's Channel and even the Atlantic Ocean if he had to. Gil Clancy wasn't just tough. He was motivated and knew what he wanted.

***

There weren't any trains in the Caribbean city of Charlotte Amalie but Emile Griffith, Jr. didn't need any because he could fly. At least that's what the vendors in its bustling marketplace swore. Obviously, street games have cultural derivations and for the young boys of St. Thomas games such as Steal The Bacon and Steal The Old Man's Bundle simply did not have the appeal of their favorite, Steal Fruit From The Peddler's Cart. He and his band of mini-pirates would come swooping down out of the sky and make off with their booty of fruits and vegetables, not because of hunger or dire need but just for the sheer fun of it. They were called many things by the peddlers, "devils" being the most complimentary.

Except for Emile. They couldn't quite figure him out. There he would be, one minute the swoopingest and fastest of the raiding party, laughing as he raced away with an armful of bananas and pineapples, then an hour or so later returning with a sheepish expression and silently helping the vendors clean up the area, lugging crates and delivering packages to nearby customers. If he was a devil, somewhere along the way he had confiscated a halo.

There was never a thought in Emelda Griffith's mind that Junior was an angel or destined for sainthood but, adding up both sides of the ledger, she was satisfied that he was not a devil. She had a pretty good boy in Emile. Emile Griffith, Jr. was born in St. Thomas, Virgin Islands February 3, 1938, the first of five children for Emelda and Emile Griffith, Sr. Next came his sister Gloria, his brother Franklin, followed by Elenore and Joyce. He had his grandmother and enough aunts, uncles and cousins living nearby to insure that loneliness would never be one of his problems. He had his share of schoolhouse scrapes but basically, he was a friendly boy, always smiling and polite to everyone – or almost everyone. Around the house she never had to ask him twice to help out. He took the job as Mother's Little Helper very seriously, just as he did as Big Brother to his siblings. To young Emile or Junior, as everyone called him, if Monday was a good day, Tuesday would be even better. There weren't any bad days.

Besides all the normal horseplay and swimming at the beach with his friends, he looked forward to the occasional evening catches in front of the house and shooting baskets at the playground with his father and Uncle Murph.

His father was a local policeman whom nature endowed with an Adonis-like physique. Young Emile didn't have to know very much about genes and heredity. All he had to do was stand in front of a mirror. At the age of eight it was already apparent that he was not just a chip off the old block – he was a scaled down model.

Then there came a day that wasn't as good as the day before.

When Emelda Griffith shouted out that food was on the table she only had to do it once. The whole family came running, like a grand new adventure was awaiting them. And, usually it was, because that's the kind of cook Emile's mother was. So when Junior sat down to his third straight meal of bananas and mango, unpeeled and uncooked, he decided to be the spokesman for his siblings and inquire whether this was to be a permanent menu.

When Mommie explained that cooking had to be a joyous experience for her and as she felt no joy because Daddy was not at home, she therefore was unable to cook, Junior pointed out that there were other times that Daddy was not at home but there was still enough joy for her to cook. That's when Emile Griffith, Jr. learned that Emile Griffith, Sr. was not coming home anymore and he didn't care about his mother's cooking because he was no longer hungry.

Emile Griffith, Sr. had packed his belongings and had gone to New York to seek his fortune. Junior wondered whether, perhaps, his father had said 'goodbye' to him while he slept. He believed that he must have because he didn't say it while he was awake. Sometimes too much knowledge can have a very negative effect so it was good that young Emile didn't know where New York was. At first he would sit in front of the house in the evening tossing his baseball in the air, all the while glancing down the road hoping, sometimes even expecting, to see his father walking down from the mountains in the distance to have a catch with him. Eventually, he put the ball away, but he didn't stop looking down the road – ever.

CHAPTER TWO

Emile wasn't quite nine years old when his mother was offered the position as cook for the Governor of Puerto Rico. With no money coming in from her husband, Emelda was now the sole support of her family. As tempting as the offer was, it was a difficult decision to make. It was only when her relatives assured her that they would care for her children that she reluctantly accepted the job. Each of the children was sent to live with a different relative with the promise they would be able to take turns visiting their mother in San Juan and she would come home and visit with them whenever she could. At first Junior moved in with his grandmother. *"That was a pretty happy time,"* he recalls. The love and warmth he felt more than made up for the leather strap she carried around as her symbol of authority. But the best times were when Emelda would return on a surprise visit. *"When my Mommie would come to visit, I'd walk in and see her sitting there and I'd flip. I'd follow her around like a puppy dog."*

He knew nothing of the Laws of Physics or Philosophy but Emile was certain that just as night follows day, disappointment follows happiness. He had become accustomed to his happy times being short run affairs, so when his grandmother took sick after he had been with her for just a few months, Emile simply packed his things and moved into the home of his Cousin Blanche, who had a much larger leather strap which was not merely a symbol. Emile was sure that whatever she had paid for it, he helped her get her money's worth.

He doesn't remember his mother even once raising a hand to him or any of the children. Everything was done with hugs, kisses and love. Maybe that's the reason Emile was so quick to help out with anything around the house. It was his way of returning the love and kindness shown him. As soon as he walked through the door of his Cousin Blanche's house he let her know that he was there to help her out anyway that he could.

It worked out very well for almost a day-and-a-half. That's how long it took for Emile to feel that not only was he being demoted from a captain to a private with the only orders to be carried out being the orders handed down to him, but also that he was a private on constant KP. Blanche lived in a small cottage overlooking Magen's Bay with her two small children. Each morning Emile would have a race with the sun to see who rose first. Generally, Emile won. There were no medals or ribbons. But there was a large metal drum. He would walk down the mountain with it each morning, fill it with fresh water and then haul it back up to the house. Exhausted, he would gobble down a quick breakfast, then take the kids to school and rush right back to carry out the day's chores. He tried very hard to be a perfectionist because his cousin demanded it. If things were not just right, he knew he would be punished. *"I would have to sit on the floor and hold two cinder blocks over my head while sometimes she'd hit me with the strap until I'd bleed. I'd hold it like that for so long that actually, some nights I fell asleep with those blocks just staying there. It's hard to believe that they never fell and landed on my head."* Cousin Blanche may unwittingly be responsible for Emile Griffith's tremendous upper body strength. If so, Emile is not sure that he wants to say "thank you".

***

The young boy never complained to anyone but whenever he could get away and be by himself, he would. It was too easy to be spotted wandering by the bay so he generally searched out wooded areas. He was sitting on a tree stump feeling bad for himself, maybe even crying – not real crying, just sniffling with a tear or two squeezing from his eyelid when he feels a hand on his shoulder. He didn't ask for help, but help was offered and he accepted it. He was young. He was naïve, and there were things he did not know about.

"If you're my uncle, where's my auntie?" He was somewhere between Blanche's and his grandmother's homes. He knew most of his relatives, but not all.

"I live here by myself. Auntie's gone. Makes for more room," he laughed and Emile wondered if he was born with all those gold teeth.

He went inside the shack that was somewhere between Cousin Blanche and Grandma's homes. He didn't like it and he wanted to leave. When the sun went down he knew that Blanche would be angry if he wasn't there to take care of the children but that's not what bothered him. He'd been late before; he'd even stayed out overnight. With Blanche, if he wasn't punished for one thing, it would be for another.

"I really got to go now. Else I can get in a lot of trouble. You know Blanche." The problem was, Emile didn't know whether his "uncle" did know Blanche. Everyone around there knew everyone else, but Emile meant *really* know, know like family.

The gold teeth shone through the smile. "When you are tired to the bone there is only one thing to do – rest. I don't know what you've been doing, but you are one very tired boy. So lay down and rest for a half hour, regain your strength, then go back to dear, sweet Blanche. And you know what. I am tired too so we both will lay down and rest."

Was it out of respect or out of fear that Emile didn't argue? He looked around. "There's only one bed."

"With no Auntie, who needs more?" Again the smile. "We are not so big that we cannot share a bed." His "uncle" grabbed him and hugged him, but it was not a hug. Hands moved to where others' hands had never been before - then terrible things happened that he closed his eyes and mind to. He knew that what had happened was bad and he knew it was wrong. And he also felt a strong sense of shame. It was something he swore to himself that he would never tell anyone else and it took him more than forty years before he broke that promise. His "uncle", no longer smiling, gave him some change for sweets. Emile ran down the road, flung the coins as far as he could, then bent over and threw up his guts.

***

Mandal was supposed to frighten Emile. "If you don't mind yourself and behave," Mommie used to warn him, "that's where you're gonna wind up, with all the rowdy hooligans!" It did frighten him, but not enough. Located outside of Charlotte Amalie, the bustling seaside capital of St. Thomas, curiosity spurred him to wander over there on a couple of occasions. He expected to hear lots of wailing and crying because that's what you expect to hear from a place where bad boys are punished until they become good. He knew that was for most boys, not all. There was no wailing and crying when he was punished. There was no sound at all. Maybe a sniffle and a couple of little, trickling tears, but no sound. What he heard from inside Mandal, though, seemed more like squeals of delight and the excited shouts of kids caught up in all sorts of play activity. For young Emile Griffith it conjured up an image not too different than Pinocchio's of Pleasure Island.

One thing that Emile did find out by speaking with a couple of the youngsters through the fence was that they fed you and didn't beat you.

Maybe it was the curiosity of discovering for himself what really went on behind the gates of Mandal, maybe it was the desire to escape the painful, regimented regime of his Cousin Blanche. Or, maybe it was the thought that if Pinocchio's father came in search of Pinocchio why couldn't his own father, who was younger and stronger than Gepetto, do the same, that motivated Junior to run off to Mandal. Since his Mommie had moved to Puerto Rico, Emile constantly dreamed of his father returning.

***

At first, Emelda Griffith would tremble with anticipation whenever she received a letter. Each of her children would relate how their days were spent, what they were learning in school and how much they missed her. Her relatives would write about what a pleasure and joy the little ones were.

14

She still trembled when the mail came but now it was for a different reason. Especially the letters from Blanche. For Emelda, a good day had been one filled with sunshine and a gentle breeze and the postman would deliver mail about her children. Now that good day wasn't complete unless the postman would pass her by without any mail from Blanche. As for the sunshine and gentle breeze - maybe it was just coincidental that a cloud bank blotted out the sun and the air was so still that sailboats might just as well have dropped anchor the day that the postman rang the bell and handed Emelda a special delivery letter.

Emelda Griffith believed that the only good news that ever came in a special delivery letter was a notification of winning the Irish Sweepstakes, and as she had never known anyone who had won the Irish Sweepstakes, and she hadn't bought any Sweepstakes tickets herself, she was not expecting any good news. She hit the nail right on the head.

It wasn't that Junior hadn't gotten into trouble before, but it was normal trouble, not special delivery kind of trouble. He'd get into fights at school, play hookey to go swimming with his friends, make too much noise playing his games. That kind of trouble he'd gotten into even before she left for Puerto Rico. But nothing like what Blanche wrote in her letter.

When Emelda arrived in St. Thomas, Blanche was crying, explaining how she had tried taking care of her cousin Emelda's son but that the devil must have taken over his soul. She wailed about how she had opened her home and heart to him and, in return what does he do? He shames the family by running off and winding up in a jail for young ruffians.

All Junior said to his mother was that he liked being with boys his age. There was no mention of cinder blocks and whippings. Neither was there any mention of the strange sense of comfort and good feelings he had living in this commune of young boys. There was an intimacy and a bond of trust and dependence that he did not experience with girls or women.

The first time he ran away and asked to be taken into Mandal, the supervisor smiled and told him it was not for boys who lived at home

15

with their parents. He had him driven home in a jeep. That night he was strapped and given his two cinder blocks to hold over his head.

The next time that he ran away he was prepared. He explained that he didn't live at home with his parents, but with a cousin who was not very nice to him. This time the supervisor smiled and gave him a bowl of chowder before having him driven home. Cousin Blanche thanked the driver and waited until the jeep was out of sight before whipping Junior, then forcing him to hold up the blocks all night without feeding him. He was very thankful for the bowl of chowder and permitted himself to dream about it while slumbering through his punishment.

He would visit with his grandmother as often as he could. She had regained her strength and his sister Joyce was living with her now. It was on a very warm Sunday morning that Emile was heading over there to go with them to Sunday Mass when he heard his grandmother screaming. Emile ran the rest of the way and found his grandmother cradling Joyce in her arms and wrapping her foot tightly in a towel that was quickly saturated with blood. She was crying and trying to explain that the little girl had stepped on a large fork that had gone right through her foot and had obviously punctured a blood vessel. The hospital was nearly five miles away and they had no transportation, nor did any of the neighboring shacks. Emile didn't hesitate. He hoisted the whimpering little girl on his shoulders while his grandmother made the towel into a makeshift tourniquet by twisting its knot with a straight stick as tight as she could until Joyce cried in pain.

The rest of what happened is just a hazy, blurred memory to Emile. He remembers trudging ahead with the sun beating down upon them. He's not sure whether Joyce passed out. He's not even sure if he passed out. What he remembers is that he was carrying Joyce and somewhere along the way she became a barrel filled with water that he was lugging up the hill to Cousin Blanche's home. Then the barrel became Joyce and Joyce became two large cinder blocks that he knew he could not drop.

"I know that boy." It was the supervisor from Mandal. He had just brought in a youngster who found out it is much better catching a baseball with a glove than with your nose.

Emile was lying face down on a gurney. His eyes were closed as he sipped water from a bottle with a long straw. It was a reflex, as he was asleep or something akin to sleep. A nurse removed his shirt and was about to rub his back with alcohol when she stopped and, together with the supervisor, looked at the red welts across his back. Miraculously, he had gotten Joyce there. They cleaned the wound, stitched her foot and were now feeding her intravenously. Everything was going to be okay – for Joyce and for Emile.

When Emelda asked how her son got to be in Mandal the supervisor said, "He knocked on the door and we let him in."

"You just let him in? My boy has family and a home."

"He seemed to like our home better. He did a lot of knocking before we opened the door for him."

"Isn't this a place for hooligans?"

"Is your boy a hooligan?"

"My boy is Christian, well-mannered and obedient."

"Why don't you ask him where he'd like to be?"

"I already did. He'd like to be with me. Next best, he likes it here."

Mommie was a smart lady. She knew Junior was a good boy. She also knew there was a good reason why he picked Mandal over living with Blanche and he didn't want her to know. She realized that perhaps it was better that she didn't know. Emelda figured that with her working in Puerto Rico, young Emile needed structure in his life. And he needed discipline, the kind of discipline his aunts, uncles, cousins and grandparents obviously couldn't teach him. Love got in the way. She was not one hundred per cent correct.

So, Mommie gave him a slap on the behind, a kiss on the forehead with a bear hug embrace and a box of freshly baked cookies when she left him at Mandal and headed back to Puerto Rico. The cookies didn't last very long but he wound up having a lot of friends in a very short time. Junior wasn't sure where he had more chores, at Mandal or at Cousin Blanche's, but at Mandal he wasn't working alone.

17

When he first got there he had an orientation meeting where the counselor explained that by following the rules and making an effort to join in and take part in all the activities and classes you can come out a real winner. Being a winner sounded good to Emile, even at the age of ten. And it was at Mandal that Emile Griffith first displayed that ability to listen, absorb and execute.

There were also activities that were not part of the regular curriculum and they did not necessarily make you come out a winner, but they did make for a strong lesson. The first time it happened for Emile was in the shower. It started with a touch.

"I thought it was an accident, but I moved to the next shower anyhow. There were just the two of us in there. When he moved right along with me I knew it was no accident. He was bigger than me and thought he could do what he wanted. That's when he tried grabbing me around like to hug me but I hit him a good shot then wrestled him to the floor with the shower water spraying all over us. The nut started smiling because he liked the wrestling part where I'm on top of him so I jumped up and when he got up I just kept punching him. That part he didn't like at all. He never bothered me again.

He wasn't the only one. There were a couple of kids in my group who liked making out and doing hard stuff, but it was different with them. They didn't push or force. It would start as friends and, you know, go on from there.

These kids were nice, so it was different. I liked them. I don't think that's what the counselor meant when he said we should take part in all activities."

Emile didn't feel as though he was doing anything wrong, but even back then he sensed it would be wrong in the eyes of some others, so he figured that it would be wise to keep this part of his life closeted. It was an instinct that stayed with him through the years.

CHAPTER THREE

Sticking to the truth, Gil Clancy was no Merlin. If he were, the very first time he made eye contact with the youngster sitting in the waiting area of the 28th Street Parks Department facility, he would have realized that here, before him, was one of such magnificent qualities, of such strength and fortitude that he would soon be sitting on a throne with an adoring world at his feet. It took Gil the better part of a week to recognize that young Emile Griffith possessed very unique talents and abilities. In his defense, it should be stated that there were no crystal balls or tarot cards at his disposal.

Gil thought someone was singing as he moved towards the locker room on the first floor. He was pretty sure that *"Are you Mr. Clancy?"* wasn't part of the lyrics of "McNamara's Band" or "Clancy Lowered The Boom" or any song that he was familiar with so he stopped and turned around. There, bouncing over towards him, was this good-looking, wide-eyed kid with a huge smile and a crop of curly hair, whose high-pitched voice came over more like music with its indelible Caribbean flavor.

"I'm Mr. Clancy."

"How are you, sir? I'm Emile and I hope I can train here for the Golden Gloves."

"Let me ask you first, why do you want to be a boxer, Emile?" It was Clancy's stock question, sort of like an entrance exam.

"Because my boss wants me to." Gil sighed and thought maybe a multiple choice question would have been a little better.

"*Because your boss wants you to.* Okay, what's the thing you would like to do most?"

The kid smiled. "*I'd like to be a ballplayer. Do you coach that, too?*"

Gil Clancy had a lot of serious youngsters to work with. He wasn't sure what to do, so he tossed an imaginary coin in his mind. Fortunately for all, it came out heads and the following day Emile Griffith returned with a bagful of boxing gear and his boss.

When Gil Clancy and Howie Albert shook hands that first time in 1956, they had no idea that it couldn't have been a more solemn nor bonding act than if a priest or rabbi had presided.

"Why are you encouraging him to box when the kid wants to be a ballplayer?"

"Let me explain something, Gil. Emile is a pretty good ballplayer. He was the varsity catcher for his high school team. I think he hit slightly over .300 in his only season because he left school in his junior year. The only way this kid will make money in baseball is by selling peanuts and popcorn for Harry M. Stevens. Let's look at him in the ring now."

Gil looked and he fell in love with Emile and Howie.

There is the story of this horse that shows up at the New York Yankees spring training camp with his agent. The Yankee manager asks, "What are you doing here, Horse?" And his agent replies, "He is here for a try-out."

"You gotta be kidding me."

"I kid you not", says Mr. Agent. "Just give a look-see."

Well, the Yankee manager, being very fair-minded, as all Yankee managers are presumed to be and also as it is an open tryout besides which he is a most curious individual, agrees. His 25-game winner ace pitcher is on the mound in an inter squad game when the Yankee manager decides to put Horse in as a pinch-hitter. Everyone assumes this will be one great big yawner as Mr. Agent calls out, "Okay, Horse, grab a bat and do your stuff." With which the not overly excited Horse picks up a bat and moves up to home plate. Ace Pitcher goes into his full windup and lets go with the high hard one which does not go SMACK into the catcher's mitt. Instead, there is a resounding CRACK as Horse swings his bat which crashes against the nearly 100 mile-per-hour fast ball, sending it on a long, arcing journey so far out of the ballpark that it is never again to be found.

The Yankee manager, along with everyone else in the ballpark, cannot believe what he sees, which in this case does not make him a non-believer. In fact, he is already trying to solve the problem of how he is going to outfit Horse when he turns and sees his soon-to-be new cleanup hitter standing at home plate and looking, along with everyone else, at his ball sail off into the great unknown.

"Run, Horse, run," the Yankee manager screams but Horse just stands there admiring his work. So the manager turns towards Mr. Agent, "What's with him? Why doesn't he run?"

Mr. Agent just shakes his head. "What did you expect? If he could run he wouldn't be here. He'd be in the Kentucky Derby."

Well, Gil Clancy and Howie Albert were more fortunate than the New York Yankees. They had the horse who could do it all.

Although speed, power, reflexes, balance, instinct and ability to learn do not always a great fighter make, there is no arguing that they certainly make for a good starting point. Another necessary ingredient to complete the package is motivation or desire, which, for a time, Clancy was not quite sure about. Again, there is the comparison of Poppa Gepetto searching for his pleasure-seeking son, Pinocchio. Only now, instead of Gepetto calling out for his wooden blockhead son, "Pinocchio!" there is Gil Clancy, calling out in a plaintive wail, "Emile, Emile!"

Clancy is definitely more fortunate than Gepetto, though, as he does not have to carry his search into the belly of a whale. But he does cover a lot of territory walking through all the areas of the 28th Street Recreation Department, which for Emile Griffith serves very well as a substitute for Pleasure Island.

Gil's boxing program began at three PM. Emile was never late. In fact he would be there three or four hours early. Well, not exactly there. First he'd put in a couple of hours of ping-pong which would be followed by an hour or so of a pick-up basketball game then a couple of sets of handball. All of that, of course, works up quite a sweat. So, it's understandable that such strenuous activity would be followed by a relaxing swim. And Gil did understand. That is why he always knew if he didn't find Griffith in the game room or on the basketball court he could find him in the pool.

Instead of getting discouraged or frustrated Gil chose to count his blessings – there was no football field. He warned Emile that he had to cut out all these other activities, that by the time he got to his workout he was already drained. Emile smiled and said "Okay". The next day when Emile wasn't in the gym by three-thirty, Gil didn't bother yelling out his name. He simply made his rounds of Emile's stops-along-the-way (it was no longer difficult finding him) and brought him up to the gym. Getting angry with the youngster was not an easy thing to do. Besides that big innocent smile cutting you off at the pass, he was simply tasting life's pleasures and enjoying them to the utmost.

Gil wondered how much Emile would enjoy his pleasures if he had to, in some way, pay for them. He decided to find out. The price tag on Emile's pleasures was a tough, seasoned pro named Roger Harvey who Clancy instructed to take Emile to school and really bang him up but to concentrate on the body. The more Emile went to the gym and took his lickings from Roger Harvey the more appealing ping-pong and swimming were becoming. Emile's competitive juices were flowing like a river and there was no holding him back. He was not willing to pay the price for a day of fun and games. The gym became his second home and Gil Clancy, with a Masters Degree in Physical Education, showed that he had obviously stayed awake during his psychology classes also.

Even when Emile was playing so much ping-pong that he could have considered trying out for the Chinese National team, once he got to the gym he was totally focused. Clancy didn't make it a habit to roam the corridors searching for straying boxers. The truth was that Gil Clancy was a taskmaster. A fighter without strong work ethics was a fighter without Clancy. But Emile Griffith was in a totally separate category. The moment he stepped through that gym door there wasn't another fighter that worked with the determination, tenacity and energy that he did. But all that determination, tenacity and energy added up to was "High Hopes"(2) and Emile Griffith was no "silly ol' ram" trying to punch a hole in a dam even though he did go on to become one of the best damn punchers in boxing.

Howard Albert took it with a grain of salt when he was warned that smoking cigars was a hazard to his health and well-being. He would smile and say, "I don't even inhale. What can it do to me?" He found out on a cold January night at St. Jude's on West 20th Street. It was the opening round of the 1957 Golden Gloves, Sub-Novice 147-lb division. He not only inhaled smoke but almost swallowed his whole cigar as he watched his stockroom boy who wanted to design hats bounce out of his corner at the opening bell and knock out his opponent with a left jab.

The guy got off the floor, shook his head and was back to normal in about a minute, a lot quicker than it took Howard Albert. Fortunately, George Albert, his father, who was sitting next to him and was able to enjoy Emile's victory a lot more than the now bug-eyed, blue-tinged Howard, enthusiastically pounded his son's back as a congratulatory gesture. It was a gesture that very possibly continued their father-son relationship for many more years. Howard was very appreciative.

He and his father made their way to the aisle as Emile and Clancy left the ring, heading for the dressing room. Emile was all smiles as he saw them and held up his left hand in victory. "How'd you like that, Mr. Albert?"

"I was all choked up, Emile."

Gil Clancy had been training young boxers for a number of years but had just taken over the boxing program at the West 28th Street Parks Department gym in July of 1956. Before that he had worked at the CYO gym on West 17th Street with Pete Mello, who had coached the United States Olympic Boxing Team in 1952 at Helsinki. Still, it was his job as a phys. Ed. Teacher at P.S. 178 in the Brownsville section of Brooklyn that put the bread and butter on his table. Before the echo of the school bell faded, Gil would be at his Manhattan quarters. That can be added to his list of Merlin-like feats.

One of the feats he knew he could not perform was to transform a raw, untrained, inexperienced youngster into a prizefighter overnight.

It was always shortly after the applications for that year's Golden Glove tournament came out that the program membership swelled with all these kids who suddenly dreamt the same dream. So, as there was no way to teach a kid the barest basics of the sport in fewer than a few months, he set up a hard and fast rule which, although he had never been a Boy Scout, he borrowed from their motto "Be Prepared!" which translated into "Wait till next year!"

As soon as he saw this kid, Emile Griffith, Clancy knew that some rules were meant to be bent. Emile brought with him this great natural athleticism, unbelievable physical attributes and the ability to almost immediately absorb everything that was shown or explained to him. But it was what he didn't bring with him that truly made him a near-perfect student. He came with no bad habits. He had learned nothing about boxing so there was nothing to unlearn. It is the unlearning process that is the most time-consuming aspect of training a young fighter. So, by lagging behind, Emile Griffith had a big head start.

"We had three weeks to train before the Gloves. The first thing we worked on was balance. It is the root of boxing. Everything else takes off from there – proper punching leverage, defensive positioning and the general ability to move around the ring. I never had to tell Emile anything twice. He learned at an incredibly fast rate, much faster than any fighter I had ever trained."(3) Then Clancy shook his head and smiled. "And would you believe he didn't even like what he was doing, at least not until I dragged him away from his fun and games up to the gym. Once he hit that training floor, you could see his entire mental attitude and emotional energy focus on one thing – training. I never knew another fighter who trained with the dedication and energy of Emile Griffith. He was the consummate professional throughout his career. The only offensive weapon I had time to work on those three weeks before the Gloves was the jab. That's all he brought along with him to the tournament and it almost proved to be enough."

Emile Griffith went all the way to the final round of the Golden Gloves Tournament that year, losing a close decision to a kid named Charley Wormley, with Gil Clancy, Howie Albert, Emelda Griffith and Emile's right hand looking on.

***

Junior had just decided to become a baseball player when he became a baby-sitter instead. At Mandal,they told him he was the best catcher they had ever had in his age group. It sounded good and made him feel good so he believed it. But when his mother sent for him to join her in Puerto Rico, he stashed his shin-guards, catcher's mask and mitt and was off. The nearly four years he had spent at Mandal were good ones but, when he heard he was going to be with his mother he didn't even stop to say goodbye.

San Juan was full of surprises for Emile. Besides his learning that there was a city so big and exciting and discovering kids with street smarts, he also learned that half-brothers and half-sisters were really whole persons, which he felt worked out much better for everyone. Another surprise was that his father was not there. Junior did not ask many questions but as he kept getting news in Mandal of his two new brothers and a sister, he had assumed that his father was back with his mother. When he found out that the new "whole" members of his family had a different father, which is why they were "halves" to him, he was disappointed, but not for long. Antonio Castillo, Tony, Guillermo and Karen's father, was a nice man who was very good to his mother and the children.

Junior loved the excitement of San Juan. It was in these barrio streets that he first learned the meaning of *maricon*. At first there was a fearful respect because anyone who didn't act tough, spit a lot and tell stories about what girl they did this to and that to last night was a faggot. It didn't take Emile very long to find out that not only was most of this talk just that – talk and stories - but some of these same guys would get together for "back door" sex at night. Emile was curious but not enough to get involved intimately with them because he had also seen some of the other guys go out on gay-bashing cruises. San Juan was a great learning ground and he was in awe of these street-smart banditos. Every day with his new friends was an adventure, but when Mommie, sitting at the kitchen table with the children, asked, "Aren't they cute?" Junior agreed with such enthusiasm that he immediately had his old job back as Mother's Little Helper. It was a job he did very well because he not only took his responsibility seriously but he fell very comfortably into the role of Big Brother. Tony, Guillermo and Karen, in turn, adored their big brother but after a few months Emile returned to St. Thomas and again moved in with his grandmother. He was barely back into a routine when his mother decided to make a major change in her family's life, the first step of which was to move from Puerto Rico to New York and Junior was the first one she sent for. He was fourteen and brimming with anticipation and excitement when he moved from St.Thomas to Harlem. Emelda Griffith knew that she could depend on Emile who was always there to do whatever he could to help her. She would pat her oldest son on the head and smile appreciatively, "My little Emile. You are just too good ... too good." She was right. That was a major problem that Emile had to deal with throughout the years – he was too good.

CHAPTER FOUR

When the stewardess served him lunch on the plane, even though he had just finished the box lunch his grandmother had packed for him, he didn't believe he could be much luckier than that. He was never happier to be wrong. There, waiting to greet him in the Arrival waiting area at LaGuardia Airport was Emile Griffith, Sr., his father. Junior was pretty much the same size as his father now. Even though he wanted to jump up into his arms, he decided not to. He wondered whether his father, who was working as a mechanic, and Antonio Castillo and his mother would all be living together. At the age of fourteen one develops a certain degree of tact and diplomacy so Emile remained silent. As it developed, there was no Antonio Castillo; he had chosen to remain in Puerto Rico, and there wasn't that much of his father who was very much like a traveling salesman even though he didn't have anything to sell.

Junior took to Harlem like a duck takes to being shoved in an oven. He got used to the noise pretty quickly. That was easy – it never stopped. After a while, crossing the traffic-jammed streets became fun – as long as you made it to the other side. Much tougher was the stink of garbage. He never figured out if the sanitation men dropped garbage off or took it away, because it was always there. Even tougher than that was living on Eighth Avenue in the shadow of the Polo Grounds when you're a Yankee fan. But toughest of all was listening to his mother's advice.

There were probably more kids hanging out on any street in Harlem than there were on the entire island of St. Thomas. Their favorite activities were smoking, and not necessarily conventional cigarettes, drinking anything from beer to rotgut, always wrapped in a small paper bag, shooting craps on the sidewalk and messing with anyone they considered to be messable, which included everyone but the cop on the beat. There were times when he too was included. Emelda warned her son about being careful and searching out only good boys to be his friends. Being an obedient son, he listened to his mother and roamed the neighborhood, searching for good boys.

Emile, with a sly grin creasing his face, told me, "*I found a few friends with that – you know – that limp-wrist wave and girlie giggles. They were not too helpful when it came to showdowns, which there was plenty of, but they were very good when it came to cheering.*" That's when I realized that Emile Griffith had his own selective prejudices.

"*The guys on the street were pretty rough and I was not a tough, rough kind but I wouldn't show them that I was afraid. I would stand there and fight them. There were times I decided – Oh heck, there's too many or they're too big – and then I would decide to run. I wasn't afraid. I was smart.*"

Being a teacher's pet does not always win friends but it definitely influences people and is generally quite an advantage. Being a teacher's pet in Harlem, packaged with a refusal to join a gang, and being a choir boy is about as insurmountable a burden as one could ever hope to face. Junior Griffith did not hope to face such a burden, nor did he choose to. He carried a six-inch switchblade in his pocket to protect himself from gang recruiters. He never resorted to using it. The lead tenor of the St. James Missionary Church did it all with his fists .. and a baseball bat.

On the streets, he won fights with his fists, but as the star catcher of his high school team he won respect with a bat and a glove. The Harlem warlords eventually decided that not everyone had to belong to a gang. There were different tunes.

The Reverend J.T. Alford was so impressed with Emile's voice and the gusto with which he sang that he encouraged him to consider a professional career as a singer. Emile liked the thought of that very much – almost as much as the thought of playing professional baseball. He began dreaming of combining the two, singing the National Anthem before the game, playing nine innings of good, solid baseball, then capping off the day by being the star act at a place like the Latin Quarter or Havana Madrid. It was such a good dream that Emile would go to bed at night hoping to conjure up reruns of the dream.

He was looking to showcase his talent on the diamond in his senior year, but as it turned out Emile Griffith, Jr. spent his senior year at the movies. The money that Emile's father brought in to help his mother make ends meet still left some loose ends. Actually, Emile, Sr. was at the apartment more often than the landlord, but the landlord dropped in only once a month and that was to collect the rent. Strangely, Emile, Sr. and the landlord were never there on the same day.

Junior was old enough to understand that his mother needed help and he would have gone to the ends of the earth for her. He didn't have to go that far. He went to the neighborhood movie theater and got a job as an usher for nineteen dollars a week. Sixteen dollars went to Mommie. He had three dollars left with which to take care of himself. Dropping out of school to help support his mother, there was no senior year and there were no scouts who were able to see Emile Griffith behind the plate. But Emile had no gripes. *"I was pretty lucky that I went to a small local theater. If I would have gone to one of the large theaters like the Loew's 175th Street, they showed first run movies and the same movie would be playing all week. At my theater they changed the movies every two or three days. I'll tell you, I was never bored."*

When his cousin Edigo told him that there was an opening for a stock boy at the millinery plant where he worked and that the starting salary was more than double what Emile was making as an usher, Emile Griffith saw his last free movie show.

Loud thunder and bolts of lightning crackled through the sky when Baron von Frankenstein taught his creation how to use all the parts of its body, enabling the monster to go forward, ravaging and destroying. Gil Clancy doesn't remember any thunder or lightning when he introduced Emile Griffith to his right hand – although most of Emile's opponents did. Gil taught Emile that there were other punches besides the left jab and in 1958 watched in wonder, along with everyone else, as Emile demolished every fighter in his path on

29

his way to win the 147-pound open titles in the New York, Eastern and Inter-City competition.

In the New York citywide tournament he defeated amateur stars Tony Torres, Johnny James and Ossie Marcano. His toughest Golden Glove bout was his victory over Cleveland's Vernon Vinson for the Eastern title and he went on to capture the National title by beating Dave Holman of Chicago on the Inter-City card.

Clancy was a betting man but not to an extravagant degree. Two bucks on the nose of a nag at Belmont was well within his bounds, fifty bucks on the Yankees to take the World Series was stretching it a bit. But when Junior came to him, asking for another ticket for his third-round bout of the New York Golden Gloves, this one for his father, Gil was tempted to hock the family jewels and plunge all the way. Since the family jewels consisted of a dented basketball trophy and his wife Nancy's engagement ring and wedding band, this event was taken off the board, though Gil stayed on as more than just an interested spectator.

He'd only known the kid for a little more than a year but in that time he learned that Emelda Griffith was right – Emile was too good. Before Gil knew him, Emile often visited the shop where his father worked as a mechanic and proudly told him about his baseball exploits at Morris High. He would invite him to game after game. His father never said No. It was always, "Sure, Junior, sure." At every game, as he squatted behind the plate, young Emile squinted ans strained to see through the protective bars of the catcher's mask. His father was never there.

"He was my father and I loved him. That's how it is with family. Sometimes it's hard though. Like the time I came home from school and he's in the kitchen yelling at Mommie. I didn't even know what it was about, but Mommie is yelling back and I got real scared because it looks like he's going to hit her. Love didn't count anymore – at least the love for him. I jumped between them and warned my father, "Don't you touch Mommie!" I wasn't talking like a boy anymore and he knew it. I always wondered if he wouldn't have stopped, would I have hit him? The answer is "Yes", but you know, I still would have loved him. I just loved Mommie more."

Emile looked out at the crowd. He had no trouble finding Mommie. You could hear her screaming for "Juunioor!" above all the noise.

There with her was Cousin Bernard, who had come from St. Thomas a short while ago, and Reverend Alford. The seat next to the pastor was empty. Clancy watched as the kid stared through the glare of the ring lights. He felt for him and worried about him but Emile's face was impassive. Then he turned slowly to his Irish father-trainer and smiled. Gil wasn't worried anymore. The kid was ready. He was used to that empty seat.

Sometimes Emile lied, but only to himself. He made a silent promise that he wouldn't ask his father to come see him ever again. Anyhow, with his cousin Bernard Forbes joining his mother, that was all the cheering section he would ever need. *"I never thought anyone could yell like Mommie, but it was close between those two."*

***

Howie Albert knew that if he worked very hard at it he would come up with an answer. He fingered the small bonnet with the floral pattern and dainty lace veil, twirled it, then placed it on his desk, still without an answer. How does someone who has won 51 of 53 amateur fights and has copped every Golden Glove title in his division decide to design women's hats? And it's not just that he designs them – the buyers want them.

What Howard Albert comes up with is not an answer. It is a dilemma. When he asks Emile why he is designing hats, Emile answers that it is fun. Howie points out that boxing is even more fun.

"Emile, you're ready to turn professional. You have a wonderful future as a boxer. What could be more fun than that."

"I don't think Mommie is going to let me do that."

Emelda Griffith was still shaking her head NO when she finally said "Yes." Even though Emile didn't have a more devoted or louder fan than his mother, as a profession, fighting just didn't seem right to her. She sat at the table - a most imposing figure, arms folded, mouth set in a hard, firm line - offering tea and cookies but no sympathy to the worn out team of Clancy and Albert. Emile turned the tide. *"Mommie, we can all be together. Each fight I have, I'll put aside money to bring one of the kids over.*" Howard Albert and Gil Clancy sighed in relief as Emile Griffith scored his final knockout as an amateur.

That is how Howard Albert lost a full-time stock-room boy-turned hat designer and this is how the New York City Board of Education lost a Phys. Ed. Teacher.

Inspiration comes in many different packages. For some, all it takes is a marching band playing soul-stirring patriotic tunes. For others, a title, a crown, a championship of any sort, performing in front of a special loved one or just reaching for the almighty dollar. For Emile Griffith, inspiration was almost of a divine nature – the linking together of St. Thomas and St. Nicholas in a joint effort to reunite the family of Emelda Griffith.

St. Nicholas Arena was on the north side of West 66th Street just off Columbus Avenue. A lot of prayers were made there. Some were answered, some were not. From the early 1900's to the early 1960's, it was New York's premier blue collar fight club. To Emile Griffith, it was Home, Sanctuary and Altar from which his sacrifices to the gods were made. He fought his first 12 professional fights there, all inspiring, all victories. Inspiration for Emile Griffith was an airline ticket from the Virgin Islands to New York. Each fight was another ticket, another precious gift from St. Thomas. It began on June 2, 1958 when he decisioned Joe Parham in 4 rounds and by his eighth fight on February 9, 1959 against hard-punching Willie Joe Johnson, Emile's promise to his mother was realized. Emelda's apartment may have been crowded, but her family was together.

The February 9th fight was also the fight when Emile Griffith established himself with the leather-lunged fight crowd at St. Nick's when, after being toppled by a vicious right for a 9-count in the 5th round, he climbed off the canvas and came back to stop Johnson in the same round. It was a good feeling but, for Emile, it couldn't match the joy of having his whole family back together again. It was a joy he savored for a very short time.

"*It was just before my ninth fight, it was against Barry Allison who I knocked out in the fifth round, that I broke my promise and asked Gil about* getting a ticket for my father. I just felt it wasn't complete. The whole family wasn't together, not without our Daddy. Gil just looked at me – didn't say a word. I told myself there's all different kinds of love and I knew my Daddy loved me but he was dealing with a lot, too. I understood that he never got what he was reaching for in life and here I was, a kid just getting out of his teens and I was doing things he was only able to dream about.

So, I went to his garage, not just to tell him to come see me fight, but to tell him it's okay if he couldn't make it; that it was really okay. I understood. I wish I could have said that to him. His boss shook his head and told me that he died while driving from the shop the night before and he didn't know where to reach us. He said he was sorry and wanted to give me daddy's pay. I didn't want it. I just turned and left. When I got outside, I partly ran and partly walked, thinking that maybe I was on the same streets as my daddy was when he died. It made me feel close to him and I wished we didn't stop doing the things we did when I was a little kid. He never got to see me do anything."

Sadly, Emile's father missed a lot.

After his first 12 fights at St. Nick's, Emile Griffith fought his thirteenth professional fight headlining the show at Madison Square Garden, scoring a 10-round victory over Kid Fichique. Now, after the fancy trappings of Madison Square Garden he couldn't figure out why he was back in a cold drafty dressing room in the bowels of St. Nick's waiting to fight a guy who sounded more like a 5 o'clock kiddie TV show than a fighter – Randy Sandy. Emile couldn't help it. He didn't want to act as though he was spoiled and unappreciative. But, when Clancy told him to get up and start loosening up, he asked, "What for?"

Gil gave him a what-for that was very descriptive and easy to understand which gave Emile just enough motivation to start getting his body ready, but his head was somewhere else and Emile Griffith learned that when you fight a crafty veteran two fists alone may not be enough. He left his dressing room entertaining himself by making silent rhymes in his mind – "Randy Sandy, Fancy Clancy, Howard the Coward." He returned forty-five minutes later, a much wiser young man with his first professional loss – a split decision by a single point. There was no more complaining about his dressing room. Randy Sandy no longer made him think of a marionette, and he knew what he wanted to be when he grew up, a championship prize fighter. Emile Griffith had just grown up.

***

The brightest lights Emile saw growing up outside of Charlotte Amalie were the flickering tails of fireflies but the neon world of Broadway was the magnet that drew him, soothed him and enchanted him. Robert F. Wagner, Jr. may have been the mayor of most of New York but 42nd Street between 6th Avenue and 10th Avenue belonged to Emile Griffith. He strolled it all hours of the day and night, stopped to kibitz with anyone and everyone and was even seen to bend down and clear away litter. Why not? It was his street.

However, not every day was reserved for laughter and joy, though. He was standing outside the Flame Steak Restaurant on 42nd Street when this light-skinned black guy with very bulky muscles and a high-pitched voice that didn't go with the rest of him stopped and stared at Emile.

"Hey, how are you doing, champ?" He spoke very properly, with perfect enunciation.

"I'd have let you call me that last week, but not this week," Emile smiled. The hurt from the Sandy fight was still there.

"Hey, man. Climb out of that hole. Everybody says that was your fight. Anyhow, around here you're always Numero Uno. But what are you doing standing in front of a dollar steak house?"

Emile turned and looked at the red-lighted electric sign behind him. "A dollar-nineteen," he corrected.

"I know a lot of nice people who would love to meet you. Come on with me. It's right down the block."

Emile hesitated so the guy with the lion's body and canary's voice softly said, "I'm Lugo", took him by the hand and led him into a world that was new but at the same time familiar and comfortable. He knew the people, perhaps not by name, but he knew them. When he ran from the harsh world of his cousin Blanche, he had found friends at Mandal who knew how to comfort and soothe him. He seemed always able to find a place of his own and friends who were able to comfort and soothe him whenever the world became painful, and difficult. Besides the kindness and kinship he found in these shadow-alley bars and tucked away meeting places, Emile found another reason for making them his haven.

"Whenever I used to go into a bar, there'd always be some guy who felt he had to show the world how tough he was by challenging "the champ." I never ever had that happen at a gay bar. They were just nice to me and respected me. I was able to relax and not have to put on any fake face."

So he moved between two worlds and at different times, felt at home in each.

Emile had the ability to keep his worlds completely separate. It was very much like this guy entering a telephone booth as Clark Kent and emerging with a totally different identity – Superman. Within his Gay world clubs, Emile was at home and interacted with other gay men, cross dressers, transvestites, male impersonators. He let his hair down, singing, dancing, clowning and being a lover. He developed lifelong relationships there, some of which he has maintained until this day.

Once he exits that world, an impregnable barrier drops and seals it off. Emile Griffith, the prizefighter, is in the gym, donning his headgear and gloves, prepared to climb into the ring and practice the brutal business of pounding away with both fists against a sparring partner returning fire, as Gil Clancy looks on alternating shouts of admonishment and praise.

The two worlds of Emile Griffith have no common base. They are both "home" to him.

CHAPTER FIVE

Not many fairy tales are without a castle, a queen, a brave young stalwart and his lady fair. Whether this was known to Emile Griffith is not an absolute but he did not deviate from the course.

The queen was ever-present. Emelda Griffith may not have had a wardrobe of elegant gowns, she was not bedecked in fine jewelry and there were no footmen or servants at her beck and call. None of these were necessary. For Emile Griffith, Emelda reigned his kingdom. His quest was to obtain a castle for her. In order to do this the gallant warrior went off to battle after battle after battle. If he didn't carry the colors of his lady fair into the arena for the world to see, it was only because it would not have been looked upon with favor by the New York State Athletic Commission.

There were no battles to be fought on Sundays. Emile Griffith enjoyed going to church although his was not "that old time religion". The mezuzah he wore around his neck in later years was not standard adornment for a Methodist. It was a gift from his co-manager, Howie Albert. Emile enjoyed singing in the choir, he enjoyed listening to the sermons and, most of all, he enjoyed being near Esther Taylor. Not only did Emile think that she was the prettiest and sweetest girl around, but her grandmother, who happened to be his mother's friend, baked the best cookies of anyone he knew. It seemed that Emile was in love with everything of that woman's – her cookies and her granddaughter. Gil told him that as a fighter in training he had to stay away from sweets. "I was sort of worried so I said to Clancy – 'That's only the cookies you're talking about, right?' When he said 'yes' I felt pretty good." So, Esther Taylor became his lady fair.

There were those who believed that Emile's true desire was for the cookies; that Esther Taylor was strictly a public relations ploy to camouflage Griffith's lifestyle. When told of this, all Emile does is shake his head and say, "I never knew so many people knew more about my personal life than I did."

As for Emelda, it took a few more conquests but the queen never doubted that Emile's promise for a castle would be realized. She believed that *fairy tales can come true.* Emelda Griffith sat as close to the ring in the Miami Beach Convention Hall as anyone could without being a member of the press. Chris Dundee, the promoter, was a wise man who had learned from other's misfortunes. Emile Griffith's punching prowess and attack were highly regarded; Emelda Griffith's were legendary. Sometimes, due to runaway emotions, at others times, in response to disparaging remarks about her son, she had resorted to pounding on backs, crushing fedoras and even employing a swinging pocketbook as a lethal weapon. Safe haven was anywhere behind her. Chubby Checker, as Emelda was lovingly referred to by her children, was not constructed for turning around in the tight space between rows of an arena. The high level danger zone was to be seated in the row and seat directly in front of hers. By seating her in Row 1 with a wide walkway and no row of seats in front of her, Chris Dundee's liability insurance was probably a lot less expensive.

It was April 1st, 1961 and Emelda Griffith could not believe that her boy was fighting for the World Welterweight Championship. She read the newspapers and heard the talk; there was no way that Emile, who had been fighting fewer than three years, was ready to fight for the title. It couldn't be done.

That's all that they kept saying about her boy. He couldn't do this, he couldn't do that, he shouldn't even try. A little over a year before she remembered their saying that no fighter with only 16 bouts under his belt should be in the same ring with Gaspar Ortega. They had also said that nobody could scream the way Emelda did for ten rounds. They were right. She lost her voice somewhere in the 7th round. Emile went the full ten, thrashing the game but outgunned Ortega from pillar to post in Madison Square Garden. He outboxed, outpunched and outmaneuvered the wily veteran in an action-packed fight that made believers of the Gillette Cavalcade of Sports TV audience as well as the hardnosed, cynical Garden regulars. Over the past year she had heard all the things Junior couldn't and shouldn't do but, in the meantime, she had watched him beat Jorge Fernandez twice, give the left-hooking Cuban slugger, Florentino Fernandez, a boxing lesson and knock out that boy from Africa, Willie Toweel. After all of those things she had heard that he couldn't do that he did do, there was something that he *definitely* shouldn't and couldn't do and that was fight Luis Rodriquez, who had never lost a fight either in Cuba or the United States.

"I've been scared," Emile reminisced, *"I mean deep down, knee-trembling scared, only once in my life, and that was because of a guy named Luis Rodriquez. The first time I fought him, in New York in December, 1960 – I thought I was going to shake to pieces.*

I wasn't much more than a raw kid then and this Luis – his fans called him El Feo, which means the Ugly One – was a hell-tearing hombre with thirty fights behind him.

Before I got in the ring that night I was trembling and kicking the ground with nerves.

Once I climbed through the ropes I calmed down, and when I saw that chunky Cuban coming at me I thought: Well, this is it, Emile, you got to stand up and be counted or get wiped off the face of the earth."

If Emelda Griffith had paid for her ticket she could have asked for her money back because she did not use her seat. She stood up all night yelling and telling her boy what to do and Junior, who was always obedient, listened to her and did what everyone said he couldn't do. That night, Luis Rodriguez learned something. He learned how to lose a fight.

It's not that Emile went through the year without learning any tough lessons. He learned to beware of invitations to sleepovers. Four Friday nights after the Ortega fight, Emile beat up on West Coast sensation Denny Moyer's belly, winning a ten-round decision. That's when Denny politely said, "Come on-a my house ... "

Maybe Emile was remembering that when Rosemary Clooney made such an offer she was going to "give you everything". Well, Emile graciously accepted Denny's offer and went out to his house, Portland, Oregon, not really expecting everything but neither did he realize that his host was expecting, if not everything, at least a nice present. When Emile came empty-handed, Denny still wound up with a surprise package, which was presented to him by the judges, a gift-wrapped decision. Howie Albert says, "It was more than a gift. It was highway robbery. Emile floored Moyer twice and gave him such a beating that if he was a rug he would have been completely dust-free. Even though it was Denny's home town, when they announced the decision for Moyer, the crowd booed for almost an hour after it was announced." Emile Griffith learned that when you go to play in someone else's backyard make sure you at least bring along a box of cookies.

***

Emelda tried to calm herself. Her Junior – fighting for the World Championship! She thumbed through the fight program, waiting for her boy and the champion, Benny 'Kid' Paret to enter the ring. Instead of it calming her, she became more upset because on the cover there was a picture only of Paret, and he wasn't even as good-looking as her boy. But when she flipped over the first page and saw a full page photo of Emile she felt a little better. It was a bigger picture than the one of Paret on the cover. Then she quickly scanned the Herb Lowe article about the fight opposite Emile's picture and she shuddered. She slowly read and read again Lowe's analysis of Paret:

> *"A look at this recent training session revealed a bad habit of dropping his hands when crowded on the ropes. This with an aggressive young man like Griffith, might be disastrous for Paret."*

It made her feel so strangely uncomfortable that she wanted to throw the program away, but she decided to roll it up and put it in her pocketbook because it had such a good picture of Emile. Anyhow, she thought that she would read it after the fight and laugh at the part that made her feel so queasy.

With the world title at stake, Gil Clancy expected to have a charged-up, energetic Griffith on hand. He did. But Emelda wasn't in the ring. The loudest crowd noises came from the section right behind her, pleading with her to sit down so they could watch the fight too, even though there wasn't nearly as much activity from both fighters as there was from Emelda, who was swinging both arms while pleading with Emile to fight.

> *"... the challenger had been a reluctant tiger – uninspired and uninspiring – who consistently ignored his corner's exhortations to 'stand off and hit.' Nine-tenths of his night's work ... was nothing more than a leaning contest."*
> – *Edwin Pope, Miami Herald 4/3/61*

Gil Clancy, Syd Martin and Howie Albert were shouting themselves hoarse trying to awaken Emile from the trance he was obviously in. The fight started with Paret charging out, throwing his usual windmill assortment of punches, almost all of them bouncing off Griffith's shoulders, arms and elbows. Griffith stayed in his defensive shell, occasionally throwing a counter right just to remind Paret he was still there. Referee Jimmy Peerless was the hardest working guy in the ring, constantly prying the two fighters apart. At the end of 12 rounds Emelda Griffith was way ahead on the scorecards of all the fans. The three officials had it dead even between Emile Griffith and Benny Paret.

Actually, the fight was won by an openhanded right hand slap. This was followed by two sizzling left hooks, but it was the slap that really turned it around. When Emile Griffith dropped on his stool at the end of the 12th round, an exasperated Gil Clancy screamed at him, "Don't you know you're fighting for the championship of the world? Get out there and start fighting!" With that he slapped Griffith in the face. Emile was shocked but he was also now wide awake. Just about a minute into the 13th round, Paret started a right hand lead. This time, instead of smothering the punch, Griffith sprang like a panther, unleashing a tremendous left hook flush on Paret's jaw, following it with a double-up of that hook right on the temple. As Paret was already heading towards the deck, Emile put the icing on the cake. He threw an overhand right hand like a baseball from the outfield and Paret was down for the count. As the referee cried out "TEN!" Emile's exuberance took over. It had almost become a tradition for him to jump joyously into the arms of his manager-trainer Gil Clancy after each victory. There is a classic photo of Emile Griffith doing a backwards somersault after winning the title. It ain't so. As Emile Griffith launched himself in the air to embrace Clancy and wrap his legs around his waist, he realized in mid-flight that it was not Gil Clancy's arms he was headed for. He was in a direct flight path for referee Jimmy Peerless who stood wide-eyed and bewildered at the human projectile sailing towards him. Somehow Emile applied brakes in mid-air and came to a screeching halt, falling to the canvas on his butt and rolling over backwards.

Meanwhile, Emelda, now the proudest and most excited mother on the planet, with pulse racing, heart pounding made her way, like a blocking back, through the throng of reporters and security people surrounding the ring. She climbed the steps, lurched forward crying, "My baby! ..." and fainted dead away. As she fluttered towards the canvas, Clancy, who never caught the other Griffith as was intended, caught Momma in the catch of a lifetime, carried her, with great effort, to Emile's corner and sat her on the champ's stool where she was fanned by Emile's corner people with large towels, while the new champion strolled around the ring by himself.

The queen got her castle shortly after the Paret fight. It was a large 10½ room house on the corner of Colfax and 110th Street in Hollis, New York. The new champion paid $50,000 for it. At first, eight people were living there: Emelda, Emile, his brothers Franklin, Tony and Guillermo and his sisters, Eleanor, Joyce and Karen. Gloria, who was married and had five daughters, had her own apartment in the Bronx. Her husband, Wilfred, and Emile were good friends. *"He was pretty much a fun guy,"* Emile smiles, closing his eyes to give himself a better view of what was. *"We did a lot together. He'd stop in at the gym and watch me work out, always kidding like he's rooting for the other guy when I'm sparring. We'd hit a movie together, play stickball in the schoolyard. But the most important thing about Wilfred was that he was good to my sister and the little girls. It wasn't easy for a young guy taking care of such a large family so I helped out however I could. Best way was giving him a batch of fight tickets to sell. Wilfie was a street guy, knew the crowds and always picked up a nice piece of change peddling tickets to my shows. I felt extra good because I knew that a good cut of that change was going for my little princesses. And then I get the call ..."* Emile can't control the break in his voice. *"You think you're doing the right thing, you want to do what's best. Sometimes it just doesn't work."*

Wilfred, Emile's friend as well as brother-in-law was shot dead on a Harlem street. He was holding one fight ticket in his hand. The rest were gone. So was his money. Emile was heartsick for his friend who he had tried to help out, his sister who was widowed at the age of twenty-one and five nieces who became "my babies". Eventually, Gloria moved in with the children and became the family cook and housekeeper.

Once his family was housed and relatively comfortable, Emile wanted to make sure that they all received an education. *"I didn't have the chance to complete my schooling. It was important to me that all of my brothers and sisters got a proper education. I was so proud when Franklin went to the Hampton Institute. I swore that if he were to graduate on the same night of a big fight for me, I would choose to be there to see him get his diploma. There would be nothing more important in my life."*

As time went on, however, a strain developed in the relationship between the two brothers. Franklin became increasingly critical of Emile's lifestyle and his choice of friends. Some saw it as his being protective and concerned for his brother. Others saw it as a fear of being stigmatized, because of what he considered Emile's questionable behavior, a fear that it was a reflection on him. Rather than being appreciative of the fact that Emile paid his tuition at the Hampton Institute, Franklin complained, instead, that Emile had stopped paying the tuition before he completed his education.

"Sure I stopped paying his tuition," Emile explains. *"He dropped out of school and got married. Then when he feels good and ready he decides*

to go back still expecting me to pay his way. When someone gets married you are now a man and you are responsible for yourself and your family. Maybe it would have been different if we were getting along better. Who knows?"

CHAPTER SIX

Howie Albert was happy. Emile Griffith saw the championship as a faucet that spewed money and he turned it wide open. Whatever there was to get for his family, he wanted to get, but he wasn't leaving himself out. His mother came first, his siblings next, then came Emile. The world of fashion beckoned and Emile heeded its call. Hip-hugging trousers, suede boots, gold bracelets, chains and an assortment of rings made the champ an trendsetter, innovator and the talk of the town, in good ways and bad. But Howie Albert was happy because he convinced Emile to invest $12,000 in a mutual fund and hoped it was the beginning of the young champion's securing his future.

Benny Paret cut a better deal. West Coast promoter George Parnassus wanted to put together a rematch between Griffith and Gaspar Ortega in Los Angeles but Benny Paret had a contract guarantying him a return bout for Griffith's first defense if he lost the Miami fight. A deal had to be negotiated and the Kid was in the driver's seat. He was paid $20,000 to sit back as a spectator.

So Emile Griffith, who did not fare too well following the "go-west-young-man" advice of Horace Greeley the first time he accepted Denny Moyer's invitation, decided to give it another try. The California sportswriters wrote about the aggressive style and tough hide of Gaspar "Indio" Ortega, who had never been stopped in over 80 professional fights.

And they expounded about the millinery skills of Emile Griffith.

They quoted Ortega as saying that Griffith never hurt him in their first fight and that he was confident he would turn the tables this time around.

They quoted Griffith as saying, "*The Jackie Kennedy pillbox will remain in vogue; she's done a great job of 'selling' for the millinery world. But hats will come in a greater variety of shape and materials than ever this year. We're featuring carabou, ostrich, novelty braids, feathers and velours. With the bouffant coiffure still in vogue, look for higher pillboxes.*" Emile's interview certainly did not follow the Great John L. Sullivan, "I can lick any man in the house" approach.

Eyebrows were raised. So was fan interest. The boxing world was starting to wonder. There were locker room whispers among the fighters and speculation among the fans. This enigmatic fighting machine frequented a shadowy world, wore the clothes of an alien fashion cult, and he had a side profession as a hat designer. The last piece completed the picture. When Emile stared out from the ring of the Olympic Auditorium the night of the fight, he saw more Mexicans than Daniel Boone and Davey Crockett saw at the Alamo. Their millinery interests were limited to sombreros.

On June 3, 1961 Emile Griffith achieved greatness. Gaspar Ortega wept. He did not weep in shame. The brave-hearted Mexican gladiator had nothing to be ashamed of. After the first two minutes of the fight it was obvious that it was Griffith's destructive arsenal of punches against Ortega's courage. Courage and honor forestall the inevitable, but punches score the knockouts. Emile's attack was relentless. He battered Ortega to the canvas twice in the seventh round and persisted with the merciless attack throughout. Referee Tommy Hart considered stopping the fight in the seventh and eighth rounds but he knew how desperately the proud Ortega wanted to win the title in front of his fanatic countrymen. In 83 fights, Gaspar Ortega had never been stopped. Hart let the game but thoroughly beaten fighter continue. Finally, as the twelfth round began and Ortega clutched the ropes to hold himself up before another Griffith onslaught, the referee stopped the fight. It was not a fight. It was a butchering. While the Griffith dressing room quietly celebrated a shared dream of far-reaching fistic horizons, Gaspar Ortega, in his dressing room, cried for twenty minutes for a shattered dream.

The raised eyebrows and the snide locker room whispers were put to rest, for a while at least. Flashing fists and the demolishing of a tough Mexican warrior didn't fit the foppish image previously conjured up.

When the street corner jockeys and the boys in the balcony brigade put a fighter on a pedestal that, in itself, is an achievement. But when the matchmaker at Madison Square Garden jumps on the bandwagon, then a star is born and the dollars are ready to flow. Teddy Brenner did not try to hide his feelings about Emile Griffith. From the moment Junior turned pro, Teddy opened the Garden doors to him and took a special interest in his career.

Before the Ortega fight the smart boys were all skeptics. There were plenty of believers but their last names were all Griffith. It was as though every fight Brenner set up for him was like throwing a kid with a slingshot in against an army of club-wielding Goliaths. Every time he climbed through the ropes, Griffith was the underdog. They didn't know he was a modern-day David.

Now, after his spectacular performance against Ortega, Brenner began working on arranging a bout with Sugar Ray Robinson. It never came off. This did not make Griffith unhappy because Robinson was his idol. But the marquees at the old and current Gardens belonged to Emile Griffith who wound up fighting more main events there than any other fighter in history. He was fast becoming a matinee idol and a TV star, but he was not an easy person to keep the spotlight on. Very often the spotlight wound up focused on an empty stage.

"Teddy Brenner would have a press conference and photo op set up at a midtown restaurant," Howie Albert remembers, "and everyone would be there with pencils and pads, tape recorders, flash bulbs ready to pop, that is, everyone would be there except Emile. He organized this Little League baseball team, the Griffs, which had Emile pretty choked up because the kids chose their own team name. He outfitted them, paid for all their equipment and coached them. What's more important, posing for pictures and promoting your next fight or getting a bunch of street kids ready for a big game? The truth was, Emile didn't need much additional promoting. His face was on the tube almost as much as Ed Sullivan's. Emile's kind disposition, gentleness and love of everyone came across and made his television exposure stand out."

Emile's eyes search the heavens like he is looking for a meteor to streak by. "Howard, Howard, Howard." He makes it sound like the refrain from a song. "If we are talking about TV exposure, we all made our debut together." The first time Emile fought on TV was the first Ortega fight at the Garden in February 1960. Emile needs help and he does what he always does in such a situation – he turns to Clancy. After all, what are trainers for? The smile is already creasing Gil's face.

"I have to admit, Howie stole the show from Emile. We're resting at the Belvedere Hotel the afternoon of the fight when we smell something burning. Howie is sound asleep so Emile and I start checking all over, closets, drawers, under the bed. By now we're sure the hotel is burning down so we run out in the hall and start knocking on doors to warn everyone. That's when we remember that Howie didn't want to wrinkle his slacks for his big debut so he took them off before he stretched out for his nap and put them on top of the floor lamp. We run back to the room, telling all the hotel guests not to ring the fire alarm, and there's Howie's pants, smoldering away on top of the lamp with a gaping hole right where you wouldn't want a gaping hole to be. You had to see Howie that night, continually stretching the back of his sweater trying to cover what used to be the seat of his pants. Fortunately, they didn't have ratings in those days, but that is what I call TV exposure."

"Nobody's perfect," Howie concedes. "As it turns out, it's the only pair of pants I ever burned. We were young and impulsive back then, but those two were lunatics. I was the only sane one. They would needle each other over everything from who was better looking to who could do this or that. They walk past a basketball court and Gil would challenge Emile to shooting fouls. Then Junior has to get even so he challenges Gil to a race in the pool. Ping-pong, tennis, whatever they saw, Gil insists he can beat Emile and Emile swears no one can beat him at anything. Okay, I think I'm used to everything from these two when I see them do something that makes me consider having the two of them committed. It's less than two weeks before the rematch with Paret and Emile just finishing a grueling training session. We're walking on Ninth Avenue when Gil and Emile are doing one of their "I can do anything better than you can" routines. This time it's who can run faster. You live with nut jobs, you get used to them. So, I'm walking along, ignoring them, hoping people on the street don't associate me with them when I see something I cannot believe. The two of them are running full speed down the middle of Ninth Avenue with the traffic honking horns and swerving to avoid them. Would you believe it? The welterweight champion of the world racing headlong into New York traffic like a kamikaze pilot neck and neck with the only person in the world as crazy as he is, and this two weeks before a title fight. Even though I will never forget it, I can't remember who won the race."

Emile never lacked confidence but he did have certain apprehensions. When Gil told him that they were going to invade the middleweight division after the Ortega fight that was fine with the young champion. The weight difference didn't bother him at all. What bothered him was that Yama Bahama, the hard puncher from Bimini, rhymed just like Randy Sandy did.

Walking from his Garden dressing room that July night, Howie Albert saw that Emile's usual upbeat bounce and energy were missing. Trying to be helpful, Howie pressed the wrong button. Not looking to demean Yama Bahama but wanting to perk his fighter up he said, "Just think of him as another Joe Schmoe, Junior."

"Joe Schmoe? Can't you get me fighters that don't rhyme."

The only poetry in the ring that evening was provided by Emile Griffith. Even though Bahama, the Bimini Bomber, did not enjoy the beat, he did hang around for the full rendition, despite his left eye having been sliced open in the second round and a leaping right that sent him reeling and wobbling in the seventh. It was Griffith's eighth straight win.

Then came the rematch against Benny 'Kid' Paret, a fight in which there was no rhyme or reason. Benny Paret was born in Cuba a year before his Caribbean neighbor, Emile Griffith. They grew up within blocks of each other in New York City and fought their first title bout in Miami.

Benny, whose full name was Bernardo Paret y Valdes, was a shy, quiet young man. One of six children, at the age of twelve he went to live and work on the farm of friends of his parents. At the age of thirteen, he began boxing as an amateur and turned pro at seventeen. His father encouraged him. His mother was worried that he would get hurt. He promised her he wouldn't. She believed him. He married Lucia Hernandez in 1959 and she soon gave birth to a son. Putting food on the table was no problem; he was managed by Manny Alfaro, a Bronx grocer.

Emile knew Benny from the neighborhood. There would be a wave and a short greeting. No big hug or a "How's the family?" Just two fighters seeing each other in the crowd and being polite. "Actually, it was more than just being polite," Emile reminisces. "It was sort of like a sense we were traveling a path together."

On the night of September 30, 1961 there was no wave to one another in a crowd. They were alone in the center of the ring in Madison Square Garden. Emile stared at Paret, still trying to figure out what had taken place earlier that day shortly before they got on the scale. Paret was on the other side of the room talking to some of the press people. Griffith caught a bit of what was going on and didn't like it. He heard Benny doing an exaggerated imitation of his high-pitched voice. He winced as he watched him do a limp wrist parody with a flourish, swishing his hips and pointedly glanced over at him. It was obvious to Emile that the neighborhood rumor mill whispers hadn't gone unheard by Benny.

And Emile did not just shake it off or ignore it.

"I did something you should never do before or during a fight. I started thinking of other things and staring hard at Paret at a time my mind should have just been on the fight. It stung me more, I guess, because no one ever made anything about it or ever said anything to me – except my brother Franklin. I had my girlfriend Esther and I had my boyfriends. That's the way it was and that's the way I liked it and this was the first time anyone made fun of me like that."

As the referee recited his instructions, the Kid countered Griffith's hard stare with a wide grin. A slight hesitation before the handshake and an hour later Emile Griffith no longer felt like being polite.

"I wuz robbed! There was no polite way to put it. Eighteen out of twenty-two ringside reporters score the fight for me and two judges see a fight no one else does."

Griffith came out fast and dominated the early rounds throwing crisp combinations. In the fourth round he had Paret reeling from two solid left hooks and only the bell saved him from being knocked out. If Paret had an outstanding trait, it was his heart. His ability to throw punches never matched his ability to catch them. He would take three to give one. And most of the time, that's what he did. He stayed in there with Griffith, taking punches but staying on top of him, pressuring with a body attack. He didn't shy away from using his head and elbows, either. If you scored for tenaciousness and capacity for absorbing punishment, then Benny 'Kid' Paret was in any fight he ever fought. Somehow, that's how judges Tony Castellano and Artie Aidala scored it.

"The day after the fight I woke up in a world of disappointment. I had beaten Paret again but lost my title on a split decision. What made it all the worse was that Paret's manager, Manny Alfaro, said they weren't going to give me a rematch. My momma cooked my favorite foods and my girlfriend Esther was so loving and tender, but nothing made me feel better and I knew it wouldn't until I got my championship back."

CHAPTER SEVEN

Rather than beg Paret's manager, Manny Alfaro, for a rematch he had sworn he wouldn't grant, Gil Clancy wisely kept Emile in action leaving it to the public to demand the fight. It was up to Emile to have them clamor for an encore performance. He did his job well. After knocking out Stanford Bulla in four rounds on a windswept tennis court in Bermuda a month after the Paret fight, Emile returned to New York for a Christmas week fight against the skillful Cuban veteran, Isaac Logart. Originally scheduled for Madison Square Garden, to accommodate a Ranger hockey game the fight was moved uptown. What more appropriate scenario could there be? A Christmas fight at St. Nick's! Somebody's stocking was going to be stuffed. Emile Griffith had an option. He chose to play Scrooge, not Santa Claus, and won a hard-fought victory over his wily opponent at St. Nick's during Christmas week. It made for a pretty nice Christmas present, but it didn't compare with his birthday present.

February 3, 1962, Emile Griffith's 24th birthday was celebrated in his home, St. Thomas. The fight wasn't much. Johnny Torres ran for ten rounds and Emile Griffith chased him for ten rounds, winning a lopsided fight-footrace.

"Forget the fight," Howie Albert says. "Everyone else did. It was the event. Emile Griffith's return to his home and his birthday. The kid was a national hero. The governor declared it a local holiday – like Columbus Day, Lincoln's Birthday. They named a park after him – 'Emile Griffith Park' and awarded him the island's Medal of Honor, which was originally given to the Governor who wrote the first charter for the Virgin Islands. And I found something out. Confetti only looks like shredded paper. It must really be very hard stuff because as it sailed down during our parade and hit Emile, I saw him cry."

Emile enjoyed the swaying, rocking motion of a train racing through its underground maze. He was able to close his eyes and relax, something he was never able to do in a taxi. When he promised Gil that he would take a cab into the city, he wasn't lying; he was just avoiding a fight. The one he had scheduled with Benny Paret the next night at the Garden was the only fight he wanted to have on his mind.

This kid Matthew insisted that he come along with him, carry his small suitcase and gym bag and make sure nobody bothered him. Matthew had become Emile's self-appointed body guard. It was like a guy carrying a .45 needed a BB gun. Not quite eighteen, Matthew came to the gym with his uncle about a half year before when Emile was training for the second Paret fight, and before long he became as much a fixture as the punching bags and medicine balls.

There are those who collect string, those who collect rubber bands, others tinfoil. There is always someone to collect anything that's to be found on the street. And they genuinely like and usually take very good care of what they collect. Emile Griffith collected people.

He genuinely liked and took very good care of his collection. He wasn't much for rubber bands and string. Emile Griffith was for flesh and blood, lost and searching, down and out, and for any stray that licked his hand there was a pat on the head, a place in his heart ... and home. Fortunately, or unfortunately, Emelda's sensitivity and sensibility levels were pretty much the same as her son's. Emelda's household was a household where the underdog became the favorite.

From the first time he saw Emile in the gym on 28th Street, Matthew was in awe. It wasn't the sculpted, muscled body, the power that exploded from the rippling biceps or the obvious toughness of the fighting machine in the ring. Matthew was from the streets. He knew what rough and tough were about. And it wasn't the warm, friendly smile, the gentle sound to his voice or the kindness in taking the time to sit down and talk with him. Matthew had no conception that toughness and compassion can join together. So foreign was it to the youngster that he couldn't understand the dynamics. He was the stray mutt who was there to protect its protector. He would snarl and growl and bite if he had to. Emile took him home and Matthew became part of Emelda's brood. In fact, Emile moved into the new house on Colfax Street with Matthew before the rest of the family had. Matthew told his uncle that Emile was his "new pop."

"New pop" may have been acceptable but it wasn't quite the way Franklin saw it. From the first time he met Matthew he let both the kid and Emile know that, unlike his mother, he was not welcoming the relationship as he saw it. What Franklin saw was a jealous, possessive kid who wanted anyone and everyone to know that Emile was his man. Neither Emile nor Matthew let Franklin's attitude bother them at first. "At first" didn't last nearly as long with Emile as it did with Matthew. Emile knew that others would be feeling the same as Franklin and doing the right thing was very important to Emile. He remembers nights when Matthew would climb into his bed while he was sleeping and he would have to physically restrain him. Then Matthew turned eighteen .... no longer any need for restraint.

Other than brother Franklin, Gloria was the only other person in the family who seemed to take note of Emile's lifestyle and his growing list of boyfriends. Instead of being angry, though, Gloria teased her brother and the teasing was good-natured. When they were still living in St. Thomas as children and thrn when they first moved to New York, she would call him Anti Man. To his other siblings, Emile was their big brother, their champion who they loved and adored and accepted as he was. There was no judging. They accepted him and his friends as did their mother.

Over the years, Emelda Griffith saw her son bringing home a steady stream of companions. Many of them slept over in Emile's room and were warmly welcomed by Emelda.

"When it came to Emile, mother was in denial," Gloria explained. It was deeper than being in denial. God help anyone who made any put-down remarks about her son within hearing range of Emelda.

****

They got off the train at 42nd Street even though they could have taken it right up to the Garden and a short block from the Belvedere Hotel where Emile was quartered. It was his usual routine. He didn't stop in at any of his now familiar haunts; just walked by and waved occasionally to a friend. From the doorways of some of the bars and shops along the way there were words of encouragement and good wishes. No one approached. Matthew did not permit any invasion of Emile's privacy at this time.

When they reached Broadway and 48th Street, Emile stopped at the entrance of the Belvedere and told Matthew to go home. Gil and Howie had seen the kid hanging around the gym. Emile had told them that Matthew was helping him out. He didn't explain further than that. He waited for one of them to ask how the kid was helping out. They didn't. Maybe, he thought, it would have been easier if they had. Emile Griffith was much braver in the ring. He watched Matthew digging his hands in his pockets as he headed back to the subway. Then he entered the lobby and headed for the elevators. The anticipation of the coming event quickened his pulse and his nostrils flared. As he rode to his floor his thoughts were of a night of celebrating after regaining his crown. Getting off he shook his head, remembering how Mommie always told him not to think of dessert before finishing your main course.

March 23rd was a typical blustery March day but Emelda Griffith had the bedroom windows wide open as she prepared to get ready to go into the city to watch her boy win back the championship the next night. For some reason she couldn't stop perspiring. It was only natural for a mother to be concerned about her son but it wasn't Emile she was worried about. Since Paret had taken that bad beating in his fight with Gene Fullmer the past December, she occasionally had these uncomfortable feelings. She opened the drawer where she kept the program she had brought back from the Miami fight when Emile won the title. She kept thinking about what was written in that program

"... with an aggressive young man like Griffith,(it) might be disastrous for Paret."

***

There are certain memories that are better erased from one's consciousness. Emile Griffith would be very accepting of that, but his recollections of the events of a March day back in 1962 remain vivid, playing over and over again to an audience of one. They have become the fulcrum on which his life has pivoted. Thinking back is not necessary. It's just a matter of closing his eyes ...

Things sometimes happen at weigh-ins. It's usually just a quick ceremony. You strip to your skivvies or skin, step on a scale and heave a happy sigh when you hear you made the weight. Then a doctor presses a cold stethoscope to your chest, looks down your throat and takes your blood pressure. That's followed by flash bulbs going off as the photographers ask the main-eventers to smile and square off in various boxing poses. But every once in a while there is a weigh-in where smiles are missing and you never get to the boxing pose. However, the flash bulbs do go off.

On March 24, 1962 there was such a weigh-in.

Benny Paret came from Cuba and I came from St. Thomas but we both wound up living in New York, Benny in the Bronx with his wife Lucia and their little boy while I lived in Harlem. There were times we would see each other on the street or at a boxing function and he would always wave and smile and I would do the same. To me Benny 'Kid' Paret was an okay guy. I called him a friend – up until that day.

It was just mid-morning, about eleven o'clock, but still I was hungry. Boxers were always hungry at weigh-ins, except for heavyweights. They didn't have to worry about making weight. So, when I walked into the New York State Athletic Commission office with my managers Howie Albert and Gil Clancy, my main thoughts were about a two-inch thick steak. It didn't take very long for me to lose my appetite.

Taking a punch on the jaw hurts – no question about it, but that kind of pain doesn't last very long. A physical punch passes much more quickly than an emotional one. Also, maybe it's because you are usually prepared for a physical punch. I sure had my guard down for what I took, though.

Someone said, "Emile, please step up on the scale," which I did. All I was wearing were my underpants and sox. A couple of photographers were taking pictures and I was just about to back off the scale when I heard Gil Clancy say, "Watch out!" He didn't shout it out and it wasn't like a strong warning or anything like that, but it was enough to make me turn around and there was Paret almost right up against me making these stupid, suggestive motions with his body. I looked down at him from the scale, still not sure of what he was doing. He grinned at me in a spiteful, disrespectful way, pointed his finger. "Hey, maricon, I'm going to get you and your husband!"

Maybe it's worse when someone you know and consider a good person does something really lousy to you than if it is a stranger. All I know is it felt like he stuck a knife into me. If Clancy didn't jump right in and get between us I was ready to go to it then and there, without gloves, without three minute rounds and no referee.

"Save it for tonight, Emile," Clancy said as he wrapped his arms around me. "Save it for tonight. That's what he wants to do, get you mad and out of your fight plan."

Well, if he wanted to get me mad he did a very good job of it because I don't ever remember being madder. It's not so much what he said. I can handle that. You know, nobody ever came up to me and asked me anything or said anything to my face. If they did, I could handle that, too. But what he did was treat me like garbage. I am who I am. And I am quite happy being who I am. If Benny Paret or anyone else thinks I am different than they are, that is alright. I can also feel that they are different than I am. That doesn't make me a better person, just as it doesn't make them better than me. It's not only that Benny didn't treat me with respect. He tried to insult me and make fun of me in front of everyone. Yeah, I was mad, I was very mad right then. Mad, embarrassed and humiliated.

Gil and Howie walked with me from the Commission office to McGinnis' where I had a cup of hot beef broth. I had learned from Clancy that there wasn't a better or quicker energy picker-upper than beef broth. Stopping at McGinnis's had become part of our regular pre-fight routine and that's what they were trying to get me back into. I was still shaking and I didn't know if it was from anger or hurt. Whatever, that's what they were trying to get me out of.

We took a brisk walk to the Belvedere Hotel with Gil telling me to suck in lungfuls of the crisp March air. By the time we got to the hotel I was beginning to feel better. I wanted to think that Benny 'Kid' Paret wouldn't do that on his own; that his cornermen pushed him into playing head games. But I felt myself getting wound up again so I turned on the TV and started watching a Charlie Chan movie. I like Charlie Chan, the way he would solve mysteries with the help of his Number One son. They probably solved this one but I'm not sure because I couldn't concentrate. I kept thinking of Paret.

Gil noticed how fidgety I was and he knew what was bothering me. I'm sure it bothered Gil and Howie, too. But they would never say why it bothered them except to say Paret was trying to get me mad to break my concentrating on the fight. They never talked to me or asked me about deep-down personal things – I mean about who I spent my time with or things like that. It wasn't their style. Anyhow, they only saw me with women. I didn't hide or sneak, but I didn't flaunt it either. Gil and Howie and a lot of people I was close with lived in one world. I lived in two. I guess I just sensed who would be comfortable with it. With Gil and Howie, we just all accepted each other. We were like family and we just felt we were all good people. That was all that mattered – being a good person.

Gil told me to stop dwelling on what happened that afternoon, that I should be used to Paret's games by now and reminded me how he played the same card just before our second fight. I remembered. It is something you don't forget. I kept remembering as we left the Belvedere Hotel and headed for the Garden.

****

Benny Paret packed his bag by himself and walked to the kitchen where Lucia stood at the sink, trying to think of the day after the fight. Maybe a walk in Central Park wheeling Benny, Jr. in his stroller. It didn't matter to her whether the man walking at her side was a champion or a grocery clerk. In many ways she would prefer the grocery clerk. She did not enjoy the world of prizefighting but she was part of it. Only as a wife – not even a spectator. She married the man, not the sport.

As they entered the park at 106th Street, Benny was wearing a part-time smile. It was sort of an I-can-fool-you-and-fool-myself grin. Lucia thought back to when that smile was much more real and always there. That was before the Fullmer fight in December. Benny couldn't fool her. She knew him too well. She also knew that he couldn't fool himself, no matter how hard he tried.

Benny Paret never backed away from a fight but neither did he ever walk into the ring with a make-believe smile before. Benny never mentioned to Lucia what had taken place at the weigh-in earlier that day. Taunting and teasing was a relatively gentle form of gay-baiting in most of the Caribbean cultures. Not that he didn't intend to hurt and embarrass Emile, but to Benny "Kid" Paret, it was just the way things were, in Cuba, over here, almost anywhere in the world – places he was never at or never even heard of. However, there were more important things on his mind now. He had been complaining of headaches and he told Manny Alfaro, his manager but Manny said it was too late. No pulling out. There was big TV money on the table.

So they walked through the park and watched little Benny, Jr. giggle at the antics of squirrels dashing off with peanuts. Benny smiled at his son. It was a real smile and it made Lucia feel very good.

CHAPTER EIGHT

The spot on the canvas kept Emile in check. It could have been dried blood, it could have been some cornerman's ointment that spilled over at a long-ago fight. Whatever it was, Emile concentrated on it. He was used to large crowds. They didn't bother him; in fact they usually picked him up and spurred him on. But now he was looking to blot out everything around him – the crowd, the noise, even the people in the ring. Everything but that brownish spot on the canvas. It became a little universe of its own; with no one or nothing to think about other than … it.

Gil ordered, Emile listened. If he didn't, Clancy would growl, shout, shake him and if he had to, whack him – all with great love, affection and devotion – but not tenderness. That was reserved for outside of the ring where it worked a lot better.

So, when Gil ordered him not to think about what Paret had done or about anything that would get him upset and out of his game plan, Emile listened and actually transported himself to this soundless, peopleless place where there were no feelings of anger, hate, love – no feelings of any kind. A spot on the canvas did not evoke any.

It was Syd Martin, one of Emile Griffith's cornermen, who shattered the small, new universe and brought Emile back to the world that took all of six days to create. Emile didn't see Paret's second who kept mouthing the Kid's *maricon* insult from across the ring, taunting and baiting Griffith, trying however he could to get him worked up. Emile was busy in his own little world. When

Syd Martin's foot came down on that spot on the canvas that world ended.

"What the hell is wrong with you?" Martin rasped, marching across the ring. "You ought to be ashamed of yourself!"

The cornerman backed off a step and shrugged, "Hey, amigo, I'm just juicing up my man, you know."

Syd Martin knew and so did Emile Griffith. His mouth set in a grim, hard line and his jaw muscles tensed. The Calm was gone. It was time for the Storm.

Emile Griffith was a pouter. Anger very rarely came to the surface, partly because he liked people and he could not conceive of people not liking him in return and, although sensitive to criticism and negative innuendoes, he could never believe they were directed at him. Because of this uncertainty, he couched his anger in a pout. Emile Griffith the great pouter was now beyond the pout.

You can never tell how a jungle cat is feeling. It pursues and lashes out. There is some instinctive sense, rather than any sense of emotional impetus, that leads to a methodical pattern of stalking and striking. But, again, you can't tell for sure. It's just a guess. Only the cat knows for sure; and sometimes, even the cat doesn't know.

Emile Griffith bounced forward. Unquestionably, there was a bell. Emile didn't hear it, he wasn't listening for it, he didn't need it. For him, the fight had started hours earlier. All the crowd sounds blended into one Babylon-like mélange and the ring lights, overheads and popping flashbulbs formed a huge, glaring spotlight that served to fuel his drive to slash at and destroy his prey.

He moved side-to-side, feinting, then lashing out at a prey that wouldn't back away but chose to take whatever was thrown at him and strike back when he could. Griffith's strength and determination was too much to contain. As his confidwnce grew, he increased the momentum of his attack.

Then it all turned around. The world tilted crazily and the lights became a whirling kaleidoscope. It was no longer stalk and destroy. Just survive. The hunted became the hunter.

Emile's eyes tried to focus. At first it was a blur, but now he was able to make out the number SIX on the balcony scoreboard across from him. He shook his head in an attempt to clear it as Clancy kneaded his thigh muscles, getting the blood to circulate and pump life and energy back into him.

It was towards the end of the sixth round when a cocky, confident Griffith changed the weaving, stalking attack to a peacock-like prance. He never saw the arcing left hook that landed flush on his jaw and spun him so that he landed heavily on all fours. It was a mixture of warrior's instinct and the sight of Benny Paret standing on the opposite side of the ring, hands on hips with a smug smile, sneering at him that enabled him to gather the strength to pull himself up at the count of eight and finish the round.

Clancy didn't have to shout or lecture him, but he did. Emile knew there was no room or time for relaxing or posturing in the ring. The stalking, snarling cat was now the wounded cat.

It took Griffith two more rounds to fully recover. In the seventh round he still couldn't get out of the way of Paret's left hook, but in the eighth round he felt the resiliency returning to his legs. In the ninth round Emile was clearly outboxing and outpunching Paret. It was a rough fight with plenty of fouls, but no one was penalized although Ruby Goldstein issued six warnings along the way. In the tenth round Griffith was scoring heavily, and for the first time Paret seemed to be tiring and returned to his corner blood-spattered. Emile was in command. Sometimes for Emile Griffith being in command is not the best thing.

Clancy watched Emile downshift in the eleventh round. So did approximately fourteen million people who were watching Gillette's Saturday Night Fights, a direct descendant of the Friday Night Fights, right up there with Ed Sullivan and Milton Berle as American TV institutions. Not everyone watching was a diehard fight fan, but there was not much channel-changing. Even though it was evident that Griffith had a comfortable lead, it was a competitive fight all the way. Much of this due to Paret's toughness and durability. He was there to trade punches and he was not a shrewd bargainer. He'd pay the price by taking as many punches as it took to get in a couple of his own and there was no quit in him. He was still dangerous. Dangerous and crafty.

Gil Clancy never drilled home a lesson with more intensity in his days at P.S. 178 than he did in that 60 seconds between the eleventh and twelfth rounds on the night of March 24th, 1962 in Madison Square Garden as his face hovered inches from his fighter's. He warned him that he couldn't afford to get lazy or careless. "If you catch him, keep punching. Don't let up! And don't let him fool you. You know he loves to play possum and soon as you hold back – Bang!! Just stay on him and punch!" Emile listened and became a better student than he ever wanted to be.

There are certain moments and events that become frozen, calendars and clocks stop, minds lock in and store them in a personal memory vault and they become a common, mental archive – a happening for everyone to share.

Emile Griffith came out for the twelfth round with Clancy's message serving as an infantry bugler's call to battle. His left hand targeted Paret's claret-flowing nose, hard jabs found their mark again and again. And then the catlike lunge forward and the smashing right hand flush to Paret's chin. Paret staggered backwards and Griffith was on him, driving him into the ropes. His right hand, his heavy artillery, was all he was using now. The force of his attack drove Paret's head between the middle and top strand of ropes.

Griffith was fighting in a frenzy fueled by his corner's message to "keep punching ... don't let him fool you..." or an anger so strong that it drove him to a peak of furious, uncontrolled violence rarely seen in a prize ring before or since. The result was horrifying to a witnessing world. More than fourteen million people watched as within the space of a few, short seconds twenty-one full-force blows, rights and lefts, pounded the hapless champion, whose upper body was outside the ropes, his arm tangled in the middle strand. It all happened so quickly that Referee Ruby Goldstein, who was behind Griffith as the attack was launched, never had the chance to respond. As he jumped in, the final punch was a left to Paret's unprotected jaw. A limp body slid slowly to the canvas, his right arm still wrapped around the middle strand of the ropes. It was a moment frozen in time forever, a moment when if anyone had the power to turn back the clock, it would be done.

There was no sense of victory, no feeling of euphoria. Winning or losing had little meaning. The new Champion was announced but Emile doesn't remember whether he even heard it. He trembled as he saw the ring physician, Dr. Alexander Schiff, try to revive or get some response from the inert Paret to no avail.

The Garden security people formed a v-wedge and carved a path for Emile and his cornermen to his dressing room. When he got inside he sat on the rubbing table and couldn't stop himself from crying.

"I was so afraid for Paret but I was afraid for myself, also. I was feeling a terrible guilt because the truth was, I was angry at him. And seeing the way he was now, I didn't want to feel that I had any anger towards him. I was angry at him, but it wasn't hate. It was nothing like hate. At that moment, I could not even recognize that there was a difference between anger and hate. I broke down, crying, asking myself if I could have been so angry that I wanted to kill him. I had to admit that I hated him so much for what he said but I really didn't hate him – the person – Benny Paret."'

Anger and Hate travel a very short parallel path. When they split they take completely separate routes. Anger can turn around, Hate cannot. Anger forgives, Hate doesn't. Anger dissipates, Hate simmers. The person controls Anger, Hate controls the person.

Reluctantly, and with deep regret, Emile Griffith acknowledges that on that tragic night he was an angry person. But hate was never part of his make-up.

Emile's only vivid memory of the fight was Clancy telling him to keep punching, but he doesn't have to rely on memory. It's all there on a video tape cassette to haunt Griffith forever. And how many times has he cringed at a social gathering when thoughtlessly someone replays forty-five minutes that he wishes could be carved from his life.

They rushed Benny Paret to Roosevelt Hospital and operated that morning to remove the pressure on his brain. Griffith went to the hospital, but they wouldn't let him in. Comatose, the Kid hung on for nine days. He never heard the Ten Count but it was over. Emile was not permitted to attend the funeral.

"They never gave me the chance to say 'I'm sorry.' I wanted so bad to say it. I had to say it, but I was never able to. Except to a mirror – to myself. Benny's wife, Lucy, she's a nice lady and I understand how she feels about me. All these years I am never able to tell her how sorry I am because she won't see me. She can't handle that. I don't think it's hate or even anger or blame. It's just that I am the one who killed her husband. I am a bad memory. But she also knows it could have been the other way around. It is a rough business. We are not bankers or clerks. No, I don't believe she hates me and my hurt is nothing compared to her hurt, but, God, I wish I was able to say to her how sorry I am. And not just to her. The little boy – that is the worst hurt of all. I kept thinking of him growing up without a father and I would close my eyes and see him sitting on a stoop tossing a baseball in the air, waiting for his father to come home to him."

But there was hate and Emile felt its sting. The Cuban/Latin fans adored their *campeon*. Benny "Kid" Paret was the matador who stood fearlessly in the center of the arena, ready to face any onslaught. His courage and *machismo* carried them to frenzied ecstasy. Now, gored to lifelessness, blame had to be cast.

"It was like the Old West," Howie Albert recalls, "Except they didn't have telephones back then. Emile couldn't walk down the street without being threatened or cursed at and we stopped taking phone calls. We holed up in the New Yorker for a few days and lived on Room Service, not letting Emile step out into the street because the way some of those lunatics were carrying on we were afraid they'd get hold of a rope and form a lynch mob."

Reverend Alford visited his lead tenor and told him how important it was for him to turn to God and to understand that there is a reason for everything. Emile tried but found that advice impossible to follow.

"At first I just accepted that God was too busy to concentrate on a prizefight, even if it was for the championship. Sure, I wanted Him to come down and breathe life back into Paret and let me just be myself again but He was everybody's God, not just mine or Benny's. I didn't feel deserted by God

– not yet. It was when He started spreading blame and punishing the wrong people.

Gil got a call from the owners of the Concord Hotel in Kiamesha Lake in the Catskills. That's where I trained for all my big fights. They heard what was happening and invited us to stay there as their guests until things cooled down. So, we all went up there. Me, Gil with his family and Howie with his. We're all happy to be away from the city just then when Howie's kids, Barbara and Eddie, come down with chicken pox. Okay, this is not so terrible. Kids come down with colds, kids come down with the mumps and kids come down with chicken pox. That is all natural, but then what happens ... oh, God!"

Howard Albert left the Concord and drove back with his wife Irene and the children to their home on Long Island and Gil packed Emile off for a vacation to St. Thomas. It was like trying if A doesn't work, go to B ...

"When we got home I called the doctor because Irene was feeling feverish and was wheezing. He told us that she, too, had chicken pox. I remember gently teasing her that only kids get chicken pox. Then I went out for a few minutes to bring back coffee. I don't think I even knew how to boil water – but I learned. I had to. It was maybe 15 minutes later that her lungs filled with fluid and my beloved Irene was gone. It was April 15th, less than two weeks after Benny Paret had died."

Emile rushed back from St. Thomas and fell into a deep depression, believing that everything happening to those around him was blanket punishment for Paret's death. He and God were now estranged.

It wasn't until the finger-pointing and the blame started spreading and shifting elsewhere that Emile was able to get back to any form of normalcy.

A TV first, that's what it was. Fourteen million people watching a World Champion beaten to death. The Roman Coliseum with Augustus Caesar pointing thumbs down never had network television coverage. Maybe the media moguls were trying to make up for a missed opportunity. They ran and reran the tragedy over and over. In slow motion and in real time, as though to make certain that those last horror-filled, violent moments were emblazoned on the minds of a mesmerized public. Animal cruelty, domestic violence, child abuse and Ban the Bomb all took a back seat to the new *cause celebre* – Ban Boxing!

> *"Several thousand persons filed past the body of former welterweight champion Benny (Kid) Paret, 25-year-old Cuban who died after a savage ring beating, at a Bronx funeral parlor yesterday.*
>
> *At the same time, seven New York state legislators were appointed to a special committee that will investigate boxing to decide if it should be banned in the state. Hearings will open in New York tomorrow.*
>
> *There were moves to end the sport in Canada and Sweden, and Rep. Abraham J. Multer, D-N.Y., called for congress to ban radio and television broadcasting of fights. Multer said this would make them unprofitable. He called the sport "public slaughter".*
>
> *The Havana press reacted furiously to the death, accusing American "commercial interests" of causing it."*
>
> *-Newark Star April 5, 1962*

Nat Fleischer pointed out in the June 1962 issue of Ring that boxing's "record for deaths is far below that of football or auto racing.

In 1960, 27 football players were killed in the United States. In 1961, 39 died, among them 28 high school boys, six collegians, one an Annapolis player, one serviceman and three sandlot gridders. This terrible record was for our country only and within a space of less than three months, while in boxing, worldwide, only ten fatalities were listed during the entire year."

To Emile, this storm of anger and protest vented in a different direction was an insane form of consolation. Everyone tried, in his own way, to comfort him. His mother cooed to him like he was her infant son again. His cousin, Bernard Forbes, who adored him, stayed with the crestfallen Champ like his shadow, just being there for him. Gil used every type of psychology from tender loving care to tough love. Even Howie, mired in his own personal tragedy, tried to help his young charge through this terrible time. He gave him a mezuzah to wear around his neck and Emile wore it proudly throughout his career.

The only places outside of his home he dared to venture to after returning from the Concord were his now familiar retreats along 42nd Street and Eighth and Ninth Avenues. It was Emile's refuge, his comfort zone. Here he found companions who didn't intrude but permitted him to ease his pain by reflecting in silence or speaking from the heart.

However, since the Paret fight, Emile found that the spotlight had become too large for him to escape its glare. Even those who previously knew nothing about him outside of the ring were looking on with voyeuristic appetites at what they deemed to be an incongruous scenario.

Matthew was his self-appointed security force. He would accompany Griff from the Hollis home to Times Square, making certain that no one bothered the champ until they arrived at their destination. Then he would stand off to the side in a stance somewhere between *ATTENTION* and *BATTLE STATIONS READY*.

When nothing seemed to ease the pain, Emile began calling his girl friend Esther every day, telling her how he was thinking that maybe it was the right time to get married and find a farm somewhere outside of the city where the two of them could lead a quiet life. He would ramble on about no more boxing, no phone calls from anyone but their families, which, of course, included Gil and Howie, no more bright lights and no more Times Square. Just the two of them, chickens and cows and a quiet life. Esther was smart enough to let him talk himself out and Emile was smart enough to realize that's what he was doing – talking himself out. But he couldn't fool either one of them. Emile Griffith was not a chicken and cow person. Nor was he a person in love as much as a person seeking an escape.

"Crazy thoughts from a crazy person." That's how Emile puts it now. But a year after the fight, a by then clear thinking, post-traumatized Griffith poured out his heart. `(excerpts from Emile Griffith's first person article in BOXING & WRESTLING April 1963)

"I lived for March 24, 1962, the night of that third (Paret)fight. But I don't have to tell you I'd virtually give my life if only I could buy it back. I won back my title by knocking out Paret – but I lost virtually everything I had ever gained in life. Benny Paret died as a result of that fight and the injuries he must have carried into it – unknown to the authorities – from previous beatings.

I was once again champion of the world – a world I thought I never again could look in the face.

... I wanted to quit the ring for good – right after the Paret fight. I told my managers I could never fight again. That I had wanted to knock Paret out because of the things he had said about me before the fight and to prove I had been robbed of the title in the second bout. It would be stupid to deny all this.

I wanted to win more than anything else. But anyone who said or wrote that I wanted to kill Paret was just vicious or stupid or both. I won't tell you what some of the people wrote me in the months right after the fight.

My managers would not let me read ninety percent of the mail. But the letters I did see, called me an 'animal who belonged in a cage.' A 'murderer' and a 'sadist'-and said they would avenge Paret by poisoning me-and my family. Things like that.

Cops who analyzed most of this mail told me it came from the professional 'crank' letter writers. They showed me a few and explained that the tiny, cramped hand-writing was common to all mentally disturbed people who wrote this sort of thing.

Albert and Clancy told me to forget about quitting; about fighting or anything else for the next few weeks and to stay close to my mother and family. I have three brothers and four sisters. They knew what was going on in my mind. Except for my mother, they said very little about it other than it had been a terrible accident.

My mother, who is a real fight fan and who has been so very proud of my success, told me to ask God for help. She said: 'Emile, you must realize, in order to commit a crime you must plan it and know what you are doing. You must realize that this could just as well have happened to you. You must know that Benny Paret would tell you this, himself-if he could.'

... Then, just as it was the mail and what it contained that was breaking me, the other kind of mail – saved me. It was a lifeline thrown by complete strangers − men and women who had lived with suffering and who opened their hearts to help me.

I got letters from guys in jail; from doctors and lawyers; all kinds of letters from people all over the world. I got one letter from a little orphan boy who said I would always be his favorite fighter; and from priests, ministers, rabbis and nuns.

One letter came from a fighter I had knocked out a long time ago. A boy named Willie Toweel. 'Champ,' he wrote. 'I know how you feel. I accidentally killed a man in the ring one night. It almost ruined me until I realized it could have happened to me. Accidents happen every day. You have to learn to roll with the punches in this life. Good luck.' That was the gist of it. It was post-marked − South Africa.

A well-known surgeon wrote me he had a personal interest in boxing and was a member of the Oregon Boxing Commission. He told me that many times he had become so discouraged he wanted to quit his profession.

'I felt this way many times when I had a patient die on the operating table,' he wrote. 'I, too, felt all was lost − and that I should quit. Then I thought things over. Life must go on. What would I accomplish if I did quit? Forfeit all the gifts I had been given to practice my profession? Look at all the good I could still do − which would be lost to the world if I should throw in the sponge. You owe yourself and your family too much to quit because of an accident. You did not will this thing. Like life, it must be faced − and conquered.'

A truck driver wrote: I have a fine wife and six kiddies. One day a little boy ran under the wheels of my truck and was killed. I was inconsolable for weeks. The guys I worked with − men who had been involved in serious accidents − came running to my side. They told me to consider my obligations to my family. What would happen to them if I continued to brood, to drink or to run away from my responsibilities? It took a little time but they were right. I had to accept it. You will, too, champ ...'

... It has been this kind of straight talk − from my good friends, in and out of the ring, and the prayers and understanding − and, of course, God's help − that has enabled me to get back my spirit. I honestly intended to quit the ring, for good, the week after Benny Paret died. But what good would it have done? It certainly would not have brought him back. It would not have erased him from my conscience.

I had just bought a new home for my family in Hollis, L.I. If I quit the ring that would still have to be paid for. And what of my obligations to the many fans who have been so good to me?

… I want to continue to fight – and to win.

I will try not to look back – ever.

It is all behind me …"

It wasn't – and probably never will be but Emile told himself it was. Positive thinking, self-delusion – whatever it was, it was enough to get Emile back to the gym.

The hostility between the two battlers was obvious from the opening bell.
(New York Daily News L.P. used with permission.)

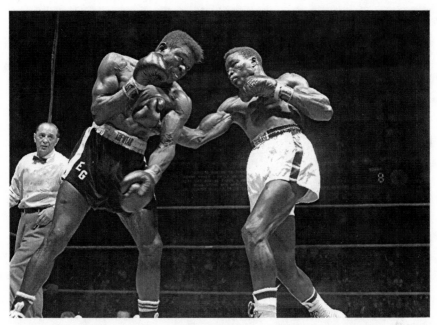

Griffith was the aggressor but Paret continued to fight back.
(New York Daily News, L.P. used with permission.)

Paret's knockdown of Griffith in the 6th round turned the fight around.
(New York Daily News, L.P. used with permission.)

So swift and devastating was Griffith's 12th round onslaught that by the time Referee Ruby Goldstein intervened, the damage was already done. (New York Daily News, L.P. used with permission.)

The crowd watches in horrified silence as Paret's handler's minister to him. (New York Daily News, L.P. used with permission.)

The new champion, Emile Griffith, appears visibly shaken as ring announcer Johnny Addie raises his hand in victory. Cornerman Syd Martin and trainer Gil Clancy look on. (New York Daily News, L.P. used with permission.)

CHAPTER NINE

"My first thought was, I am so glad to see him. Benny stood there at the foot of my bed smiling at me. Didn't say anything. Just smiled. I got up – I wanted to shake his hand, maybe hug him, but he was gone and I'm standing there, now wide awake. I know I must have been sleeping but he kept popping up in front of me everywhere I went during the day. Howie, Gil and Sid, they all told me they were daydreams, hallucinations. Okay, I'm sure they were right but for me it was real. Benny Paret was there."

Gil Clancy was hurting for his young fighter. After a month of brooding, mental self-flagellation and seeking some sort of safe haven, Emile was still floundering on a sea of recrimination and self-pity. He needed a life-line. Gil told him to come to the gym, just hang around, maybe exercise a little. He encouraged him to spend more time with his Little League baseball team, The Griffs. For Emile Griffith, kids and baseball were a happy world to be part of. He became the Pied Piper of Chelsea, followed by his youthful legions wherever he went. He played stickball with them, lectured them and visited their homes.

In the gym, Clancy had him work with a few of the younger fighters, but Emile didn't put the gloves on himself. Not until Gil placed his arm around Griff's broad shoulder and said, "It's time, son."

It was the better part of an hour for Griffith to do the usual ten minutes of work it took to get into his ring togs and wrap his hands. When he finished he was perspiring as heavily as if he had been working out for hours. He walked over to the heavy bag, eyed it, turned and walked away. Gil sent him back. He took two or three half-hearted swipes at it. Luckily, the bag didn't swing back.

Gil then put him in the ring with a kid named Jackie Kelley. Griff moved around tentatively, getting a feel of the canvas under his feet, occasionally lobbing, not snapping, a lazy left hand. He then threw a right hand. It landed and Griffith climbed out of the ring. His first day's workout was finished.

Gil knew his man. There was no question in his mind that Griff would show up the next day. So when Emile walked through the door Gil continued what he was doing, making no fuss over the Champ's arrival. Emile went over to him and, with hands in pockets, said sheepishly, "Sorry, Gil, I left my locker key at home." Gil looked at him and nodded. "You just may be the first naked fighter to work out in this place."

Emile tilted his head, faking a contrite look. "Can't we play ping-pong instead? I'm dressed for it." At a dollar a game, Gil had no illusions of becoming rich, even after winning three straight games. He intended playing only one but Emile refused to quit as a loser and blasted his way to victory in the fourth game. Gil insists he threw it in order to get back to the kids in the gym. Emile swears he just wore Gil down with his smashing forehand. He did admit, though, that ping-pong was not his main game. Gil agreed and waived his two dollars in winnings. He had his fighter back.

Emile Griffith could have believed that he was living a fairy tale. It was easy to believe when you're a raggedy kid from some remote island who comes to a great kingdom and winds up wearing a crown. All fairy tales may be "Once upon a time" but "Once upon a time" does not always end with "happily ever after". It was easy to believe until what Emile Griffith called "the accident", which was now four months in the past but stayed with Emile every minute of every day.

He couldn't forget it even if he wanted to, and he didn't know if he wanted to. The specter of Benny Paret wouldn't fade. People didn't permit it to fade. They kept it linked to Emile Griffith. Wherever he went, it followed him.

Whether it followed him or he brought it with him, there they were. After four months away from the ring, in the desert kingdom of Las Vegas, Emile Griffith was going to show the world that he was able to get past the Paret tragedy and to resume his career as welterweight champion of the world.

Las Vegas should have been Emile's kind of town. The garish lights of the strip glowed and danced even more brightly and crazily than the neon world of Times Square. If people slept, it was a secret. It seemed that everyone kept the same hours as the bats and the owls, but they made a lot more noise. The noise, the action and the vibrant life of the casinos ordinarily would have drawn Emile like a powerful magnet.

But he chose shadowed corners and, preferably, the solitude of his room. He knew the questions. They were always the same. They were usually asked politely, innocently and even with compassion but Emile heard it only one way – "How do you feel after killing Paret?"

He was in the desert to corner a jackrabbit. Ralph Dupas was a slick, always moving, clever boxer whose fight plan was more to stay out of trouble than declare war. Nobody ever put him in a paper bag, but if they had he probably would have remained there because no way would he have punched his way out. At 26, he had filed for bankruptcy. He had been fighting professionally for twelve years and had 115 fights behind him and minus twelve thousand dollars in his bankbook ledger to show for it. He needed a big money fight desperately. It would have been if it had been held in his hometown of New Orleans, but New Orleans did not allow mixed-race fights. As Emile Griffith was black and Ralph Dupas was white, they could not fight in New Orleans. A couple years before, they could have. Some of the local citizenry stated that Dupas was "a Negro". He claimed he was white. He won his "race", but the fight ...

They said Emile would be reluctant to throw his right hand. He wasn't. It just didn't land. They said he'd be hesitant to charge in and corner his man. He tried, but it was like trapping a raccoon, which bounces to the left, to the right, then retreats, snarling, baring its fangs and swinging out with paws that are more effect than substance.

For the first six or seven rounds, Dupas' hit-and-run style kept him in the fight but Emile never let up on applying the pressure. As Dupas' tank slowly ran down, it seemed that Griffith's battery kept recharging, and in the fifteenth round he finally landed the right hand flush and all the things Dupas generally thinks about in a week became recycled in one resounding instant. Griffith won by a wide margin and took his usual joyous victory leap into Clancy's arms. He knew that he didn't only beat Ralph Dupas, but he had beat a second person in the ring that night. His name was Emile Griffith.

Once he had his machine revved up, Clancy didn't want to turn the motor off. He wanted to make sure he had Emile Griffith running smoothly on all cylinders. They traveled out to Tacoma, Washington two months later to fight Denny Moyer. It was two years since Emile and Moyer split back-to-back fights in New York and Oregon. Now Moyer was looking towards a middleweight title bout either in New England against Paul Pender, recognized titleholder in New York, Massachusetts and Europe, or in Chicago against Gene Fullmer, National Boxing Association middleweight champion. Denny didn't have to travel. Emile made sure he stayed at home. Even though he came in weighing 156 ¼, about ten pounds over his best fighting weight, Emile, with his speed cut and looking somewhat sluggish, kept up a relentless body attack, packaged it with a snapping, solid left jab and wore his man down while turning his face to a bloody mask.

Clancy was relieved. Emile let his fists fly. There was no holding back. Now for the real test. It was time to go home.

Howie and Gil tried to keep Emile's mind on things such as his training and his girl friend Esther. Esther may have seemed an anchor of stability to his managers. There were no "two-way streets" in their comprehension. Having a nice girlfriend precluded any other type of relationship. They even got to know the batting averages of every kid on his Little League team, the Griffs, but they couldn't shield him from the world. Not when almost every reporter interviewing him asked the focal question, "How do you feel about the Paret fight?" It got to be so bad that Emile sometimes got physically sick before an interview.

It was mid-September, 1962, just a few weeks before Griffith was to fight Don Fullmer, Gene's younger brother, in Madison Square Garden. Emile walked into the gym with two cuts on his face. They weren't bad enough to cancel the fight, but they gave Clancy a good scare.

"What the heck happened to you? Were you in a fight?"

"No, I was in no fight, Clahncy." He was mimicking, which was Emile's way of being bitchy. "I cut myself shaving." He went on to explain that he shaved without using the mirror because he kept seeing the image of Benny Paret's face alongside his own. "I see him in my dreams at night and during the day he's still there with me. I want to say – 'Benny, I am sorry', and sometimes I do but I know there'll be no answer."

Gil Clancy was not a guy who gave in to emotional jags. A tear rolling from his eye would be caused by a windblown cinder, a lump in his throat from swallowing his food wrong. So he reached out to this youngster who was now like a son to him, gripped his shoulder very hard and decided that it would be a good idea for Emile to take his show on the road. He knew that you can't run from a ghost but you can stay away from the people who keep making the ghost reappear.

Emile's excitement at hearing that he was going to fight Teddy Wright in Vienna, Austria was so great that Gil and Howie were afraid his head was not in the Fullmer fight at all. While they worried about Emile's concentrating on Fullmer, Emile's major worry was whether the people in Europe would like him. Then he worried about whether he would get to go to Europe when Gil told him that if he lost to Fullmer or got cut, the fight in Vienna was off.

"Just make sure that you use a mirror when you shave from now on." Clancy warned.

"You are one mean man, Clahncy. You probably would enjoy taking candy from children."

It was Griffith's first time back at the Garden since the Paret fight. He had one request and it was granted. He didn't want to be in the corner that Paret used that night in March.

For ten rounds he chased Don Fullmer around the Garden ring. Whenever he caught up with him, Fullmer grabbed and held on for dear life. The hardest-working person in the ring was the referee, Arthur Mercante, who was drenched in perspiration from prying Fullmer apart from Griffith, who won a lop-sided but dull 10-round decision. There was no time for a victory celebration because they had to be at the airport the next morning. Emelda Griffith was a much better grabber and holder than Don Fullmer ever dreamt of being. When his momma, who climbed into the ring for her traditional victory hug, let go of her Junior, he checked all his ribs to make sure he was still in one piece. She admonished Howie and Gil for taking her boy half way around the world but offered them a bag filled with peanut butter and jelly sandwiches that Gil suggested she give to her grandchildren.

Emile was already packed and ready to leave for Europe with his two managers and Syd Martin. He was determined to shave carefully as he looked into his medicine cabinet mirror.

The Emile Griffith-Teddy Wright fight was supposed to be for the world junior middleweight title and originally was going to be recognized by all sanctioning bodies but at fight time only the Austrian Boxing Association recognized it. The European Boxing Union and the World Boxing Association refused to permit a current champion to fight for a second crown.

Without a title on the line the ultra-modern Stadhalle which held close to 15,000 was only about two-thirds filled. When someone remarked that Vienna's world-famous Lipizzan stallions, which dance and perform to music draw a larger crowd, Emile commented, having watched their routine, "They're good but I dance better, I know more steps and I can sing. They can't."

Emile did something else that they couldn't do. He could fight. It was only Teddy Wright's longer reach and his instinct for survival that enabled him to last the full fifteen rounds against the ever-aggressive, savage hooking champion.

There was another guy on the card who could also lay claim to being a better dancer than the great white stallions. Forty-two year old Sugar

Ray Robinson, fighting his first preliminary fight in twenty-two years, knocked out Diego Infantes of Spain in 1 minute and 15 seconds of the second round, saving and flashing his dance routine for night-clubbing a little later.

That night Sugar Ray Robinson and Emile Griffith, with two statuesque blonds as their companions, hit Vienna's trendier clubs and tapped out some rhythmic steps far removed from a Viennese Waltz. No great white stallions ever had it so good.

Jack Singer had a dilemma. Here he was in Las Vegas bad-mouthing a guy who had been one of his best and most loyal customers at his bargain basement Times Square steak house, the Flame Steak. Emile Griffith had just arrived from Austria with a belt that had little more value than to hold up his pants and was now ready to take on Jack's Argentine warrior, Jorge Fernandez. Formal introductions were not necessary as they had fought twice before, both fights at St. Nick's arena almost two-and-a-half years ago. Griffith got the decision in both fights but the first one was so hotly disputed that it caused a major riot. As far as Jack Singer was concerned, the second fight was just as big a stinker. He had some most unkind words to say about Griffith and asked the Nevada commission to watch out for dirty tactics. This despite the fact that Emile testified that there was such a thing as a truly good steak for $1.19, which was the product that enabled Jack Singer to provide room and board for his stable of fighters from home and abroad. "It even comes with a salad and a baked potato," the champ confirmed.

How does one denigrate such loyalty? Jack Singer was certainly tougher than any of his steaks. Obviously, Jorge Fernandez wasn't. He lay on the canvas going, "Ooh, ooh, ooh ..." in the ninth round, refusing to continue after taking an accidental low blow. The fight was awarded to Griffith. Jorge Fernandez wasn't even rewarded with a screen test for his performance.

It was a Griffith crowd so no one was disappointed. He had become the darling of the Strip. Nancy Sinatra and Tommy Sands were among his most stalwart fans, wearing matching "Emile Griffith" sweaters. Nancy had even brought Emile to her parents' home in Hoboken, New

Jersey for dinner. Her mother, Dolly, was there to console and comfort Emile after the Paret tragedy.

Emile Griffith captivated people wherever he went. Nobody was too important for him to approach and chat with, and no one was too insignificant or trivial for Emile to include in his group or in conversation. Emile enjoyed everyone as long as they enjoyed being with him. It was the Griffith mystique.

For Griffith, Las Vegas was close to being the perfect town. No clocks, day and night were blended as one. He starred at the crap tables, where everyone was his friend except for the dice. In the nightclubs, he was called on stage to be introduced and, sometimes, to entertain. Shyness surrendered to showmanship. With an infectious smile warming them up, he sang and danced his way into his audience's heart. He loved the spotlight because he loved to be loved and everybody loved the guy in the spotlight.

Meanwhile, Clancy's bicep measurements increased by almost an inch, he claims, from the vigorous exertion of continually hauling enamored young ladies from Griff's bed. Clancy says it was similar in principle to Charles Atlas' Dynamic Tension program, but a lot more interesting. It wasn't that Gil was a killjoy, but, after all, his fighter was in training. Whether Emile's playmates got there by invasion or by invitation, Clancy did not know. All he knows is that his champion did not seem unhappy.

"That was the toughest thing in the world for me. God, I loved that man Clancy and Howard, too. They were more to me than any father could have been. I could not hurt them. Maybe if I felt Clancy would smile the same way pulling a guy out of my bed like he did finding a girl there – I don't know – I might have acted in a different way. So many times I wanted to say, 'Meet my boyfriend … my partner ….' They saw Matthew clinging to me and hanging out with me all the time. Other people around us – guys in the gym, family and friends – they all saw us and knew. But Gil, he saw what he wanted to see. I don't think anyone, except maybe Mommie, meant more to me than Gil. And I wasn't going to hurt him, no matter what. I also think to myself, wouldn't it be funny if, all along, Gil knew and couldn't talk to me about it. Maybe not funny; sad!"

I know, I'm the one who made my life more difficult, I'm the one who was afraid to be honest. But I was so sure that the two people I cared about more than anyone else wouldn't be able to deal with the truth."

What Clancy eventually found out was that ever since the Paret fight, Emile's cousin Bernard, in an effort to keep the champ's mind away from the tragic outcome, kept a steady stream of girls flowing into Emile's hotel room. Emile never locked the door.

Las Vegas was a world of bright lights and Life. As long as he didn't sleep, there was no room for ghosts.

CHAPTER TEN

The last composition Emile Griffith remembered writing was his 10th grade report, "What I Did On My Summer Vacation" and here he was, in a hotel room in Pittsburgh trying to write an acceptance speech for having been voted the 1963 Fighter of the Year by the Boxing Writers Association.

He had taken a book of great speeches from his local library in Hollis to use as a guide. "Clahncy, you were a school teacher. I need some help. How about this one? *'Friends, Romans, countrymen, lend me your ears.'*"

"That's for a funeral, not an acceptance speech."

"I'm glad you weren't my teacher. Nothing I read to you is good. One speech you tell me is to free the slaves, another one is what you say when you are being hanged as a patriotic spy for your country, now, a funeral ... Did anyone ever pass in your class?"

"Okay, Emile, then just say 'Thanks.' It's easy to memorize also."

"I need something a little longer to show appreciation, don't I, kind sir?"

Gil, who is thumbing through the local papers, doesn't bother looking up. "Okay – 'Thank you very, very much.'"

"It will be a lot more enjoyable dealing with Mr. Hurricane Carter tomorrow night than with you, Clahncy!"

The bright lights of Pittsburgh did not tempt Emile as those in Las Vegas did. Sparks and bursts of flame shooting from chimney stacks of steel mills did not hold his interest the way the neon world of the Strip did. This saved Gil a couple of dollars. He did not have to spend money for a leash to keep Emile from straying. And it gave Emile the opportunity to concentrate and possibly turn out his best composition since 10th grade.

He could have started his Fighter of the Year acceptance speech by relating how he got a great Dane for his 25th birthday present on February 3rd. Actually, Chris Christensen was not such a great Dane. He was no dog. He was a good, tough Dane who had held the European welterweight championship, but was simply not in Griffith's class.

Emile, who felt uncomfortable in Copenhagen at first because "*I was the only person in the whole city who wasn't a blond and didn't ride around on a bicycle,*" didn't take long finding plenty of comfort zones, like Tivoli Gardens, sipping a Sinalco soda pop at Frascati's, or just taking in the sights along Vesterbrogade.

Chris Christensen, although he wasn't looking for it, also found a comfort zone, the canvas in the middle of the ring at the Forum Hall. Actually, Griffith arranged it for him. He pounded the willing but outgunned Dane savagely, beating him to a bloody mess. After dropping him for the third time in the ninth round, Emile looked towards the referee, Robert Seidler, but the referee wouldn't stop the fight. Visions of "the accident" danced before Emile's eyes and he stepped back. He didn't want to throw another punch. A towel came sailing into the ring from Christensen's handlers. It was over. Emile walked to the Dane's corner and hugged him.

Gil and Howie did everything they could to shield their fighter and Emile struggled, trying to put it all in perspective. They sailed across an ocean hoping the change and new faces would help keep his mind off "the accident", which is how Emile referred to it, unable to even mutter Paret's name. As hard as they tried they could not keep Emile in a vacuum and there were guys out there who made life miserable for the kid. A typewriter and a meat-axe have very little in common. Yet, there are those who cannot tell the difference. They can do a hatchet job with either one. Completely ignoring the inner torment and pain he was going through, they branded him with ink that burned just as much as any hot iron.

February 4th 1963, Desmond Hackett, who may have been beating the drums for an Emile Griffith-Brian Curvis fight, blindsided Griffith in the

London Daily Express. He was not bound by any equivalent of the Marquis of Queensbury rules or any sense of fair play to keep his punches up.

'*Emile Griffith, the fearsome-looking welterweight champion of the world, turned on a fighting show of brutality, and indifferently clubbed 36-year-old Dane Chris Christensen into ninth-round defeat here yesterday.*

Griffith belabored the durable Dane so mercilessly the referee stopped the fight in the same second that the white towel of surrender came in to save Christensen from further senseless, pitiless slaughter.

Having completed his dour destruction Griffith contemptuously rippled his mighty muscles as though defying the whole of Denmark to take away his world titles.

... Griffith shattered Christensen without feeling much more pain than he would have endured during a rather stiff workout.

In the evening he entertained at a victory celebration party he had ordered before the fight.

How fearsome is Griffith? Should (Brian) Curvis be kept away from this man who knows no pity and who will cripple or destroy those who seek to take his titles?

Griffith cunningly concealed this animal aggression today or, if he did not, Curvis will have a victory choir of 60,000 saluting his world championship in Cardiff Arms Park in mid-June.

... My opinion is that Griffith, who has the odd off-fight job of hat designer, revealed a frightening streak of ring sadism. He appeared to enjoy mauling the brave and ageing Dane.

There were times when it looked as though the next coldly exploded hook would be the merciful end for Christensen. Instead Griffith danced away on easy gliding feet, only his eyes betraying his remorseless urge to inflict more punishment.

He completely ignored the demands of his manager: "Don't fool around, get in and pin him."

... I thought and hoped the fight would be over in the first round. Christensen may have been inviting an early and possibly

less painful execution, but he committed the folly of clubbing Griffith's dark expressionless head.

Griffith obviously does not like this sort of treatment. He glowered and blasted back with hooks that sent the Dane tottering back like a novice on stilts.

Griffith grimly carried on with the thrashing and during the early rounds the dull thud of pain-packed punches blasting against the Dane sounded ominously like a scaffold being erected.

In the third round Griffith drilled in a right to the head that compelled Christensen to take a count of eight.

Griffith may have been attempting to conceal his true menace but he painfully showed he could be a cruel fighter. He shoulder charged, held, grabbed and charged in head first.

But the inevitable came in the ninth and I was relieved when it was over.

Curvis is young and powerful and may be a shade impetuous for a man like Griffith. But a hurt Griffith is a mighty dangerous animal.'

Howie Albert kept this article for over forty years. "Here was a guy who even turned Emile's reluctance to throw any punches because he didn't want to hurt his man any more into an act of sadism. He resorted to the vilest stereotypes – 'Griffith's dark, expressionless head' – and his distortion of facts bordered on the libelous. All we could do was share some of the pain. It wasn't enough."

*** *

Emile was having a lot more trouble with his speech than he ever expected. That was partly because he had nothing to write with. He thought better while chewing on something and the only thing he had to chew on was his pencil, which had now become not much of a pencil at all.

"Maybe I should not mention the California fight with that ugly man, Rodriguez. What do you think, Clahncy?"

"I think that being that they're all boxing writers, there's a good chance they know about it whether you mention it or not. Anyhow, that was a good fight to lose."

It was three days short of one year since the tragic fight with Paret when Griffith dropped his title on a close decision to Luis Rodriguez in Los Angeles. Two-and-a-half months later, June 8th, 1963, Emile Griffith made history at Madison Square Garden against the same Luis Rodriquez, by becoming the first man ever to win the welterweight championship three times, a mark he could never have achieved without losing the previous fight. The fight was also historic as it was the first fight utilizing a fourth strand of ring rope and the fighters wore 8-ounce rather than the customary 6-ounce gloves. So, ironically, Emile Griffith, whose disastrous fight with Benny Paret brought about these new safety regulations, was the first fighter to participate with the new code in place.

Irony seemed to go hand-in-hand with action and surprises in Griffith's encounters with Rodriquez. There was a special irony to the night Griffith lost his title to Rodriquez at Dodger Stadium in Los Angeles. Following that fight, Sugar Ramos knocked out Davey Moore in a featherweight championship bout. Emile was back in his hotel room when he heard that Davey Moore had died, almost one year to the day of Emile's fight with Paret. He looked at Gil but didn't say a word. Clancy was glad. There were certain questions that simply had no answers. They packed their suitcases in silence. It was time to move on.

After a relatively easy win over veteran trial-horse Holly Mims, Emile journeyed to San Juan, Puerto Rico and decisioned local favorite Jose Monon Gonzalez. Then he got the call telling him that he was voted Fighter of the Year by the Boxing Writers Association and he's been working on his speech ever since.

It's not that Emile Griffith didn't believe in Santa Claus. A grown man, especially a World Champion must conduct himself in a certain manner. So, the day before the fight – December 19, 1963 – after a light workout at the gym, Howie Albert, who likes to check out ladies' hats wherever he goes, stops off with Emile at Kaufmann's department store where there is a much longer line of children waiting to see Santa Claus than there is for ladies hats. Howie turns and asks, "Why don't you hang out here while I check out some hats?"

Emile gives Howie that impatient look he conjures up so easily. "What should I do, sit on Santa's lap and ask him for a present?" He doesn't realize that he is speaking louder than he intended. One by one, the little heads on the line turn and stare at Emile. The Kaufmann Santa, sitting on a raised platform, smiles and asks, "Well, would you like to come up here and see what Santa can do for you?"

Emile smiled politely, shook his head and walked away with Howie to look at some ladies' hats. He did not get a Christmas present.

It's not known whether Rubin "Hurricane" Carter visited Santa Claus but he definitely got a very nice Christmas gift and he didn't even wait for Christmas Eve to enjoy it.

On December 20th, Emile Griffith heard only one bell and it was not a jingle bell. It was the bell sounding the start of the first round. It was the only bell that was needed that night. He remembers coming out quickly and scoring well with the left hand. He knows what happened after that because he read about it in the Pittsburgh Post-Gazette the next morning. He knows that he climbed off the canvas at the count of nine after taking a hard left hook to the head and he also knew, both from the newspaper and trying to chew his toast, that it was a very hard right to the jaw that floored him again. He got up but the referee wrapped his arms around him, which was okay with Emile because there was no way the fight could have gone on anyhow, the way the whole arena was swaying and tilting.

Emile Griffith learned a new word. It was *chagrin*. And he learned how to deal with it. Three weeks after the Carter fight, Emile walks from the dais table to the lectern at the Americana Hotel in New York when he is officially announced the recipient of the Edward J. Neil Memorial Plaque for the Boxing Writers Association Fighter of the Year. The acceptance speech that he had worked on for so long and so laboriously had long since been reduced to a reasonable facsimile of confetti. There's a lot of throat clearing and har-umphs as this slightly uncomfortable audience cannot imagine what the first Fighter of the Year in the Boxing Writers Association's history to have been flattened between the time he was voted the award (December 4, 1963) and the night of its presentation (January 12, 1964) could possibly say.

"Ladies and Gentlemen," he sang out with his Caribbean-flavored dialect, *"a funny thing happened to me on the way here. I met a guy named Rubin Carter and he looked down at me and said, 'Get up, Griffith, that ain't no place for the fighter of the year.'"* The ballroom went wild. Emile Griffith was a far better extemporaneous speaker than he was a speech writer.

"Now I have some awards that I have to give out to my managers Gil Clancy and Howard Albert and my cornerman, Syd Martin. They are extremely uplifting awards. In fact they will be known as the Uplifters of the Year and that is for lifting me off the canvas in Pittsburgh without ever dropping me once."

He may have been the Fighter of the Year to the rest of the world, but to Gil and Howie, Emile was still the kid they had to take care of. They wanted him to forget the Carter fight so they took him as far away from Pittsburgh and New York as you can get, to Sydney, Australia to fight an opponent as different from Carter as could be found, clever, slipping and sliding master boxer, Ralph Dupas. Maybe it worked and maybe it didn't. Dupas had been Emile's first opponent after the tragic Paret fight so Emile knew who he was, but it seemed as though he was seeing Carter. He fought with a fury and purpose that shocked the capacity crowd of 10,500 in the arena.

He hammered the game but completely outgunned Dupas to the canvas three times in the second round with the crowd screaming at referee Vic Patrick to stop it. With less than a minute left in the third round Griffith unleashed a thunderous overhand left that caught Dupas flush on the chin and sent him crashing to the canvas where he lay motionless, his face covered with blood. Any thoughts or images of Rubin "Hurricane" Carter were gone. Emile wouldn't go to his corner. He stood outside the cluster of medics and ambulance men who now surrounded the still-inert form of Ralph Dupas. Howie Albert gently tugged at his elbow to bring him back to his corner but Emile shook him off. He stayed there for five minutes. Life, expression and motion returned to him seconds after it did to Dupas. As the New Orleans veteran was helped to his feet, Emile's chest heaved and his head nodded slightly, as though he was giving thanks to someone or something. He was asked if he was thinking about Benny "Kid" Paret. He said "no". Emile Griffith usually told the truth – but not always.

CHAPTER ELEVEN

Emile Griffith was not the kind of guy who would call out, "Mommie!" every time he was in trouble. But if he did, he would not have been in trouble for long because Emelda Griffith was one Momma who took very good care of her boy. She was Emile's Chubby Checker, but when this Chubby Checker did the Twist it was more like Shake, Rattle and Roll.

Allen Rosenfeld, Ring Magazine's former Detroit correspondent, remembers on a visit to New York, going to the Tavern-On-The-Green in Central Park for dinner and seeing Emile Griffith come in with his mother. Just as he was about to walk over and introduce himself, a couple of wise guys at a nearby table gave a wolf whistle and said something about Griffith that disproved the fact that they were truly wise guys. It wasn't uncommon for malicious whispers and cutting remarks to be said behind Emile's back, but only a major league blockhead would say anything loud enough for Momma to hear.

"I never knew a pocket book could do so much damage," Rosenfeld recalled. "What I remember is that those guys did not stay for dessert."

***

Emelda Griffith liked airplanes very much. She just did not like to fly in them. She preferred the train and as they did not have a train that went across the Atlantic Ocean she did not join Emile in Italy when he fought Juan Carlos Duran, which was probably a very fortunate circumstance for the present-day Roman Empire.

The Italian sportswriters played up the angle of a "killer" puncher, graphically detailing the Paret fight and packaging it with Griffith's crushing knockout of Ralph Dupas just a month before. Anticipating a show equal to some of the Christian vs. Lion spectacles at the old Colloseum, the Roman gentry put their lire on the line and filed into the Palazzo dello Sport with bags of food, fruit, vegetables and bottles of chianti to further their evening's pleasure. But what they saw was more like a chariot race without chariots.

Juan Carlos Duran ran backwards and sideways very fast, even faster than Emile could run forward. As the referee, Fernando Pica, was much slower than Duran, the only one he was able to communicate with was Griffith and as he did not speak a language that Griffith could understand, he resorted to a sign language of sorts. He kept rapping Griffith on the back of the head. What this meant was open to interpretation, but the referee was definitely the only one scoring points. Besides being very angry and yelling what you knew had to be bad words even without understanding them, the Italian fans went home hungry because all of their scrumptious fruits, vegetables, and even their bottles of vino, wound up being heaved into the ring.

Near the end of the seventh round, Pica, the referee, ankle-deep in garbage, waved his arms and announced in Italian, "I suspend this fight because it isn't safe to go on." Even though Griffith was well ahead on all scorecards, the fight was declared no contest.

"I was so upset, I didn't bother to shower, which made Clancy more upset than me because I smelled pretty bad. He said it was anchovies and he was probably right because it seemed like every cat in Rome followed us back to the hotel. I guess it's better to get hit with an anchovy than with a bottle.

Now, I don't need anyone fighting my battles for me but we hardly got inside when the phone rings and it's my Momma who tells me she has been calling and calling from our house in Hollis to find out about the fight and if I am all right. I assured her I was fine and that I did not lose. "Oh, so how did you win, knockout or decision?"

"Well, Momma, I didn't say I won."

"A draw? You must have been tired, Junior."

Clancy took the phone from my hand. That man can be such a troublemaker. When he finishes telling her what happened, she is trying to figure how to get right over and is making all kinds of threats and promises. I tell her I can take care of myself and explain to her to stop blaming it on Mussolini because he is already dead. She shouts at me that I cannot take care of myself, that I should come right back home and I am never to go back to that place again!

About some things, Momma does know best, so I took her advice and went right back home."

Emile's Momma was waiting for her boy but it was late at night when the taxi brought him in from LaGuardia and she had dozed off when she heard, "Somebody is sleeping in my bed!" Emelda jumped up and the first thought in her befogged mind was, "My God! It is Goldilocks!"

She raced down to the basement to where the commotion was coming from and saw Emile standing over his bed, his suitcase still in his hand. "Who are you?"

The smiling face that lifted up from the pillow answered in a sing-song very much like Emile's. "I am so happy to be meeting you. I am your cousin Winston."

"Junior," his mother cut in, embracing him in a bear hug as she spoke, "I'm so glad you are home, my baby. Meet your cousin Winston Wheatley. He has come in from St. Thomas to spend a weekend here with us." It turned out to be an extraordinarily long weekend, lasting three years.

Emile originally had a choice bedroom on the main floor. As he kept bringing over his brothers and sisters from St. Thomas he moved to the attic and when his sister Gloria moved in with her five chidren, Emile wound up in a small room in the basement, just a few feet from the door that leads outside, making it very convenient for Emile to leave and find a place where he can sleep in his own bed in peace and quiet.

If you live in New York, finding peace and quiet usually entails crossing a river, so that is what Emile did. He crossed the Hudson and there, directly opposite Manhattan – whose bright lights spanned the river but whose sounds didn't – was the city of Weehawken. To Emile it meant sleep, peace and privacy. To visitors, it generally meant shock, awe and wonder. Weehawken was in New Jersey but Emile's pad made you think that you were lost somewhere in the Montmarte section of Paris. Red carpeting, a circular bed, French Provincial sofas, walls decorated with cupids and closets filled with enough pairs of hip-hugging pants, frilly shirts and heavy gold jewelry to make one wonder whether Madame DuBarry was expected for dinner.

Madame DuBarry obviously was not expected for dinner, although she would probably have been a most welcome visitor. Such was not the case for her presumptive host, Emile Griffith.

Emile was not a sophisticated shopper when it came to the local A&P and since he liked his tea sweet, it was important that he have an ample supply of sugar on hand. He did not. As Emile hadn't read Shakespeare's "Hamlet", he did not know to "neither a borrower nor a lender be."

He knocked on plenty of neighbors' doors, but couldn't get his tea sweetened. As no door was opened to him, he thought that it was strange that no one seemed to be at home in the building, and it really gave him cause to wonder until he noticed that the peephole openings moved. Whenever he passed or saw a neighbor, either in the hallway or in the elevator, he smiled and greeted them. No response was forthcoming.

It wasn't until he spoke with the building janitor, who was of Jamaican extraction and the only other non-caucasian on the block, that he began to grasp the situation. "How come nobody in this building knows I'm alive?" he asked.

"Oh, they know you're alive, okay," the janitor answered as he pushed his mop along the terrazzo lobby floor. "They just never had no one like you living in the building before. You do see you're different than them, don't you?" he grinned. "Maybe they just got to get used to you."

Emile nodded his head slowly. "Uh-huh. I see. So that's it."

A couple of days later when his momma came to visit him with his sister Gloria and asked how he liked his new home and new neighbors, he explained to her, "None of them have spoken to me yet. They have never lived with a welterweight champion before. I suppose it will take some getting used to." For a while Emile made sure to buy his own sugar but with his infectious smile and friendly disposition it didn't take long for his neighbors to accept this welterweight champion among them.

"I missed seeing my Chubby Checker every day, but those days we didn't see each other we would talk on the phone four or five times. Gil and Howie were investing my money in mutual funds and I think they were smart enough to buy Bell Telephone for me."

***

Not too many guys with thick crests of wavy red hair worry about going bald. Howie Albert was an exception because he found it very difficult to restrain himself from pulling out handful after handful of his hair every time he sat down and tried explaining to his stockboy-millinery designer-turned World Champion that the two sets of keys in his pockets opened the front door to a house in Hollis and an apartment in Weehawken. Neither one of them opened the door to Fort Knox. Counting his four sisters, three brothers, five nieces and his mother, he had an extended family of cousins and such that brought the total number of people who were Emile Griffith's "dependents" to seventeen.

"I didn't mind when Emile treated himself to a wardrobe that was so large it just about needed its own apartment. He's entitled. He works hard and deserves to see the fruits of his labor. But he was like a quartermaster. He was clothing an army and paying for the educations of his brothers, sisters, and nephews. His mother was decked out like the Queen of Sheba. I loved Emelda, even though she was buying hats from other milliners! I told Emile that the arithmetic didn't work. You can't spend more than you got coming in. Gil and I wanted to invest in a future for him but Emile's smile can fool you. He's as stubborn as a mule."

"If my Mommie needs money or wants to buy anything, I want her to have it. She is the queen in my family. That's what my money is for!"

Howie Albert kept a big ledger book on Emile but he would explain, "One ledger book wasn't enough. You needed two for Emile – one for what he gave from his pockets and one for what he gave from his heart. No matter which ledger book you went to, Emile Griffith was no piker."

Emile had just finished training and was getting ready to walk over to Macy's and buy a complete Hawaiian wardrobe to bring with him to Honolulu for his fight with Stan Harrington when his cousin Bernard Forbes entered the gym.

"I don't know," Emile said, shaking his head either in admiration or wonder, "first you are my number two cheerleader, then you want to take my title from me and now you are a movie star?" He is referring to the fact that Bernard is wearing a pair of dark glasses in a gymnasium that last saw sunlight just before the roof was installed.

Bernard walked over and hugged his cousin in a strong embrace. Emile noticed that from behind the glasses a tear was trickling slowly down his cheek. Bernard Forbes adored his cousin. He wanted to emulate him in every way, so he started putting on boxing gear in the gym and copying all of Emile's moves. At first, nobody paid much attention, but that didn't last for long. Gil started working with him and in a short time, people would gather around to watch when "Emile's shadow" climbed into the ring to spar.

Maybe Emile was watching too, but not closely enough. At least not the evening that Clancy sent Bernard in to spar with him. To this day Emile says he would have loved to have seen the right hand that dumped him to the "Oohs" and "Aahs" of the trainers and fighters in the gym. That's when Bernard Forbes decided to become a prizefighter, with the full blessings of Gil, Howie and Emile.

Bernard made his pro debut at Sunnyside Gardens less than three weeks after Emile's loss to Hurricane Carter. He won by a second round knockout and went on from there to roll off six straight wins. Everyone was saying that a new star was born. Nobody thought too much of the accidental thumb he took in the eye on the way to his last victory. It caused some headaches and blurry vision. When it didn't clear up in a few days Gil sent him to see Doctor Edwin Campbell, the Athletic Commission doctor.

"Maybe I should consider being an actor," Bernard smiled, "because I ain't goin' to be doin' any more fighting." Doc Campbell brought in an opthamologist to examine him and they concurred that he had a detached retina and his boxing career was over.

Now it was Emile's turn to have a tear course down his cheek. He never was very good at hiding emotion, except when he was the injured party. "I know why you're doing this, Bernard. You just want to let me hold onto my crown. Just stick with me. We're a team." And Emile took care of Bernard from that day forward. It wasn't that Bernard couldn't take care of himself, Emile just wasn't going to take chances. There was the time they were visiting St. Thomas to relax, stretch out on the beach and have some fun dancing at the local clubs in the evening. One man's fun often unleashes another man's demons. Bernard, always sociable, glib and often at his debonair best when with a pretty, young damsel was merely doing his thing, but this time with the wrong damsel.

Emile backed away from the bar and saw a group of not very pleasant-looking guys turn and follow Bernard and the girl when they left for a walk on the beach. It was obvious that one of these guys had some sort of exclusive with the young lady and was mad enough to spread his anger around for all his buddies to share. Emile didn't count. He was too busy. Bernard had nothing better to do since his cousin was doing all the work, so he did count. There were seven, then there were six, five, four ...

A lot of sand was stirred up, the only sounds were the thwacking of bone on bone, some oohs and ahs, a few grunts and then the clapping of someone's hands.

"Well done, Cousin," Bernard smiled at the only other person left. "You got to be careful with those fists. Let me look."

He ran his fingers over Emile's knuckles. Emile grinned, "And you've got to watch what girls you chase after."

"How? You know I've got bad eyes!" Then he embraced his cousin who he knew was always there for him.

Even after Emile retired, he had Bernard Forbes work with him training young fighters. Whatever Bernard needed throughout his life, Emile made sure he had. This type of extravagance Howie Albert did not object to.

While Howie tried to protect Emile from Emelda and himself, Emelda was there to protect her son from everything else. But a big, tough, loving and a bit overbearing momma can only do so much. She couldn't protect Emile from dreams and visions, if that's what they were. To Emile they were real.

At various times he would see Paret at the foot of his bed; he saw him in the solitude of his dressing room after training. He would tell Gil and Howie about it and he would tell Emelda. He even told the press at first, but eventually he learned to say that it was all in the past and that he was okay now. The truth was that the images of Benny Paret were with Emile Griffith for much of his life. It even extended beyond Benny Paret. There was the day that Emile came into the gym shortly before leaving to fight Brian Curvis in London. He had this beatific smile on his face when he walked over to Gil and told him that he had been driving around his old Harlem neighborhood (besides his wardrobe Emile developed a penchant for Lincoln-Continentals) before coming to the gym. " .... and as I turned a corner I saw two little colored boys standing on the sidewalk.

The smallest was about seven and right then I got a feeling I'd seen him someplace before.

I drove around the block and when I got by him again I said: 'Hi.'

He said, 'Hi," and got in the car. I was ready to tell him he should never get in a stranger's car but I didn't feel like a stranger and maybe he felt the same.

I asked him his name and he said, 'Benny Paret. What's yours?'

Looking right at him I said: 'Emile Griffith.'

He didn't blink or nothing, and I felt that it was the same with him as it was with me - it was like magnets – we just knew.

He sat there fooling around with the car, and when I said I've got to be going he put his arms around my neck and hugged me. I hugged him back. I couldn't see him clearly then because my eyes were filled with tears. For years, how I've wanted to say, "I'm sorry" and now I was finally able to, but how do you explain to a seven year old. So I just whispered "I'm sorry" as I hugged him. I couldn't help crying as he got out of the car."

In November, 2003, Benny Paret, Jr., who was living in Miami with his mother Lucia, came to New York for the filming of Dan Klores' documentary of the Griffith-Paret saga. For Emile it was a reunion; for Benny, a first meeting. He had no memory of their prior encounter, although Gil Clancy says that it was no daydream or imagination as he went with Emile on subsequent visits to see young Benny Paret, Jr.

There were nights where Emile couldn't go back to sleep after seeing Benny Paret at the foot of his bed, so he'd drive from Weehawken to the house in Hollis. Momma would then cradle his head and comfort him but she couldn't keep the image of Benny Paret away.

CHAPTER TWELVE

There was something else Mommie couldn't help Emile with. That's because there are certain territories that are strictly off-limits to a mother.

Emile came back from Hawaii with a half-dozen over-ripe pineapples which they wouldn't permit him to take through customs, seventeen Hawaiian leis – one for each member of the household – and an authentic hula skirt for Emelda. He knew to get the largest size they made, but Momma said he should have known to get two of them; that she could have sewn them together and then, maybe, just maybe, it would have fit. "You're dealing with the Equator, Junior," she emphasized, pointing to her waist, "not a Pole."

The Hawaiian press beat the drums, trying to convince the Islanders that Stan Harrington's big punch and the fact that Griffith's style was made to order for Harrington should make it a very tough fight. They may have convinced a lot of people, as a record crowd turned out at the Honolulu International Center, but Stan Harrington was not one of them. For Harrington, Emile's tremendous right hand flush on his nose in the fourth round was much more convincing. He contemplated it from a prone position and decided to do so for more than ten seconds. He was very happy to be able to get up and pose with Griffith for some post-fight pictures. He was even happier to say "Aloha."

Gil Clancy's training methods were not always orthodox or by the book. There was such a large number of the press corps sitting around the tennis courts at the Thunderbird Hotel In Las Vegas, you'd think that Bill Tilden had come back to play Don Budge. Not that the two players out there were uninteresting, but it was a surprise to some of the guys on the boxing beat that with Griffith's fight against Luis Rodriguez less than a week away, there he was, racing back and forth on a tennis court under a sizzling afternoon sun. And instead of his trainer jumping in and putting an end to it, he was the guy on the other side of the net.

Afterwards, wiping his face with a towel, Clancy explained that the movements on a tennis court were very similar to those of a fighter in the ring. It was stop and start, side to side, backwards and forward, turning from the hip, getting your power from your legs. Much more beneficial than plain roadwork.

Someone asked Emile how long they "trained" on the tennis court, pointing out that they had been playing for more than two hours.

"That depends. If I'm winning, we just keep playing on and on. If Clahncy should happen to take the lead, which does not happen very often, he'll come up to the net and say, 'Okay, Emile, I think you've had a good enough workout for today.'"

"There was nothing Emile attempted that he didn't excel at, especially if it involved athleticism," Clancy explained. "Whether it was tennis, ping-pong, baseball, basketball, he simply had that natural instinct and ability to pick it up almost immediately. It was like a mother bird tossing her young ones from their nest to teach them to fly. It just came naturally. And it was not limited only to sports. You put him in front of a microphone to sing or out on the dance floor, whatever he did, he mastered it quicker than anyone else I've ever known."

"Don't forget hat designing," said the red-headed guy in slightly tight-fitting white tennis shorts walking onto the court.

"And who are you?" asked one of the younger reporters who did not know Howie Albert.

Emile smiled a devilish grin. "He's the ball boy. That way I don't have to over-exert myself."

Playing along, Howie bent down to pick up a ball and lost his job before it began when the seam on the seat of his shorts ripped open.

The toughest part of tennis for Emile was the scoring. When Gil would call out fifteen-love, Emile would ask what the score was in numbers. Gil would explain that "love" was nothing. Emile found out that this applied to more than tennis.

When he came back from Vegas, after another hard-fought split-decision victory over Rodriquez, he took stock of his personal life. He walked around his Weehawken pad and shook his head. His bed was unmade, just as it was when he left; it wasn't easy making a round bed. He felt a little better when he went to his clothes closet and counted out his seventeen mod suits, and a neat mountain of slacks and sweaters. All that glittered in his night table drawer was gold, from his swanky four hundred dollar watch to the rings and cufflinks that he fingered lovingly. But there were still some dishes and silverware in the sink waiting for him for over two weeks.

Matthew, who had been living with Emile's family while he was away for the Harrington and Rodriquez fights, came over and started straightening out the apartment. Emile hadn't kept it a secret from friends or boxing reporters that he and this sweet kid Esther were going steady but he also had let them know that he wasn't ready to settle down. Now he was thinking of changing his mind and he told Matthew.

"What are you looking for, a wife or a maid?"

"Are you crazy?" Emile snapped. "We love each other. With all my traveling and running around, it's not fair to her."

"Man, you are full of shit!"

Whether Emile was or wasn't became moot.

Momma was the first one to find out. "What do you mean, she said 'No'? Is that girl out of her mind?"

"It's not exactly that she said 'No'. Her grandma, your friend, was the one who said 'No'. She told Esther that I am too dark-skinned."

"Now, ain't that the damndest kind of prejudice you ever heard?" Emelda fumed. "You can't even take it to the NAACP. Don't that girl have no backbone?"

"I guess her grandma is the boss. What she says, goes. I mean, she wasn't nasty or nothing. She said I'm still welcome for tea and cake whenever I want."

"What – you mean she didn't say you had to use the back door? I just don't believe it. That sweet little girl Esther, don't she know what love is about?"

Emile thought back to his tennis education with Gil and smiled wryly, hugging Momma as he whispered hoarsely, "Love is nothing, Momma. Love is nothing."

Maybe forty years dulls the memory because when you tell Emile that it must have really hurt, he shrugs and says, "No. Not really. That's life. Anyhow, I don't chase after what isn't willing to chase after me."

Emile was pretty good at covering up and he didn't have to be in the ring to do it. He found himself drifting back to his favorite spots along 42nd Street where he always seemed to feel safe and at home. All the while that he and Esther were a visible twosome, the petty talk and back-room gossip had pretty much faded away. Now people began talking again.

Emile Griffith never lurked in the shadows with a collar pulled high around his neck. He never sneaked inconspicuously through a side door when no one was looking. He found a world of people that he liked. When he was down or depressed they knew how to raise his spirits. They knew when to give him his space and they knew when to comfort him. It was Emile's perfect world and everyone in it was good. That's what he believed and that's how Emile was. People and places were good until and unless they proved otherwise. But he gave them that head start. They started out good, which meant that he could eat, drink and make merry, then lay his head down on the bar and drowse off without a thing to worry about. Fortunately, he had a Kathy Hogan to watch over him.

The bars that Kathy tended may not have been palaces, but Kathy Hogan was, without question, the Queen of 46th Street. Bars changed, names changed but the clientele remained pretty much the same. She catered to a mainly Gay crowd – but through it all, she ran a pretty tight ship. However, on the best of ships, an occasional rat will always find its way on board. She didn't want any rats nibbling at Emile. Whether he instinctively gravitated towards her, or Kathy had some dormant maternal feelings that surfaced for Emile, she became his watchdog, protector and Fairy Godmother. When Emile's head rested on the bar and he sailed off to slumberland, Kathy would gently take his cash, remove his jewelry, any expensive coats or jackets he might have come in with and stash everything away for safe keeping. Kathy Hogan, who knew there was no such thing as a perfect world, or a perfect watering hole, made Emile's world as close to perfect as could be.

Emile's attitude never changed. He always held onto that one simple criteria for judging people – if they were nice to him, then they were good. Nothing meant more to Emile than a sincere pat on the back and a warm smile. Emile Griffith walked through the front doors of his midtown haunts to be with people who cared for him. He, in turn, cared for them.

He used to get defensive when asked about who he hung out with. Three days before the Paret fight, Milton Gross, New York Post columnist who spent a lot of time with Emile, asked him about the rumors that were going around about him.

"People tell my managers they see me with the wrong people," Griffith replied. *"If I am stopped on the street and a person asks me a question, that doesn't mean I am with him. Gil and Howie and I know I don't do anything wrong."* – Boxing Yearbook 1963 Edition

Howie Albert always understood Emile. The problem is, he says, too many other people don't. "A boxer projects a certain image. It's like a strong stereotype. A boxer is not supposed to be a good, gentle soul, who can even cry at sad parts in movies or over someone else's problem. He's supposed to have a low, rough voice and talk with "dese" and "dems", not a high-pitched musical voice with some kind of English accent. Who ever heard of a boxer who kisses the hands of ladies when introduced to them? He's more at home playing street games with a bunch of raggedy kids than hanging out in a poolroom or bar with the guys. Maybe if he acted like a gangster or a bum, he'd get more respect, or at least they'd understand him more."

Over time Emile's attitude changed. There was still denial but it was softer and not nearly as emphatic. There seemed almost to be a need for Emile to explain.

"Let people think what they want. All of my friends are good people. If I hang out with a Chinese friend and I tell you he's a good person, that doesn't make me Chinese.

It doesn't bother me what some people think about me anymore. I have nothing to prove, or nothing that I want to prove. When I was living the good life back in the 60's, some friends suggested that I shouldn't wear tight fitting hip-huggers or the frilly shirts that I like or sandals, so maybe people wouldn't talk. I said, They want to talk, let them talk. If I turned away from things I liked, then I'd really be a phony. People talking doesn't bother me. What does bother me is when I see young kids who are teased and beaten up, some of them even thrown out of their homes by their own parents because they are different in a way that they can't even help."

You know that Emile Griffith means every word that he says because as he speaks his eyelids flutter in an unconscious effort to hold back the misting tears. It is difficult to correlate the petulant, slightly breaking voice housed in the same body as fists that flash out with venomous, destructive force.

You can try very hard to understand Emile Griffith and sometimes you may even think you do, but then you realize, No, you only think you understand him. He just doesn't add up. Among people who thought they knew Emile Griffith very well was Emile Griffith. And he was wrong.

The one person that he ever deceived or lied to was himself. It wasn't intentional. He'd look in the mirror and where there was a frown, he'd see a smile. He took in Matthew and befriended homeless street kids because he said they needed someone to care about them when, in fact, no one searched for love and compassion more than Emile. Dogs, from Dobermans to poodles, were treated as part of his family, not just as pets. Emile's emotional outpouring was not restrained by convention or tradition.

Howie Albert and Gil Clancy knew how important it was to keep Griff's mind away from any personal problems or stress. They figured that the best way to keep his mind away was to keep his whole body away. It was a strategy they employed since the Paret fight but now they had shifted to high gear. Emile Griffith's suitcase was becoming covered with exotic stickers. He was a true globetrotter.

Emile was two years old when Adolph Hitler's Luftwaffe began bombing England so he had no idea how tough those Brits were as they stood up under blitzkriegs and heavy-duty bombs. That slice of history was happening at a time when going to kindergarten was still a far-off dream to him.

True, there is no comparing a prizefight, even one of championship caliber, to a World War and certainly, Emile Griffith was no madman seeking to conquer the world. To the contrary, he was attempting to defend his crown. However, in doing so, he did invade the United Kingdom and as all who did before him, he learned what gutsy Welshmen and Englishmen were all about.

Brian Curvis was in the Garden with British promoter Jack Solomon the night of the last Griffith-Paret fight. Eerily, since that night each fighter has been haunted by an image. The vision of Benny Paret stayed with Griffith while the vision of "a killer" was emblazoned upon the memory of Curvis. "I have a date next week with a killer ... Emile Griffith, welterweight champion of the world," he wrote in an excusive article in the Sunday Mirror (London) in September 1964.

He went on to explain that his anxiety was not for himself, but for his bride of six months, Barbara. The daughter of sportswriter Leslie Bell, Barbara Curvis was a petite, extremely attractive young lady who could not stand seeing anyone get hurt, most of all, her husband.

"I see through to Barbara's anxiety and she knows that when she worries I worry. ... Barbara doesn't like to see anyone hurt, not even my opponents."

Barbara Curvis let it be known that she wouldn't be at the fight nor would she be watching it on television or listening to it on the radio.

"I get so tense. The atmosphere at Wembley is terrific. In fact, it's frightening. The worst part is not the fight. It's just when the lights dim, the spotlights come on, here's the fanfare and then that sudden, awful hush. It seems to last for hours.

"Once the fight starts , it's not quite so bad. But oh ... those punches. I'm sure I feel them far more than Brian does ...

"Listening to it on the radio I think is even worse. If the commentator says Brian has a small cut, you immediately think it's a great big gash. Your imagination runs away with you.

"So I'm not going. Friends are taking me to a quiet hotel to take my mind off it." – South Wales Evening Post 9/18/64

Emile Griffith was able to contend with almost any situation he was confronted with in a ring. Reading newspapers and hearing reports on radio and television is well outside the confines of the roped-off squared circle. That's where Emile was vulnerable.

Brian Curvis was the first southpaw that Griffith ever encountered, but Emile's only concern was not for himself. It was for a pretty little Welsh housewife who pictured him as a killer and feared for the well-being of her husband. So he crossed the Atlantic and presented Barbara Curvis with a hat that he personally designed for her and then went out and beat the Hell out of her husband.

Brian Curvis was gallant and resilient but completely outgunned, outmuscled and outfought. A very competent, thorough, workmanlike Griffith gave the British and Empire welterweight champion a thorough drubbing, dropping him three times in winning a lop-sided decision. It went the full 15 rounds only because of Curvis' stout heart and perhaps Emile's thinking of the worried Welsh housewife walking the lonely streets of Middlesex, unable to bear watching or listening to her husband's struggle.

After the fight, Emile expressed himself very nicely in the dressing room when he turned to Howie and Gil and asked in true wonderment, "How foreign is this country?"

"There is no degree of being foreign," Howie explained academically. "To us, if you are not from America, then you are a foreigner. Why do you ask?"

"How come every time I knocked him down, they start singing?"

Howie and Gil looked at each other and it was Gil who answered, "You gotta remember, Emile, this is a foreign country."

***

It had nothing to do with Frank Sinatra being there to root for his favorite, Emile Griffith. It was simply the Welsh way. They sing at weddings, wakes, marching off to war and prizefights. Junior felt it was a very nice touch and would even have joined in but pointed out that it was not easy singing with a gum protector in your mouth.

The Griffith entourage was not a large one. It consisted of Emile, Gil Clancy, Howie Albert, cousin Bernard Forbes, Syd Martin and the Sinatra family. At least, it seemed as though the Sinatras were part of the group as one or more of them always seemed to be around. If it wasn't Frank, there was daughter Nancy, Tommy Sands, Frank, Jr. and Frank's mom, Dolly, who had her kitchen door wide open for Emile.

The week of the Curvis fight they'd be sitting at a table in the Stork Club next to the Piccadilly Hotel where they were staying, with Gil and Frank, who was there on a singing engagement, exchanging Jack Daniels-backed advice while Emile looked on, sipping a cup of sweet tea. Howie was quite impressed at the way Emile was becoming oh, so very British in such a short time as he watched him hold his teacup with his pinky extended.

Frank Sinatra had always dreamt of being a fighter. Emile Griffith had always dreamt of being a song-and-dance man. They probably would have been very happy switching bodies. Sinatra would have had no trouble slipping into Griffith's, but there was no way that Emile would ever get those shoulders into what housed Ol' Blue Eyes.

Frank let it be known on numerous occasions that he would have liked to buy into Emile Griffith's contract but it was never even a consideration to Gil and Howie. Junior was family, not a chattel. They were always close friends with Sinatra but Gil and Howie did it their way.

A 21-year old Griffith stops Ray Lancaster at Academy of Music, 1959 (from Emile Griffith's Personal Library)

Emile with Gaspar Ortega and a few of Emile's millinery creations- June 1961 (from Emile Griffith's personal library)

Griffith alters flight plan to avoid crash landing on Referee
Jimmy Peerless after dethroning Paret April 1, 1961
(From Emile Griffith's personal library)

The new champ buys family a house in Hollis, New York- 1962
(From Emile Griffith's personal library)

Emile's Weehawken pad (From Emile Griffith's personal library)

*A GATHERING OF GREATS: Manuel Gonzalez and
Emile Griffith (with gloves) surrounded by Willie Pep, Barney Ross,
Rocky Graziano and Sugar Ray Robinson - December, 1965
(From Emile Griffith's personal library)*

A master of song, dance and Punch! - 1966
(from Emile Griffith's personal library)

Mommie lifts her new champ after regaining title from Nino Benvenuti
September 1967 (From Emile Griffith's personal library)

Emile Griffith Park, St. Thomas, VI
(from Emile Griffith's personal library)

*Emile staggers Tiger in 9th round of middleweight title bout. Emile won
championship with 15 round decision - April 25, 1966
(from Emile Griffith personal library)*

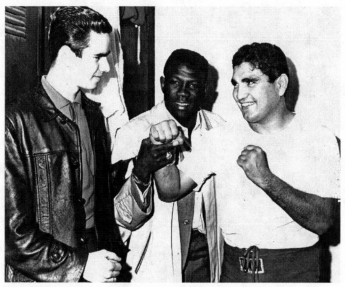

*Emile with Matthew (l), his bodyguard and companion - 1966
(from Emile Griffith's personal library)*

*Griffith regains title from Nino Benvenuti - September 29, 1967
(from Emile Griffith's personal library)*

Griffith and Benvenuti at International Boxing Hall of Fame,
Canastota, NY June 2004
(Photo by Lisa Ross)

Emile primping on his wedding day - May 7, 1971
(from Emile Griffith's personal library)

Emile and his ward Luis Rodrigo in 1981. Emile adopted Luis in 2004.
(from Emile Griffith's personal library)

Brother Franklin readying Emile for his wedding - May 7, 1971
(from Emile Griffith's personal library)

Wedding Party - Joe Frazier (Best Man), Mercedes's sister Ulla (Maid of Honor), Mercedes and Emile - May 7, 1971 (from Emile Griffith's personal library)

Emile with his Godson Giuliani Benvenuti and Giuliani's dad Nino at WBC convention, 1983 (from Emile Griffith's personal library)

Emile, his daughter Christine, Howie Albert and Gil Clancy - 2004
(photo by Lisa Ross)

Emile Griffith, vice-president of Stonewall Veterans Association (2nd from left,
son Luis (2nd from right) - March 2006 (from Emile Griffith's personal library)

Emile and Storme DeLaviere, famous female vocalist and male impersonator of the 1950's-60's (Photo by Lisa Ross)

Emile, vice-president of Stonewall Veterans Association, getting ready for Gay Pride Parade with president Williamson J Henderson (l) and SVA member Storme DeLaviere -June 2007 (© Hal Weiner 2007)

Emile in a rather unique pose at entrance to Lesbian, Gay, Bisexual and Transgender community Center in Manhattan
(Photo by Lisa Ross)

Emile and Mike Tyson
(from Emile Griffith's personal library)

CHAPTER THIRTEEN

Howie Albert was considering making a purchase. "I was seriously thinking about buying Emile a red cape, taking him to the top of a tall building and saying – 'go fly.' And you know what? Chances are he would. I was getting to believe there was nothing he couldn't do.

The ring was one thing; that was his home, so we were never shocked at what he could do there. The first time Gil ever put a tennis racket in his hand was when he was training at the Concord Hotel in Kiamesha Lake, New York and a little old lady who saw him make a great backhand return gasped, 'Nobody told me Arthur Ashe was here!'

He's sitting at a table in the Latin Quarter when the emcee asks him to take a bow, then says – 'Come on up and sing a song for us, Champ,' and Emile says – 'I can't sing.' But they drag him up and he winds up taking requests and making curtain calls!

A couple of guys from the gym take him to Roseland Ballroom after training one night and he's standing at the side like a wallflower when a pretty young thing comes over and asks him to dance. Before you know it the entire dance floor clears for him and his partner who he's twirling around like he's a cowboy and she's his lasso.

So, it's only natural when he says to me and Gil – I want the middleweights, we listen to him. I still think I should have gotten him that red cape."

Junior's idea to move up to the middleweights actually took seed right after his return to England for the Dave Charnley fight. At the time, Joey Giardello had the middleweight title. Giardello was neither an incentive nor a deterrent. He wore the crown and Emile wanted it. It took almost another year-and-a-half for Emile to get his wish. By then, Dick Tiger was the guy wearing that crown and Griffith's desire to grab it was somewhat muted. Dick Tiger was one of his favorite people. But they were both fighters and a work day was a work day.

It wasn't that when Emile looked in the mirror he felt he was shaving Dick Tiger's face, but he did relate to him very strongly. He respected a guy who recognized his responsibilities and priorities the same way he did. Both had large families that were put first and provided for to the best of their abilities. Emile's group of seven siblings, his mother, cousins, nieces and nephews gave him a potential dependent write-off of seventeen while Dick Tiger was not exactly a slouch, taking care of his wife, back in Lagos, Nigeria, with their five children and a sixth on the way. Each wore a crown in a world where royalty was rewarded. For Emile, boxing was his only real source of income; Tiger had a group of small apartment buildings and various business enterprises in his homeland. There was also another great burden that Emile carried that Tiger did not – that was Emile.

Emile Griffith wore clothes that enabled him to cross Broadway and 42nd Street without a traffic light. He had approximately 50 suits, all color by Technicolor, costume jewelry, gold chains and so many diamond chips that he could never get lost at night; he shone in the dark and jingled as he walked. All his clothes were tailor-made for his body, and anyone wanting a referral to his tailor had one very long wait as Emile had him working overtime.   Referrals from Dick Tiger may not have been any easier to get because it did not seem as though his clothes came from any store, unless you considered the Salvation Army to be a retailer. Tiger carried unpretentiousness to an unimaginable degree. His suit often looked as though it served a dual purpose, pajamas and business attire. Looking at his shoes, it might be assumed that they were very strong shoes at one time because it appeared that Tiger had walked across the Sahara desert in them. As different as Tiger was from Emile, he was Emile's kind of guy.

Although Emile was serious about his flamboyant appearance, boxing was his serious business. But Emile Griffith had long before set his sights on the middleweight title. Most people assumed that after his very brief encounter with Rubin Carter in Pittsburgh, Griffith would be content, and much better off, sticking to guys his own size. Emile sometimes took advice but he usually had to be slapped in the face to make him listen. Junior had never argued about the stoppage in Pittsburgh – only Emelda had done that. The stoppage had not made him at all apprehensive about going after middleweights. He chalked up the Pittsburgh fight to having been caught cold by a perfect punch, something he was confident would not happen again. Confidence was what it was all about, and Emile Griffith was brimming over with confidence.

Being British, the Brits did what Englishmen do; they exhibited exceedingly good manners and invited Emile Griffith back only two months after his demolition of Brian Curvis. Rather than bloody rare beef, they chose to serve the welterweight champion a lamb, Dave Charnley, the British lightweight titleholder.

Emile's most vivid recollection of that visit was that the week before the fight he was presented to the House of Commons. With a large contingent of the British boxing community in the gallery, never was so much cauliflower assembled in that august Chamber as when Emile Griffith, smartly attired with the help of a Carnaby Street tailor, rose to address the House. "I am deeply honored to be here. It is the greatest thing that ever happened to me apart from winning the world title."

The British boxing fans' most vivid recollection of Emile's visit was that the fight was something like big, bad Bluto hauling off at a Popeye without any spinach. After pulverizing and bouncing poor Popeye Charnley off the canvas for eight-and-a-half rounds, Emile Griffith, who does not like being compared to Bluto (he liked Howie's red cape idea much more) hauled off with a left hook that started almost from the floor and actually sent Charnley catapulting head over heels across the ring. This was one time Popeye never got his can of spinach.

So awesome was he that night that many boxing fans felt that it was that fight that ignited a flaming spark of desire in Emile Griffith to move up to the middleweight division. Emile's recollection is that he simply ran out of welterweights.

Emile Griffith returned to the States with a strong sense of dedication. Desire had transformed to purpose. Purpose had become hunger. He had set his sights on a goal that he was determined to attain.

Sometimes you can focus so strongly on a target or dream that everything else is put out of your horizon. That's exactly what happened when Emile went to Houston, Texas to fight Manny Gonzalez. He may have heard Gonzalez's name when it was announced, but the person he was thinking of was the middleweight champ. Manny ran and tried to stay out of trouble for 10 rounds. Emile forced the fight and chased after his man, but it seemed like a "So what if I catch him" effort.

Scoring well to the body but unable to corner and destroy Gonzalez, Griffith heard the bell sounding an end to the ten-round non-title bout knowing that he had won the fight. It seems that everyone agreed with him except for two people, but they happened to be two-thirds of the officials judging the fight. Emile already knew that when you are a visitor in someone else's backyard, you are not necessarily treated as an honored guest. For a globetrotter, it goes with the territory.

Emile proved his point when they did a curtain call performance eleven months later at Madison Square Garden, this time with the title on the line. It was pretty much the same chase-and-try-to-catch-me fight as their first one. Emile had nothing to prove, but he thought he did. The boxing world knew that what had happened in Texas really hadn't happened. Jimmy Cannon of the New York Post told it like it was.

"The people who gave Gonzalez the decision over Griffith in Houston that night could have been social workers. They couldn't have based their conclusions on the skills of the pugs."

It turned out to be a much more enjoyable evening for Emile Griffith and Sugar Ray Robinson than for Manny Gonzalez. For Griffith, the joy was in sweeping just about every round and being able to say "I told you so" in a most convincing, if not exciting, fashion.

For Robinson, it was an emotional farewell to boxing as he stood in the center of the Garden ring wearing a short white terrycloth robe, listening to the cheers of an adoring crowd while the living ghosts of his past encircled him, sharing the moment. There was Bobo Olson, Gene Fullmer, Carmen Basilio and Randy Turpin. Emile's only regret, as he was becoming an accomplished showman, was that his fight with the non-combative Gonzalez wasn't more exciting as it was the first color telecast of a prizefight.

In between the two Gonzalez fights, Griffith did not have a single match scheduled at the South Pole. He fought just about everywhere else. After the first Gonzalez fight, he traveled from Houston to his first New York fight in almost two years, which his mother, Emelda, broadcast live from Madison Square Garden to the whole world – without a microphone.

Jose Stable, fighting for the welterweight championship in Madison Square Garden on March 30, 1965 did not stand a chance. If, somehow, Emile didn't take care of him, for sure Momma would. There was no way anyone was going to spoil her boy's homecoming. Stable fortunately did not have to face Momma's wrath. Part of a double-header championship fight card, Jose Torres - Willie Pastrano being the co-feature, it set a money record gate, breaking the Joe Louis - Joe Walcott record set in 1947. The spectacle proved to the New York fans what they had been missing for two years. Emile's strength and tenacity were overwhelming. Using right uppercuts to lift Stable out of his crouching, bobbing and weaving style, and exhorted by Clancy between rounds to "Stop loafing!", Emile wore down his opponent through the first ten rounds and took him apart with a steady assortment of left jabs and hooks, throwing in an occasional right cross as an exclamation point.

Greatness comes in various shapes and forms. Its mantle, which seemed inevitably to be passed on to Emile Griffith, covered more than his broad shoulders. Without the exhortations of Gil Clancy, Griffith was a great racehorse without a jockey. His was a team effort, not a one man show. Emile Griffith had all the ingredients and attributes of a great prizefighter, but those attributes had to be channeled, disciplined and directed. Clancy did more than teach Griffith the fundamentals, refining his skills. He did more than motivate him. He scared the hell out of Emile Griffith when he shouted and threatened him to take him out of his lethargy. Emile Griffith never had to worry about having hiccups as long as Gil Clancy was around to go "Gr-r-r!!"

But there were times when no amount of threats, cajoling or pleading could elicit the needed effort. Emile's inner workings were controlled by his emotions. Sometimes he couldn't shift from first gear because his sensitivities and good nature overrode his competitive spirit and fighter's mentality. He was the wrong guy with the wrong head on the right body who did what he was meant to do better than anyone else – when he did it.

After the Stable fight Emile traveled to Honolulu where he had an easy time beating Eddie Pace. That's when the gears got locked up, as Clancy remembers it.

"You don't have to steam Emile up to get his head into fighting mode, but on the other hand you can't let his emotions come into play either. Once he feels sorry or has compassion for someone, forget bout it."

Boxing writer Bob Waters quoted Gil in Newsday (November 30, 1965), "We were fighting Don Fullmer in Salt Lake City last August. Emile knows Gene Fullmer and Don and their wives. He was enjoying himself. So now it's the night of the fight. You should have seen it.

Gene's wife sings the Star Spangled Banner and Gene is the announcer. Gene, after he's through announcing everything, leaves the ring at Emile's corner. 'Hey,' he says to Emile, 'take it easy on my kid brother. There's his wife and kid sitting at ringside.' Emile looks at Don's wife and kid and waves. That's all he does all night. He just couldn't bring himself to hit Don. Emile was so bad he stunk the house out."

Emile was upset with himself, but not for long. When he got back to New York he found the Griffs, his Little League baseball team, floundering without its coach, Matthew and his brother Franklin needed a referee to keep them apart and his momma was crying that she wanted her white twins back. Until this point, the only thing that King Solomon and Emile Griffith had in common was that they both wore a crown. Junior had three weeks to close the gap.

A few extra practice sessions followed by ice cream treats at the local candy store was all the motivation the Griffs needed to get untracked. Packing up Matthew's bags and moving him from the Hollis family home to the Weehawken apartment temporarily solved the Matthew-Franklin problem. At least neither one could reach across the Hudson River. As far as momma's depression, that was big league stuff.

From his earliest days as a Golden Glover, after working out at the gym Emile would patrol the Chelsea neighborhood, play with and counsel the kids who looked up to him, not as a father figure, but as an idol they related to and respected. He was a kid, a big one, but a kid just like they were. They all tried to follow Griff's path, which was a good one, and he kept them from straying. He was there with them on the handball courts, the basketball courts, and he even started a Parks Dept. gym for the kids. When they had a problem they came to the Champ. He even became the godfather to several of them.

It wasn't only the kids he counseled. He knew a young white couple in the neighborhood who were having a rocky time with their marriage, and as a result were neglecting their eight month old twins, a boy and girl. Emile suggested that he take the twins home to Hollis so they could be taken care of by his family while the parents tried to work out their problems. After having the twins for over four months, Emelda learned to love them as her own and set up her own laws, statutes and codicils. They were her common-law children. When the parents came to "kidnap" their twins back, Emelda was heartbroken, depressed and furious.

Emile was back home so she poured out her troubles to him. His first thought was "Give a twin, keep a twin" which would have been a very Solomon-like call, but he remained silent and in deep thought. Emelda did not wait for her son's counseling. She took the train to Manhattan and confronted the parents with what she thought was a very persuasive argument. "You need more time to straighten out your lives and it's not fair to the kids until it's done." She returned to Hollis with the twins. What was really persuasive was Emelda Griffith, weighing in at 230 pounds plus, with hands on hips and a fiery glare in her eyes.

Emile explained, "When it came to being a momma, you couldn't stop my momma."

With the current problems of Emile Griffith's world solved, the Champ realized that he had never had the chance to unpack his bags. This made going back on the road relatively easy.

CHAPTER FOURTEEN

Tommy Sands found out that despite being a singing idol and movie star, life is not necessarily a proverbial bowl of cherries. In September of 1965, he found himself dealing with two major problems. The first was that after ending his five year marriage to Nancy Sinatra, he learned that there was a greater fury than the wrath of a woman scorned. In his case it was the wrath of a father-in-law, or ex-father-in-law, whose precious daughter had been scorned. And when that father-in-law happened to be a guy named Frank Sinatra, discretion becomes a major consideration.

The other problem was having to choose between two close friends, which may be an age-old problem, but when these two friends, Emile Griffith and Gabe Terronez, are battling in one of Fresno, California's biggest bouts in years, it added another dimension.

"I came up from Hollywood when Emile called and said he was fighting here. I think it will be the best fight of the year. Gabe loves to bang away and Emile loves to mix. It's a natural. Both are my friends and I hate to think they'll be batting each other around..." Tommy Sands from the Fresno Bee, September 12, 1965.

Problem number two he solves by acting like a charter member of Gamblers Anonymous. He sits at ringside going "Hooray!" for every punch that is thrown, no matter who throws it, a perk which a guy whose only money riding on the fight is for soda pop and peanuts can enjoy. Almost all the hoorays turn out to be for Emile Griffith who has little trouble putting out Terronez' lights in four rounds.

The first problem is a bit more complicated as Frank Sinatra, being a guy who sang songs and made some movies, was also a guy who came from Hoboken. He may not have controlled everything between the Atlantic and Pacific Oceans but it was widely believed that he had enough friends in high places who did. So Tommy Sands, displaying some very prudent judgment, changed his career and lifestyle and moved to Hawaii.

The loss of a singing idol barely had time to sink in when along came a replacement. Emile Griffith, the lead tenor of the St. James Missionary Church choir had graduated.

Bennie Benjamin was the first Virgin Islander to hit the big time in the American music industry, so maybe it was only natural for him to have an affinity for the first Virgin Islander to hit the big time in the boxing world. Benjamin, who had written such great all-time favorites as "I Don't Want To Set The World On Fire" for the Inkspots, "When The Lights Go On Again" for Vaughan Monroe, "Rumors Are Flying" for the Andrew Sisters, "Wheel Of Fortune" for Kay Starr and "Cross Over The Bridge" for Patti Paige was so impressed with his fellow Islander's singing ability that he penned four songs that Emile recorded for Columbia Records, "Always On My Mind", "A Little Bit More", "Everybody Needs Love" and "While We're Dancing."

Both Howie Albert and Gil Clancy are confident that if Emile had opted for a career as a singer he would have succeeded. "He was a sensation on the Ed Sullivan Show," Gil points out, adding, "Jackie Mason should have had it so good."

Joey Archer may have worn the shamrock on his trunks and robe, but the wrong guy got his Irish up. Griffith traveled from Fresno to London where he picked up his automatic UK paycheck by stopping another brave but outclassed Englishman, Harry Scott, in seven rounds. After his rematch with Manny Gonzalez in the Garden, Emile celebrated his 28th birthday by beating Johnny Brooks over ten rounds in Las Vegas. Then he got mad and madder at Joey Archer.

Only two men had previously made the jump from welterweight title to middleweight title, Ray Robinson and Carmen Basilio. Not too many expected Griffith to join them, not against the reigning king, Dick Tiger.

Tiger was simply too big, too tough, too seasoned and already looking past Griffith towards a bonanza gate with European middleweight champion and matinee idol, Nino Benvenuti. But there it was, set up on the table for him, a far better dream than the one plaguing him for the past four years, a chance for true ring immortality.

Sticks and stones are what it takes to hurt some people, but with Emile Griffith, words were enough. Especially the words hurled around by Joey Archer. He even took out newspaper ads claiming "Foul!" – protesting that he deserved the shot against Tiger before Griffith. And when some of the press rallied behind Archer, Emile was furious. Sometime during his growing up years Emelda must have told Junior, "Do not cut off your nose to spite your face. It is obvious that Emile paid no attention.

What he did was unparalleled in the annals of boxing. With his fight for Tiger's title signed, sealed and scheduled for April 25th at Madison Square Garden, Griffith did the unthinkable. He stormed into the Garden office on Valentine's Day with a message that did not speak of love. He told matchmaker Teddy Brenner and promoter Harry Markson that he wanted to fight Joey Archer in March at the Garden with the winner fighting Dick Tiger on the April date. Clancy and Albert agreed very reluctantly as Emile left them no choice. Jimmy Archer, Joey's brother and manager consented immediately. The next day the Garden Boxing Club was ready to announce the Griffith-Archer fight, but Joey Archer delivered the biggest kayo punch of his career. He refused to fight Griffith.

It was only natural to assume that Archer was afraid to fight Emile, but Griffith is the first one to deny that as Joey's reason to refuse the fight. Emile's logic was simple. "Archer afraid? He's Irish!"

Whatever the reason, Joey Archer wanted no part of Emile Griffith at that time. The man he wanted was Dick Tiger. But Emile was on line ahead of him. There was a big, long line waiting to get at the middleweight champ. Not everyone was after his crown.

Richard Ihetu, besides his immediate family, had a huge extended family of aunts, uncles, cousins and others living in Nigeria. He was the self-appointed patriarch of the clan and he took his responsibilities very seriously. Before coming to the United States in 1959, he set out to earn his family's keep in England. It was there that a British army officer, watching him training, exclaimed, "What a Tiger!" Dick Tiger was born. A tremendous counterpuncher, he had a trademark style of coming forward to mousetrap his opponent into trading punches, then countering with his own bombs, his awesome left hook being his major weapon.

Among those looking to get at Dick Tiger, and it was not within a roped-off enclosure, was a killing squad of his own countrymen. Nigeria, which gained its independence in 1960, lived under an uneasy coexistence between the Muslim north and the minority Biafrans of the Christian south. In 1965, when national elections tore the fabric of the government apart rather than unite it, a genocidal campaign was begun by the Muslims. Thousands of Christians were massacred and Dick Tiger became a marked man in his own country because of the resentment that he had made his fortune working in the United States.

This was an arena where Dick Tiger became Dick Ihetu and chose not to counterpunch. Never politically involved, he was mild-mannered and polite and would not badmouth his stalking enemy. His response to questions from those concerned with his well-being was always to say that things were fine back in his homeland.

Emile Griffith, like most people, knew it was not so. He tried to understand how it was possible for your heart to go out so strongly for a person you wanted to beat up so badly.

So the poor-looking rich man from Africa and the free-wheeling, rich living, who-cares-what's-in-the-bank Virgin Islander set up their training camps, each indelibly stamped with their individual personalities. Dick Tiger's quarters at Grossinger's were just down the Catskill road from the Concord, Emile's traditional home base training facility. Dick Tiger brought Jenny Grossinger's home style plainness and refreshing simple lifestyle down to true Spartan living, while Emile Griffith revved up the glitz and high living pace of the Concord to a jet-setter's idyll. While Tiger was early to bed and early to rise in his monastic cabin set on a mountain above Grossinger's main buildings, Griffith's elegantly appointed quarters at the Concord were very well suited for someone who danced the nights away at the hotel's posh Gypsy Room. It was the Jerk, the Mashed Potato, the Boogaloo, the Monkey and the Watusi versus ten hours of solid sleep time. It was acknowledged across the board that Emile Griffith was some dancer and a carousing night animal. But Emile was also a great fooler, and he didn't fool anyone as well as he fooled himself. He danced and he sang and he partied to fool himself. He may have fooled some others along the way, too, but there were those he could not fool – like Tim Moriarity who was covering the fight for the Jersey Journal and was watching Griff climb out of the ring at the Concord after a brisk four-round workout when he was approached by a boy who looked about 10 years old.

"'Is it true that you once killed another fighter?' the youngster asked.

"Howard Albert, Griffith's co-manager, and Madison Square Garden press agent John Condon had been conversing about three yards behind Griffith, their backs turned towards the champion. Both men instinctively whirled around, their mouths open; their eyes on Griffith.

"The 28-year-old Virgin Islander mumbled a one word reply – 'No' – tossed the towel to the floor, climbed back into the ring and started shadow boxing.

" ... Emile has tried hard to erase the memory of this tragedy, but there are always 10-year-old boys, or older fans with the mentality of 10-year-old boys, who keep asking: 'Is it true that you once killed another fighter?'"

" 'He's been trying hard to forget the whole thing, but some people won't let him,' Albert said. 'You don't mind the kids. They're so naïve – like that boy today – you have to forgive them. But it's the older people, those who should know better, who keep bugging Emile.

It's unbelievable how they keep bringing up Paret's name. What do they think he is? An animal or something with no feelings? We've told him to walk away from people like that, and he does now. But he's more like a 16-year-old who never grew up. People come up and shake his hands and Emile is nice as pie to them. Then they turn around and say, 'Paret had a wife and child, didn't he?' Honest, it's unbelievable.'

" 'Emile, he never talks about that fight,' cousin Bernard Forbes said. "But the people, they always bring it up. I know he wants to forget. For four years he's been trying to forget. But it's still on his mind."

"It could be, as Forbes said, that Emile Griffith has Benny (Kid) Paret 'still on his mind' whenever he dons boxing gloves."

Four days before the fight Phil Pepe of the World-Telegram wrote of sitting down with Emile and the ever-presence of Paret.

"Emile Griffith says he doesn't like to think about it, but he thinks about it. He says he doesn't like to remember, but he remembers. He says he doesn't like to talk about it, but ..."

No, Emile Griffith wasn't able to fool everyone, but he did fool some, and most importantly – himself. While Tiger was tucked in his bed, Emile danced the night away. Elbow benders watching from the bar in the Gypsy Room marveled at the swivel-hipped, frenzied gyrations of the Virgin Islander with the golden mezuzah flying from a gold chain around his neck. But they went out and put their money on a sleeping Tiger.

Things did not change on fight night. The dancer danced and the Tiger slept. Benjamin Franklin went out and flew a kite and Bingo! Electricity. Griffith and Tiger did not fly a kite. There was no electricity.

It wasn't so much a matter of styles, because it was not the usual Griffith style on display. The customary cocky, prancing, aggressive brashness that brings an arena to life and the fans to their feet cheering was replaced by a dancer flitting backwards, side to side, boxing cautiously behind a flicking left jab against a slow, plodding adversary who was unable to adapt to what he didn't expect. There was excitement – the kind that is created because of what is at stake and the anticipation that is inherent in a championship fight. But each round was a virtual replay of the preceding round. Nobody yelled at the peanut pusher or cold drink vendor for blocking their view.

In spite of this, there was plenty of noise and loud cheering, even though, of the 14,934 crowd, 14,925 did not do much straining of their vocal chords. The other nine fans did not need any help. Emile's mother Emelda, his four sisters, one brother, two cousins and an uncle had a decibel rating equivalent to 15,000.

"Stick 'em and run, son! Hold that Tiger!"

Like a good son, Griffith listened to Mommie for seven rounds. Then he changed his tactics, bringing the fight to Tiger in the eighth round. Confused by the switch from a retreating, defensive boxer to an aggressive puncher, Tiger got tagged by a tremendous right to the chin in the ninth round and found himself on the canvas for the first time in his career. This was the only decisive punch and round of the fight and it was on this one punch that Emile Griffith rode to the middleweight championship.

Fourteen of the fifteen rounds were so close that the officials, referee Arthur Mercante and judges Frank Forbes and Tony Castellano, who scored unanimously for Griffith, saw eye-to-eye on only five of the fifteen rounds. Emelda Griffith had a much easier time. She scored every round for her son.

"Good things happen to good sons. And he's a good son. He bought me a house!"

Emile Griffith and Dick Tiger didn't just respect each other; they liked each other. Each one was certain that he had won the fight but there was no bitterness on Tiger's part. He believed that as the aggressor he deserved the decision. "But being a stranger, I have no choice but to accept it." It was said with a gentle smile.

Griffith smiled back, just as gently. "I'm a stranger too. I'm from Weehawken, New Jersey."

Emile Griffith and Dick Tiger met in the ring one more time. It was four years later, July 15, 1970 at Madison Square Garden. Shortly after losing his middleweight crown to Griffith, Dick Tiger defeated Jose Torres for the light heavyweight championship and continued as a top-flight contender even after losing that crown to Bob Foster in 1968. Following spectacular victories against Frankie DePaula, Nino Benvenuti and Andy Kendall, he had his rematch with Griffith. The result was the same with Griffith winning a ten-round decision. Dick Tiger retired from boxing after the Griffith fight. His final fight was fought outside the ring. A year after announcing his retirement, he was diagnosed with terminal liver cancer. Concerned only for his family's well-being he gambled on an amnesty agreement with the Nigerian government to return to account for his holdings in his homeland. This he was able to accomplish but, spitefully, the ruling military regime refused to let him return to his family now living in New York or to undergo radical medical treatment. On December 15, 1971, Dick Tiger died at age 42. Thousands of mourners came to pay their respect at his graveside funeral. Emile Griffith grieved as deeply as anyone.

CHAPTER FIFTEEN

Telephones do not make up stories. It is something they are incapable of doing, but you would not know this by the way Emile stared at the white Princess phone he held arms-length away from himself, mumbling, "I don't believe it."

To which the telephone, which sounded very much like his sister Gloria, responded, "You don't have to believe nothing, Junior, but I'm telling you, you had yourself one white brother for about ten minutes, because that's what Franklin turned when that wildcat Matthew tried to run him down in the driveway. I strongly suggest you find out how fast that snazzy Lincoln of yours can get your butt over here."

Emile found out and so did the trooper who ticketed him on the turnpike. Even with the time out for the speeding ticket, his Lincoln got him to Hollis before tempers were cooled down.

Fortunately, Momma showed she was a good enough referee to sub for Arthur Mercante at a Garden slugfest. Franklin, who had become openly critical of Emile's relationships with young men, didn't approve of Matthew hanging on to Emile and Matthew didn't approve of Franklin's right to approve. This was just one area of disapproval between them. From the moment they met they enjoyed each other's company like a mongoose does a snake's. Emile tried keeping them apart. Whenever he went on the road he moved Matthew into his mother's house realizing that he was mixing a concoction as volatile and unstable as nitroglycerin. He hoped against hope that no one would stir the batch.

Franklin, who was studying law at the Hampton Institute, was pretty good with words. Matthew, who was no match in that department, did not look at the car trying to run Franklin down as a weapon. He explained to Emile, that, on the contrary, it was a completely defensive action necessary to shut Franklin's mouth.

Emile had just lost an argument with the New York State Athletic Commission in his attempt to keep his welterweight title after defeating Dick Tiger for the middleweight crown. He, Gil and Howie and almost all the press felt that he was entitled to retain the welterweight crown as long as he could make the weight, but the Commission strictly enforced the rule that says that no boxer can hold two world titles at the same time. Tired and frustrated, he wasn't looking for another argument, especially one that he recognized as a no-win situation from the start. Although Franklin's constant criticism of his lifestyle and friends bothered him, Emile accepted from family what he wouldn't from others. *"I knew I wasn't doing things and living the way the rest of my family and most of the people we knew were. But what I was doing was living my life the only way I could – the only way I was really able to. Hey, that didn't mean that Franklin had to go along with it and accept it. Where we come from you don't shout out, 'Hey! I'm gay!' and expect to get to the other side of the street."*

Franklin was Emile's brother and even though Franklin could never accept the person that he was, Emile loved Franklin. Emile also loved Matthew's companionship, but he knew that Matthew had to be restrained.

Emile drove back to Weehawken with Matthew, upset over what had happened. He told Matthew that he couldn't go around threatening people, even though he felt that he was protecting him. Emile expected Matthew to, defend his actions, or at least argue that they were justified. Instead, Matthew responded, "Okay, Poppy-man, you just take care of yourself then. I got this girl anyhow, so I guess I'll just be staying with her."

Emile felt as if he were in the ring, carefully guarding against that big right cross to the head, when you get tagged by an unexpected hook to the gut. It takes all the wind out of you and turns your knees to jelly. It's almost an instinctive act when a fighter gets hurt ... Emile smiled.

The youngster smiled back. "You been good to me, Champ. Take care." And he left.

Emile was devastated. He didn't like to be alone. When he was by himself, he didn't really feel alone. He was never alone. He was plagued by thoughts, by daydreams and nightmares.

Exactly two months after taking the middleweight championship from Dick Tiger, Emile Griffith had a very busy day doing his road work between the offices of the New York State Athletic Commission, where he and Joey Archer signed contracts to fight for Griffith's new title, and Columbia Records Co., regarding the four Bennie Benjamin songs he had recorded.

"Yesterday also, Griffith signed a lucrative contract with Columbia, which has put Emile on wax and will heavily publicize the new recordings.

Sugar Ray Robinson sang, Ernie Terrell sings and now Emile joins the ranks. ... he is being booked to appear on the Johnny Carson and Merv Griffin shows. There is rhythm in this young man, who is so many things, and an eagerness in him that makes him a completely different personality than so many others who earn their living with their fists.

But there is also a gentleness in him, which makes him a kind of paradox of our time." – Milton Gross, New York Post, June 28, 1966

If it hadn't been the overhead ring lights that bathed him in its glow, Emile Griffith would probably have wound up in the glare of a spotlight, doing whatever he chose to do before an enthralled audience.

While Emile's glamorous lifestyle captured and fired the imaginations of fans and media there were those who looked past the glitz and glitter of his storied career.

There was concern for a genuinely good person whose primary consideration was to take care of and support his large, extended family. However, this included friends and an ever-growing army of hangers-on as Emile's reputation of being a soft touch reached all the right – and wrong - ears. Whatever was left over was used to support an extragantly lavish lifestyle. This was the true paradox of Emile Griffith.

When he and Dick Tiger sat next to each other for interviews and press conferences it was a modern-day version of "The Prince and the Pauper." Comparisons were eventually made that caused many to wonder about the wisdom of his ways.

Emile Griffith has two world boxing titles, about 30 well-tailored suits, a collection of expensive paintings, two homes and 13 hungry relatives. After 57 professional fights, including 12 title bouts, you'd figure the flashy Virgin Islander was a wealthy man. He isn't.

That's the primary reason Griffith agreed yesterday to make the first defense of his newly-won middleweight crown against Joey Archer at Madison Square Garden July 13. Emile needs the money — to buy more suits, more paintings, more jewelry and to keep those 13 hungry relatives living in the manner to which they have become accustomed.

... Generous to a fault, that's Emile. In addition to caring for his large family, he is also a soft touch for any guy with a hard luck story, so he has reached the point in his career now where he must keep fighting in order to meet all his bills.

... Other bouts are being lined up fast for Emile, who needs all the money he can get his hands on to pay for those Italian silk suits — and to keep the wolf from his relatives' door. – Tim Moriarity, Jersey Journal June 28, 1966

It wasn't that Emile was blind to what was happening. Not with Howie Albert, whose concern was rapidly turning his red hair gray. Clancy's was merely falling out. They pleaded with him to stop spending money and supporting the whole world the way he was but his answer was always the same – he knew what he was doing and it was more important for his family, especially his mother, to have whatever they needed or wanted even if he went broke. That's what he said and that was the true paradox that was Emile Griffith. When emotion and intellect clashed Emile Griffith could not control Emile Griffith.

In his dressing room after the Tiger fight he was overjoyed and hugged and kissed his mother who proudly told everyone what a wonderful son she had. As the new champ beamed and his mother kept praising him to all around, Emile suddenly started screaming, "Mommie get out of here! I don't want you in here. Get out!"

Embarrassed, Emelda stammered, sulked and quietly slunk out of the room. Friends tried to calm him down but he continued shouting that it was his night and he could do anything he wanted. "Just get her out of here!"

Five minutes later an unruffled and smiling Emile looked around and asked, "Where's Chubby Checker?"

It wasn't easy being very, very good.

Sitting on top of the world was a great place to be. Emile enjoyed it. He knew that nobody stayed there forever but he had this ability of mentally cropping the whole picture. He was an expert at selective "seeing" as he had done it all his life. So Emile Griffith was able to smile a lot. He wasn't really fooling himself. It was his way of dealing with life.

Howie Albert simply couldn't understand Emile's ignoring his and Gil's warnings. They saw different worlds. In Emile's, time stood still, things never changed; he was twenty-eight forever and the money always flowed. Gil's and Howie's was a harsher place, a more real world where hair turned to gray, accomplishments became memories and rainy days followed sunny ones.

They waged an ongoing battle outside of the ring as fierce as any of their protégé's ten or fifteen round wars. No punches were thrown although at times it came close to that. Whenever possible, they would invest ten or fifteen per cent of Emile's purse. "We put it in mutual funds," Clancy explained. "Retirement is one thing Emile would never even talk about."

Clancy and Albert worried for Emile while Emile worried for everyone else. It was Emile's cookie jar and everyone he knew seemed to have a sweet tooth.

Howie Albert usually did not travel further than from his bedroom to his kitchen for a cup of coffee. Howie had remarried in 1963 and although his wife Diane preferred tea, she brewed such a good pot of coffee there was no need for Howie to make a longer trip than that. So when he calls Gil Clancy and tells him that he drove some twenty-five to thirty miles from his Syosset home to Hollis for his morning coffee,

Gil, very concerned, eases out his telephone directory and searches out the number for Pilgrim State Psychiatric Center.

Gil decides not to make the call as Howie explains that he just wanted to be supportive of Emile's brothers by patronizing the candy store that Emile had purchased for them near the bus station. It is not that Gil doesn't believe that someone who burns up about a dollar's worth of gas and drives round trip close to two hours to help someone out with a twenty-five cent breakfast special should not be quietly whisked away in a strait jacket. Because of a long-standing friendship, he is able to rationalize that his friend and partner is not a danger to anyone but himself.

"Go home and get a lot of rest," Gil advises.

"Can I stop off at your place for a cup of coffee?"

Gil takes the phone from his ear and looks at it as if he expects to see Howie in the earpiece. "I thought you just had a cup of coffee."

"No. I said I went for a cup of coffee. I didn't say I had a cup of coffee. The store wasn't open yet."

"What time did you get there?" Gil asked. "Four in the morning?"

"About ten-thirty. One of the storekeepers on the block told me they open up around noontime. I couldn't wait. My stomach is growling."

Gil decided not to have a second breakfast. He and Nancy sat and watched as Howie drank his morning coffee and explained that there was actually a method to his madness.

No matter how hard he tried convincing Emile not to throw his money away on harebrain investments, Emile's devotion to family and friends took precedence over his common sense. He paid for educations that were never completed, bought wardrobes that never left the closet and backed any idea or whim of his family without question. When he told Howie he was buying a luncheonette for his brothers, his manager pleaded with him not to touch the money that he still had invested. Emile, as always, refused to turn down his brothers' request. Howie actually felt that it was a prime location, situated near the bus station. As it turned out, the store did have some good, steady customers – all siblings of Emile.

It was with a great deal of wishful thinking – but very little hope – that Howie made his journey from Syosset to Hollis. The store depended upon the morning commuter trade to make it a success. The trade was there, but the front door was locked.

Emile Griffith had to continue plying his trade. It was the only way to keep the kitty flowing.

"It was difficult for me to understand", Howie reflects. "Whatever they did, Emile beamed. One of his brothers would start school. Emile would be so proud. He'd drop out. That Emile ignored. He only saw the positive in them. It was like that with everyone, but more so with his family. If anyone ever saw the world through rose-colored glasses, it was Emile."

There is this finger that can be pointed straight up in the air to tell someone very graphically where to go without having to speak a word. Emile Griffith had extremely small hands for a fighter, but he did have that middle pointing finger and no one would have been more justified in using it after Joey Archer's screaming for a shot at Dick Tiger's crown, then walking away from the table when Griffith offered a fight-off for it.

Emile didn't use the finger – at least not by itself. Instead he showed Archer ten fingers, balled into fists and encased in leather gloves. Less than three months after taking the title from Tiger he put it on the line against Archer and showed the tough Irishman from the Bronx, who outweighed him by seven-and-a-half pounds, that he was stronger, tougher, and faster. Archer was far from being a slouch. He pushed Griffith to his best performance since the Paret fight. Emile was the aggressor, banging away to the body, hooking, jabbing and even roughing up his bigger opponent on the inside, cutting him over his right eye and the forehead.

Even with Griffith doing his usual loafing once he had a comfortable lead, he convinced just about everyone that he had no trouble handling Joey Archer. Everyone, that is, except Joey Archer. Emile explained, "I could not stand to see a grown man cry. All his friends were crying, too, so I said 'Okay, let's do it again.'"

So they did. On January 23, 1967 Griffith retained his crown by again beating Joey Archer. The decision was unanimous, but even though Joey's face took an even worse battering than the first fight, he couldn't accept defeat and refused to shake Griffith's hand after the fight. Any chance for a Chapter Three went down the drain then and there. For the first time Emile Griffith was angry at Joey Archer.

It was a good payday for Emile as a crowd of nearly 15,000 paid in $127,119, a great gate for a fight under the heavyweight division. Actually, there would have been a few more bucks in the till but there was this good-looking Italian guy sitting in a ringside seat who got a freebie from the Garden brass. Nino Benvenuti had a translator, but there are certain things that are easy to understand just by the look in an eye or the set of a jaw. Nino, who had won all but one of his seventy professional fights, and that one a controversial loss to a Korean in Korea, wanted Emile Griffith.

CHAPTER SIXTEEN

Emile Griffith's life was a sea of emotions. He cried as easily as he laughed and taking care of someone, usually many someones, was very important to him. With Matthew living with a girl friend, Esther Taylor now a distant memory and his friends in the Times Square clubs being declared out of bounds by "that dictator Clahncy" while he was in training, Emile began brooding.

For Emile, it was just as important as loving and taking care of someone, to feel loved, needed, and wanted. He was a strong believer in unconditional love ... so he got a dog, actually two dogs. And they did love him, and he loved them in return. There was his peacocky, princely white poodle, Don Achilles and his Doberman, Lady. He bathed them, brushed them till the static electricity made them feel as though they were participants in a Pavlovian experiment. Emile Griffith was very happy because he was loved. Being loved was as much a need to him as eating and sleeping.

Emile didn't expect to hear them barking for him when he walked from the dressing room to the ring in Madison Square Garden that March night in 1967, because dogs were not allowed at the fights unless they were accompanied by a blind person. But this was his Garden, his home, his people so he did expect to hear the crowd roar for him ...

"Forza con Nino! Forza con Nino! Forza con Nino!" "Strength with Nino!" It echoed from Eighth Avenue to Ninth Avenue. Forty-ninth Street to Fiftieth. It drowned out everything else, even Mommie's screams of "Ju-u-un-i-oor!" which he heard only because he knew she was there. They had come over by boat and plane from Italy to cheer their hero on. Emile sucked it up. They were doing a good job.

He remembered Mommie warning him not to go back to Italy after they rioted and tore up the arena when he fought Juan Carlos Duran there three years before. He listened to her, but what good did it do? He didn't go to Italy, so Italy came over here.

Being thick-skinned, sneering and saying, "Okay, I'll show them!" is one way to respond to such a situation. But to Emile Griffith, it was like being in his own house with his own family turning against him. He tried, but it was like a wounded bull tries against a matador. He rushed and charged; to the clever, side-stepping, nimble-footed Benvenuti it was listless plodding. The handsome Italian moved in-and-out, a step to the left, then to the right, always snapping out the left jab, then a strong left hook to the body and the crowd roaring their own version of "Ole!" – "Forza con Nino!"

In the second round a solid right uppercut dropped Griffith. He shook his head as the crowd drowned out the referee's count. He arose, more embarrassed than hurt. But the bull did have his moment. In the fourth round Benvenuti was hammered by a solid overhand right to the jaw. Like a tree felled by a sharp-edged ax, he toppled face first into the ropes, bouncing to the canvas. It looked as though there was no way he was going to get up but, somehow, he did, beating the count of ten. After that, he was able to avoid Griffith's wild swings the remainder of the round and again in the fifth.

Emile missed his big opportunity. Benvenuti didn't give him another chance. He regained his composure and once again dictated the flow of the fight. He was the master technician and it was almost as though, on that night, Griffith was his foil. Emile's charges and lunges continued, he threw punches, because these are the things he was trained to do, but the energy, strength and vitality that was Emile Griffith was missing. Even Clancy's urging and scolding him between rounds couldn't raise him from his lethargy. Emile Griffith wasn't hurting from any blows, nor had he lost his stamina, adroitness or resourcefulness as so many boxing writers suggested. It was just the way Emile Griffith was. His crowd, his house, had deserted him. He was able to shake off some of the hardest shots in the ring, but he was also a guy who could be hurt without a punch being thrown.

When Johnny Addie, the ring announcer, called out the unanimous decision separating Emile Griffith from his coveted title, the ring had already been taken over by a hysterical mob of Benvenuti fans who had broken through the unprepared security force, trampled the press row, knocking over chairs, tables, typewriters as well as a few syndicated columnists. It was a tough crowd and Emelda Griffith did not have an easy time breaking through their ranks.

Emile went back to Weehawken somewhat wiser than when he had left. He learned that he was a much happier person being a champion than not being a champion. Someone took what was his and he wanted it back. Cousin Bernard thought he was doing Emile a favor by staying with him and walking the dogs. He didn't realize that Lady and Don Achilles were good listeners and that's what Emile needed, not lectures or pep talks. The dogs sensed Emile's sorrow and whimpered softly on occasion, passing their favorite sniffing sites at a slow, almost courteous trot while they listened as Emile unburdened himself. There was no barking and out of respect they chose not to do their usual business. It could wait.

Bernard consoled his cousin, assuring him that the three officials were either blind or incompetent and how fortunate they were to have a return-bout clause because no way did "Benny Venuti" want to get back in the ring with him. Emile smiled. He loved his cousin Bernard, but he really appreciated how smart poodles and dobermans were.

***

"Chickadee, Chickadee, fly away ...," and that's what all the little chickadees who lined the bar and the dance floor at the Gypsy Room and the crystal-chandeliered night club at the Concord Hotel did – one by one they flew away. They rouged their cheeks, brush-painted their mouths with high-gloss lipstick and shadowed their eye-lids, all in preparation to squeal in delight at the handshake, touch or perhaps enjoy a fling around the dance floor with Emile Griffith who was becoming better known at the Concord than their "house" comedian, Buddy Hackett. But there were no squeals because there was no Emile and, pretty soon, no chickadees.

For Emile, this was serious time. Clancy didn't have to set down any ground rules. This was a training camp and Emile was here to train. Whether it was designing hats, crouching behind home plate wearing a chest protector and catcher's mask, playing tennis or having a footrace down Ninth Avenue against traffic, Emile Griffith had to be the best. Clancy's job wasn't always easy. This time it was.

On September 29, 1967 Shea Stadium was starving for a hometown winner. The New York Mets were closing out a 101-game losing season and had finished 10th in the National League. If you come in 10th place in a marathon race, it is not too bad at all. In fact, unless one comes from Kenya, it is a stellar accomplishment. But considering that the National League in 1967 consisted of 10 teams, it is no wonder that so many of the faithful Met fans would leave early to beat the traffic – even those without cars.

Generally, Shea Stadium winners slept in hotels. They were from out of town. Emile Griffith, who owned a home in Hollis, was so close to Shea Stadium that he wouldn't have missed by much if he threw a baseball from his backyard to the ballpark's home plate but he had no intention of filling the bill. He smiled as he journeyed from the dressing room to the ring hearing the shouts for "Nin-o". This time they served as some elixir that started his adrenalin flowing. And it continued flowing for fifteen rounds, just like the blood from Benvenuti's recently renovated nose which Griffith smashed in the first round. Although outweighed and the smaller of the two, on this night Griffith was the stronger, tougher fighter and simply out-muscled and out-punched Benvenuti. There was no aimless lunging like in the first fight. Emile plodded forward behind a stinging left jab, never letting the Italian get off. Nino was dropped in the fourteenth, and at the end of the fight he looked like someone who was keeping company with a vampire.

The loss was not easy for Benvenuti to accept. He cried in his dressing room, feeling he had let his fans and his country down. Emile's fans, meanwhile, celebrated like only Emile's fans can, especially when following Emelda. She scooped Emile up in her arms and to everyone's amazement – and delight, carried the once-again middleweight champion around the room like a little baby. Emile didn't protest. He laughed and waved. After all, he was Emelda's little baby.

"I may have been her baby," Emile laughs, "but I didn't always do as she says. When I told her I was going to fight Remo Golfarini in Italy less than two months after I won the title back from Benvenuti, she was so mad she says she told me I was not to fight there anymore after that riot when I fought Juan Carlos Duran and she yells if I don't obey her she will not give me any more allowance. I told her, 'Mommie, you don't give me any allowance. I give you an allowance.' I waited for her to say that if I didn't listen to her she would not accept any more allowance from me. She didn't say it and I went to Rome.

There was no riot this time as Emile easily dispatched Golfarini, stopping him in the sixth round. When he returned home he was told that he would be opening the new Madison Square Garden on Seventh Avenue and 33rd Street on March 4th, 1968 against Nino Benvenuti.

***

Emile Griffith was some kind of party animal. He was congenial, he smiled a lot, give him a microphone and he'd sing, a dance floor and he'd dance. So, when Emile, who is usually the life of the party, shows up at this penthouse shindig at a midtown hotel on March 4th, 1968, and acts like a withering wallflower there had to be a good reason ... and there was.

He was not happy. In fact, he was very unhappy. Unhappy to the degree that cocktail franks, champagne and socializing did not interest him. Opening the new Madison Square Garden in a championship fight, he had just made history. Like Napoleon made history at Waterloo.

His good friend, Joe Frazier, followed him by knocking out Buster Mathis in the eleventh round of their heavyweight elimination bout, which was a good reason for throwing a party. Joe did sing and dance, eat and drink, and had his back pounded in congratulations.

Joe and Emile became close friends when Joe decided he needed someone to push him doing his roadwork. Emile, who still ran with the joyful abandon of a kid swiping fruit from the peddlers' stands in Charlotte Amalie, was asked and gladly obliged. Joe conceded that Emile ran faster and longer than he could but he didn't mind because he claimed he sang better than Emile. Realizing that Joe Frazier was a lot bigger than he was, Emile permitted Joe to enjoy his delusional fantasy.

Emile Griffith had fought his heart out earlier that night. Now that heart was broken. After the twelfth round, Gil screamed at him that he needed the last three rounds to be sure of victory and like a great stallion making a tremendous stretch drive, Emile poured it on, blasting away at the Italian's body, driving him across the ring with a relentless attack. He did what was asked of him and was certain that he came out a winner.

"When they took so much time adding and re-adding the score cards, I began getting nervous. And when they announced the decision I couldn't believe it," Emile recalls. It was hard for Emile to take this defeat gracefully. He was instructed that as it was an international event with much of the world watching, his family was not to come to the Garden waving American flags.

"So what's the first thing I see walking from my dressing room – the Italian flag being waved all over the place."

The decision that stripped Emile Griffith of his title was razor-thin and was probably decided by a ninth round knockdown that Benvenuti scored with a stunning left hook followed by a right cross as Emile was charging in. An unsteady Griffith climbed to his feet at the count of six and somehow saw a sight that made him believe his brain was scrambled. "There was Mommie, charging into the ring to save me and the police were grabbing her and holding her back. I should have been embarrassed but it made me feel good because I liked knowing my Mommie was always there for me."

A disconsolate Griffith went to the party only because he wanted to congratulate his friend Joe Frazier. Joe hugged Emile and spent a good part of the evening consoling him. "I couldn't believe how much he cared about me," Griffith said softly. Joe cared a lot and it was mutual. They remained friends, sharing family experiences over the years. When

Joe asked Emile to be the godfather to his son Marvis, who grew up to become a topflight heavyweight contender, it was as emotional and stirring a moment to Emile as becoming a champion. This was one title no one would ever take from him.

CHAPTER SEVENTEEN

It is said that the slide down from the top, once it begins, is inevitable and happens much more quickly than the scramble to get there. The subject of that slide doesn't always see it as clearly as the objective viewer. Then again, if you don't see it, it may not happen.

A few days after losing his title to Benvenuti in their rubber match, Emile Griffith went to visit his mother in their Hollis home. That's what he always did when he was feeling low. He went home to Mommie. He walked through the front door into a house covered with confetti. As there was no parade until St. Patrick's Day and that was almost two weeks away and as there was not too much Irish blood in his family he did not expect such a high degree of enthusiasm.

It did not take him very long to discover that the swirl of shredded newspaper covering the floor had nothing to do with shamrocks or the wearing of the green. If a shillelagh were available, that would probably have been put to very good use, though.

Emelda Griffith believed in every kind of freedom, from speech to freedom of the press – as long as it didn't mess with her boy. Emelda felt that some of the articles written about Emile after the fight were better suited for the obituary page than the sport page. Although Emile had dropped his title by the closest of decisions – and to Emelda it was highway robbery - to many of the boxing writers her boy was past tense. It was fortunate that only the articles were within Emelda's reach and not their writers, otherwise they, too, might have been shredded.

At the age of thirty they saw Emile's leg and hand speed slowing, his punch losing its sting and his stamina diminishing. They even wrote of his receding hairline. She hugged her son, shook her head and sighed, "Don't they know that a high forehead is a sign of intelligence?"

Ripping up newspapers may have been a good way of Emelda "showing them", but Emile came up with a better way. He took the matter in his own hands for the next year and a half, carved a path back to a title fight by winning six of seven fights from the toughest opponents to be found. The one loss was of such a questionable nature that a hearing was held to review the facts. Emile Griffith was not a fighter who looked for a soft touch. He looked to fight the best out there and never shied away from a challenge. That was his style.

Emile was scheduled to fight Andy Heilman in Oakland on Friday, June 7th, 1968. It was two days before the fight and Emile was relaxing in bed, watching Senator Robert F. Kennedy claiming victory in the California primary from the Ambassador Hotel in Los Angeles when Gil told him to turn off the TV and go to sleep. When he got up the next morning he found out that Senator Kennedy had been shot. He died later that day.

Fighting Andy Heilman no longer seemed that important. The fight was pushed back to Tuesday, June 11th. It was a 12-round elimination bout and Heilman was a hard-nosed contender but Emile, working with mechanical efficiency, won in impressive style. However, there was no exuberance.

When Emile got back from the coast, there was a surprise waiting for him. Maybe it was inevitable, maybe the thought of taking on the responsibility of married life was too heavy to handle for someone Matthew's age, but whatever the cause or reason, Matthew had returned. Emile was glad. He may not have needed a bodyguard, but he did welcome a companion that did more than just bark. Emile realized, though, that other than barking and an occasional accident when he forgot to walk him, a dog presented no problems.

"It was true that with Matthew there was always trouble," Emile smiled wistfully. *"But it was worth it. It was so good having him back. As much as*

he wanted to be with me, I wanted to be with him just as bad. Oh, there were plenty of friends I enjoyed being with, but Matthew – I really loved him. And he loved me. Yes, I was glad he was back."

His dream of having Matthew to care for – his own little family – was not a bubble. It was real, it was his own small, protective world. True, Emile had a family, but it was large and unwieldy. It was like a universe, each body interacting and dependent upon the movements and actions of the others. He loved and cared for his family, his universe. But he and Matthew – it was so much simpler; a planet and its moon, the magnetic pull of each keeping the other on its proper course. Emile Griffith was happier than he could ever remember being before.

While Matthew reacquainted himself with the neighborhood and wiled away the days playing cards with friends, Emile went to Philadelphia. He liked the soft pretzels and cheese-steak sandwiches. Okay, so they had a broken bell. He did not even mind that they made their local dandy, Gypsy Joe Harris, the favorite. After all, the Philadelphia version of Muhammad Ali had a perfect 24-0 record. He had youth and the fans on his side and a supposedly fading ex-champion to feed off.

On the night of August 6th, in a steambath called the Spectrum, Emile Griffith taught the boogalooing dancing man in white tassled shoes and red, oversized drawers what prizefighting was all about. After the fight, Gypsy Joe Harris thanked him for the lesson. Emile couldn't understand all the put-down jokes about the City of Brotherly Love.

He extended his hand to the disappointed but gracious youngster who was coping with his first loss, and predicted a long and glorious career for him. Gypsy Joe smiled at the kind words but they never came to be. The youngster never fought again. It was discovered that he was blind in one eye and had been since he was eleven years old. He was suspended for life as a prizefighter and a once promising life spiraled steadily downward until, in 1990, Philadelphia's one-time glamour-boy star attraction died a broken man in virtual obscurity.

Emile Griffith went back to Philadelphia in October and when he was trick-or-treated two nights before Halloween, it was definitely no treat. Stan "Kitten" Hayward, number three ranked welterweight in the world, was a good enough fighter when he didn't have to depend on tricks. He was not the one who rang Emile's bell. The bell that rang was a telephone call to Emile's hotel room the afternoon of the fight. Clancy answered it and the trick was whether to believe it or not. The message from an anonymous caller was that Hayward would be getting help from the officials. All Gil could do was stare at the phone and shrug.

That night in a hard-fought ten-rounder, the Kitten kept it close but virtually everyone had scored it for Griffith after he nearly took Hayward out in the final round. Referee Zack Clayton scored the tenth round, Griffith's biggest round of the fight, even. That point cost Griffith the fight. Clancy protested to the Pennsylvania State Athletic Commission and they went through the motions by granting a hearing. Of course, the decision was upheld.

Dan Daniel, in the February 1969 issue of Ring Magazine, wrote,

> *".. two judges as well as referee Zack Clayton were involved in the decision, in Philadelphia, favoring Stan Kitten Hayward over Emile Griffith.*
>
> *The Ring Magazine has received many protests from men who saw the bout as a victory for Griffith.*
>
> *No matter which way a decision goes, there always are complaints.*
>
> *But in this case Griffith's letter writing supporting cast numbers close to 100, to date."*

Although the record books show Griffith's fight with Hayward as a loss, in the minds of most, including Emile, it registered as a win, but he didn't like question-marks so in May 1969 he set the record straight when he easily defeated Hayward in their rematch held at Madison Square Garden.

It seemed certain now that Emile's most fervent wish would come true, a fourth match with Benvenuti. But Emile learned a lesson that he had learned before and he would, unfortunately, learn many more times during his life. It was a message bellowed forth some years earlier by Leo Durocher, bemoaning the nature and character of his "Beloved Bums", the Brooklyn Dodgers – "Nice guys finish last!"

After winning four consecutive fights in 1969, Emile Griffith was given another crack at the title. But it wasn't the middleweight title. Nino Benvenuti felt that Emile Griffith was too nice to fight again. He was so nice that he took time out to help Nino prepare for his fight against Dick Tiger. Nino could not repay such kindness by exchanging punches with this man. Instead he asked him to be the Godfather to his son, Giuliano, which immediately doubled Emile's list of Godchildren, headed by Marvis Frazier.*

So, instead of fighting Benvenuti for the Middleweight crown, Griffith was asked to bring his weight back down and challenge Jose Napoles for the welterweight championship. It was four years since Griffith last made the 147-pound limit. He was always a natural welterweight and felt he had no problem making the weight. In fact, he came in at 144½. As a welterweight, Griffith was always the stronger man in the ring, able to outmuscle his opponent. But it was obvious that he had drained himself as Napoles showed that he was the stronger of the two that night. It was the first fight of his brilliant career, discounting the one-punch Hurricane Carter knockout, when Griffith was soundly, decisively beaten.

One thing true about Emile Griffith was that he knew how to have a good time. He enjoyed singing, dancing, he enjoyed hanging out in exotic night spots, but among his very favorite pleasurable pursuits was fooling the press. After the Napoles fight, Emile had a very good time. Over the next year and a half, he won ten consecutive fights, in between which, he met and married Mercedes Donastorg.

The boxing writers weren't the only ones that he fooled. Tom Bogs, the Danish and European middleweight champion, was unbeaten in 54 fights and had never been knocked off his feet. He was in negotiations with Madison Square Garden regarding a title fight against Nino Benvenuti.

---

* See tribute from Nino Benvenuti page 249

Emile Griffith, an old man in Bogs' mind, was merely a stepping stone who was already considered stepped over. It turned out to be a step that Bogs missed. He fell flat on his face.

Actually, it was not his face that he fell on. Emile gave him an old-fashioned whipping, dropping him in the 6th and 10th rounds before a stunned crowd in Copenhagen.

"I sort of felt bad for him. I know what it is to have big dreams spoiled, but you should never be fighting your next fight until you have taken care of the one at hand."

Emile was wrong. In Bogs case, that's all he had, a big dream that never became real. Emile realized his dreams; they were part of his life.

After the Bogs fight he had little trouble disposing of Dick Tiger in Tiger's final bout, then beating Danny Perez in St. Thomas while falling in love. Emile had not planned to fall in love. Like so many of the things in his life, it just happened.

Christine Griffith wasn't there to see her Mommie and daddy dance into each other's lives at Bambousay, a Charlotte Amalie night club, in the fall of 1970 but she heard about it so many times from so many people that she might as well have been.

"Mom used to wear hot pants and boots and weighed 105 pounds. It was love at first sight for daddy."

It was actually love at first sight for both of them. It's just that Emile knew it while Mercedes Donastorg, who definitely did not look like the prim and proper school teacher that she was, could not believe that Emile Griffith, adored by and every Virgin Islander's hero, was in love with her. Emile claims that as soon as he saw someone who looked better in hot pants than he did his heart was won over. He had no curfew as he had just beaten Danny Perez two nights earlier, on one of his frequent visits to his root base, so he was able to dance, dance, dance all night.

It wasn't just that this pert, sassy girl looked better than he did in hot pants. She even out-gyrated him on the dance floor, which took a lot of gyrating because Emile was good. Mercedes was as at home on a dance floor as Emile was in the ring. She had moved to New York as a young girl where she went to grade school and high school and eventually became a professional dancer, performing with the June Taylor Dancers, who opened and closed the Ed Sullivan Show each Sunday night. After graduating high school she returned to St. Thomas and starred with a dance troupe called Prince Edward and his Slave Girls. She was not Prince Edward.

Gentle breezes, a star-filled sky, a large, glowing tropical moon and a beautiful face smiling up at you can have a very powerful effect. *"I knew I was in love when I started doing silly things and being over-protective. Like when I hear this guy make a remark and I am ready to take him apart. I put my nose right onto his and say – 'I'm going to teach you some manners unless you apologize to my lady-friend!' And he looks at me with eyes growing as big as the moon. 'What should I apologize for?'*

'I heard you call her a bimbo – Look at that bimbo, you said.'

'What? I said, "Look at her do that Limbo!" when I couldn't believe how low she got under the Limbo stick on the dance floor.'

Man, maybe I couldn't hear so good because of the loud music – but whatever, I felt so stupid I couldn't apologize enough. So to show him how sorry I was and that I am really a good guy, I am buying him drinks all night. He says, 'Please, it really is not necessary, but I don't take "No" for an answer. I keep plying him with liquor until one of his friends comes up to me and pleads with me to stop, that he is a reformed former alcoholic who has taken the pledge and is on the wagon."

Griffith returned to the States thinking that being in love could be a very scary proposition. He had a talk with his mother. Emelda agreed with him.

He was getting ready to fight Nate Collins in San Francisco, the culmination of an unbelievable comeback year that catapulted him to the Number One contender position in the Middleweight division. He truly believed that he was very happy to be unattached and free as the wind when Howie Albert told him that they were offered a fight against Juan Ramos in St. Thomas. "Interested?"

"Yup!"

Now he was trying to make up his mind about telling Matthew about Mercedes, remembering that Matthew wasn't exactly overjoyed when he had told him about his thinking of marrying Esther Taylor. It was a decision he never had to make.

It was early Saturday morning and Emile was still in bed when Matthew returned to the apartment with a few friends. Emile began the waking up process and was going to pack for his trip to San Francisco while Matthew and his buddies indulged in one of their favorite pastimes, seven card stud poker. It turned out that more than just deuces were wild.

When he heard the shot he dropped the suitcase he was holding and ran to the living room. He couldn't believewhat he saw. Two guys were backed up against the wall, while this other guy, Monserrate DeLeon, was sprawled out on the couch, blood spurting from his mouth and Matthew standing over him with a still-smoking thirty-eight. The kid was crying, "It was an accident. It wasn't supposed to be loaded."

Knowing that Emile wasn't in the room at the time of the incident, they let him post a $1,000 bond as a material witness. Emile left for the coast for his fight with Nate Collins, another easy win for Griffith. Even though the case was dropped and Matthew got off with a slap on the wrist, Emile knew that his little world was just a bubble after all. It had already burst. He thought back to the kid trying to run his brother Franklin down. That was strike one. This was strike two. Emile didn't want to be around for a strike three.

He didn't have to say anything to the kid. Matthew was already packed when Emile returned from Frisco. He gave Emile a gentle nudge, but couldn't look him in the eye.

"You know that girl-friend of mine. I think it's about time I grew up and let her take care of me. Know what I mean, Champ?"

Emile knew. He also knew what it was to be angry with and feel good about someone at the same time.

Matthew stayed in touch. He'd write, he'd call on occasion and Emile always lit up when he heard from him. When he spoke of him, he called him "My boy." Matthew called himself "The Bodyguard." About five, six years later, Emile got a call. Matthew was still the protector, the bodyguard. Now it was his girl friend that he was protecting. Some guy who wanted what Matthew had couldn't handle rejection. This time he was the one with the .38 and he pulled it out, ready to do an "If I can't have you, nobody can" bit. He pointed it at the girlfriend and squeezed off. Maybe Matthew was some special kind of a guy, maybe it was strictly a reflex. He jumped in front of his girl who somebody else wanted very badly, and took the bullet for her. He took it in the right temple.

Emile visited him at a rehab center on Roosevelt Island, New York. Matthew was in a wheel chair, paralyzed on the right side from the neck down. Emile couldn't speak at first. He didn't know what to say. "Hello, Poppy-man," Matthew smiled up at him. Emile reached down and clasped both of his hands. He still couldn't speak. It took him quite a while.

It was not the kind of fight that was going to enhance the storied reputation of five time world champion Emile Griffith. The guy's name was Juan Ramos. He was going nowhere and Emile got him there even quicker – two rounds to be exact. What this fight did for Emile Griffith was get him back to St. Thomas and that large tropical moon. He went home with a victory, Mercedes "Sadie" Donastorg and a great big smile.

On May 8, 1971 Emile and Sadie were married at St. Peter's Church in Monticello, New York with a grand reception at the Concord Hotel. Joe Frazier, who two months earlier had defeated Muhammad Ali for the heavyweight championship in what was called the Fight of the Century, served as best man.

Mrs. Mercedes Griffith moved from St. Thomas to the apartment in Weehawken prepared to live happily ever after with the man of her dreams. But that's where he mostly was – in her dreams. Emile would be at his training camp or making an appearance for this organization, an interview for that TV station, always something to do and someplace to go, while she remained in Weehawken. She had two dogs and four walls and she got to know them very well. As for Weehawken, she knew the super market, the dry cleaner and the drug store. That was her Weehawken. She wanted to go with Emile when he traveled but he couldn't be distracted so she stayed at home.

CHAPTER EIGHTEEN

The first thing Emile did when he got off the plane from Monte Carlo after his rematch with Monzon was call home. There was no answer. He said goodby to Gil and Howie and took a cab to Weehawken. When he got into the apartment he tiptoed because it was late and he didn't want to wake anyone. It was wasted consideration. No one was home.

It was too empty and too quiet for Emile. He didn't like being alone. Neither did Sadie. She had left a note on his night table. He read it and laid his head back on the pillow. He felt tired and for the first time, he felt old.

Growing old just happens. You don't strive for it, you don't study for it; some do prepare for it, but most just slide into it without even realizing it. For some it is a graceful transition, it is termed achieving maturity, others try to stave off the inevitable with hair dyes, lotions and youth-enhancing elixirs. It occurs at different times for different people. Athletes, especially boxers, face it sooner in life than others, the 30th birthday generally being the passport. As he reeled off win after win at the age of thirty-three, it was becoming obvious that Emile Griffith simply had no grasp of the situation – until this point.

Even after the robbery in Monte Carlo, there was an edge to him. Anger is good. It channels into desire and action. He searched for anger. It wasn't there. For the first time that he could remember, Emile felt absolutely nothing. He loosened his tie and closed his eyes, letting his thoughts and mind wander.

***

On July 26, 1971, in a fight against Frenchman Max Cohen for his tenth straight victory, Emile Griffith tied Tony Canzoneri's record for most appearances at Madison Square Garden – twenty-three. He remembers accusing Clancy of being an evil man for breaking up his honeymoon to train for that fight. Emile went on to establish a Garden record of 27 appearances that probably never will be broken.

After beating Cohen, Emile was being interviewed in his dressing room by Lester Bromberg, then writing for the New York Post.

"Well, Emile, looks like you found the Fountain of Youth before Ponce de Leon," Lester said with a smile.

Emile looked surprised. "De Leon? The boy who was accidentally shot in my apartment? I didn't know he was looking for any fountain. Is he all better now?"

Nino Benvenuti had promised Emile time after time that he would give him another title shot, but it never happened. Perhaps it was because he liked Emile too much to fight him again. The same week that Emile fought what Clancy calls one of his greatest fights against Nate Collins in San Francisco - Carlos Monzon knocked out Nino Benvenuti in the 12th round in Rome, becoming the new middleweight champ. Monzon gave what Benvenuti promised.

Emile's mind jumped to what was freshest in his memory. He was sitting in the dressing room in Louis II Stadium in Monte Carlo, too stunned to speak. He didn't have to. Gil Clancy said it all for everyone, and it was meant for everyone to hear. Griffith was the first one to step forward and acknowledge Monzon as "a real champ" after their first fight in September, 1971 in Luna Park, Buenos Aires.

When the referee stopped that fight in the 14th round, Griffith was still on his feet and able to defend himself, but Monzon was clearly ahead then and Griffith had nothing but praise for him. Since then, Monzon had been destroying everyone who climbed into the ring to challenge him. Until Bennie Briscoe lost to him by decision, he had scored eleven straight knockouts.

Emile, still having no clue about how seniors were supposed to behave, was equally effective over the next two years except for one outrageous blemish in Paris. Griff reeled off six straight wins after the Monzon fight, at times reaching back and finding the greatness that once was his. Greatness can be multi-dimensional. There are those who feel that the Emile Griffith who fought Mando Muniz at the Anaheim Convention Center on January 31, 1972 was Griffith at his best. Not just as a fighter, but as a person. Armando Muniz was the darling of the West Coast. A handsome college graduate working towards his master's degree, he was undefeated in eighteen professional bouts and seemed to be on a streamlined express to the championship. Emile, cast as the villain, a role whose lines he never mastered, lived up to that role and derailed the train. In a one sided bloodbath Emile taught the youngster enough to qualify him for a second graduate degree. But the cloak of evil-doer simply did not sit well on Griffith's broad shoulders. In the eighth round, after taking a steady pounding, a large purple mouse under Mando's left eye split, with the blood cascading down his face. What Emile Griffith did then transcends greatness, raises nobility and class to a level rarely seen in a prize ring or any sports venue. He lowered his attack to the body, refusing to damage the youngster any further and encouraged him not to quit, pleading, "Don't give up. Keep punching!"

Winning the fight had become a foregone conclusion. What was important was that Emile transformed himself from villain to super-hero, with the crowd standing as one and applauding him as he embraced the youngster at the end of the fight.

Nearly thirty-three years after that fight, October 16, 2004, Emile Griffith and Armando Muniz got together at the 25th Annual Banquet of Champions of the World Boxing Hall of Fame in Los Angeles. The memory of that night was still strong and the esteem each had for the other was gratifying to behold. Mando smiled at Griffith and before a crowd of onlookers said that even though it was his first loss, he was proud that it was to a great champion like Emile Griffith. "And I didn't mind the loss, because, really, it was an education. I learned what prizefighting was all about that night."

The travesty in Paris was quite different but didn't remove the mantle of hero from Griffith's shoulders. Emile was fighting Jean-Claude Bouttier in what was billed as an elimination bout to meet Carlos Monzon for the middleweight title.

At the end of six rounds, Griffith was in complete command, leading five rounds to one on most cards. In the seventh round, after Griffith launched a strong body attack, all blows being well above the belt to all ringsiders, Bouttier clutched his midsection and moaned and the referee simply stepped in and disqualified Griffith. Not only were there no low blows – there were no warnings. It was a carbon copy of what had happened in Bouttier's previous fight against Jose Chirino. It was a brazen and obvious attempt to assist a national sports hero but the crowd didn't appreciate it, jeering Bouttier and cheering Griffith. And Griffith got the call to fight Monzon.

So, as Clancy took it out on any and every inanimate object in the dressing room, Emile was in a state of shock. He fought the perfect fight against Monzon, pressuring him to the ropes, banging away on the inside and taking away Monzon's reach and power advantage. But this was a town where you don't pick up your chips until the croupier says they're yours.

He thought of the title that he should have had but didn't. It hurt, but there were things that hurt more.

He looked around at the empty apartment – that was a deep hurt. He felt sorry for himself and lonely – maybe even a little old.

Love and marriage don't always go together like a horse and carriage. "*I wasn't that good at being married,*" Emile admits, "*but that doesn't mean that I didn't truly love.*"

Emile did truly love and perhaps that was part of his problem when it came to being married. His heart was open to so many – family, friends, associates – that to channel that love to one person was something that he was incapable of. But the love was always there. To this day he and Sadie remain best of friends and Christine, Sadie's daughter who was adopted by Emile as an infant when he and Sadie were married, now a beautiful young woman, visits her father often and they adore each other openly.

"*Coming back from a fight or a trip was always exciting,*" Emile reminisces, "*because I knew Sadie would be there to greet me and it was nice. Then one day I come home and Sadie isn't there. Okay. I figured I take trips, so she took a trip. I waited. It was a long wait.*"

Mercedes decided to go back to St. Thomas and resume her career as a school teacher.

There's this thing with prizefighters when it comes to being hurt. They learn very early in the game that being hurt makes you vulnerable so they hide hurt. In the ring a tooth-jarring blow often results in a smile, intense pain brings looks ranging from indifference to pleasure. Emile Griffith's world was not confined to a roped-off twenty square-foot area. Whatever pain there might have been was masked by an easy smile and comforted by Mommie and his Times Square friends.

Christine Griffith, like most people, did not hide hurt. She didn't try. Over the years she's remained very close to her father, as has her mother. Although they were eventually divorced, Sadie and Emile still visit each other occasionally. She speaks of Emile fondly and explains, "Emile has his ways, I have mine. I decided we would be best friends."

For Christine, who sells clothing, jewelry, incense and cologne from her store bearing Emile's name in St. Thomas, it hasn't been quite that simple. It was a beautiful fall day in 2003 and Christine had come in from St. Thomas to visit Emile. Her voice fills with emotion as she says, "I love my father very much. Daddy used to get up 4-5 in the morning to do his roadwork and spend the rest of the day training in the gym. We didn't spend much time together, but it was precious time." Then she shook her head. "I have to come up with my own conclusion over their separation. It was nobody's fault. They just didn't have enough time together." She pauses and possibly without realizing, exhibits some resentment. "But Dad was working, why didn't she understand that? If I had a husband, I would understand." Catching herself with a sigh of resignation, she smiles reflectively, "I'm not here to take sides. I love both of them. And Mom loves Daddy very much."

She stopped to turn and look at Emile. "The best thing I got from my father was love." Christine's hand reached out to her father. "Don't ever leave me."

Emile gripped his daughter's hand tightly.

"I always want to be here to protect her – I love her so much. Sometimes I go a little crazy, though." Emile laughed, but he was laughing at himself as he thought back. *"I had this red Doberman, Caesar. Next to Sadie and Christine ... and Mommie, Caesar was probably the dearest thing to me. Christine was maybe 2, 3 years old. I just opened the door, coming back from the gym – and, oh, my God! What a sight. There is my precious Chrissie, crying and screaming in Sadie's arms, her face covered with blood and Caesar is cowering in a corner. When Sadie tells me that Caesar bit – not just bit – tore through my baby's lip, I am a wild man! I run to my closet and get my shotgun and go for Caesar to take him outside and kill him. I'm furious, I'm crying, I'm out of my mind, but not so much that I don't know what I have to do. Then I find out something I never knew before; that is how strong Sadie was. She wrapped me up with one arm as she is still holding Christine. Maybe I wanted to be stopped, but I don't think so. Anyhow, she screams at me that we must get Caesar to the vet and have him checked for rabies. They stitched up my beautiful baby's lip and over time I was able to forgive Caesar and permit him back into my home."*

Emile thinks back to his wedding at the Concord Hotel. It's a fond memory. He remembers dancing to many different tunes. Sadly, Emile found that when his marriage ended he was still dancing to a different tune. Instead of the usual commiserating and offers of advice, in Emile's case, he was not sure what people were saying or offering because it was all done in whispers. But others heard it very clearly ...

Emile Griffith's wedding was a staged affair to cover up the fact that he was exactly what Benny "Kid" Paret said he was – a maricon!

For Emile, the specter of Benny Paret never leaves. The haunting continues. He knows that it is not a ghost following him, but, rather, a slight, a taunt, an accusation made decades ago that refuses to be put to rest. It is what people remember of that long-ago March night – a championship prizefight in which one man mocked the other's manhood and was beaten to death because of it. It is a memory that distorts reality and alters truth. This is the ghost that follows Emile Griffith his every waking day.

The irony is that if the bout had not resulted in its tragic aftermath, the death of Benny Paret, Emile Griffith probably would never have been subjected to the continued disrespect and back-fence sniping insinuations. A prizefighter projects a certain image and Emile was never a perfect fit. There are plenty of men who speak in high-pitched, melodious Carribean voices, who are compassionate enough to care about others and sensitive to the point that they cry at sad events, whose movements are graceful, and enjoy wearing an exotic wardrobe. Their lifestyles are not scrutinized or questioned. But, then again we don't expect to see them climb through the ropes for an all-out fistfight. As we look at Emile's life, it is as if he straddles two worlds, accepted both and usually – but not always, was accepted by both.

Emile made no effort to hide the fact that he not only frequented the bars of Times Square but considered them his second home; many of the regulars were his close friends and confidants. But his answer when questioned about why he was there, consistently and without rancor was, "They are my friends. People want me to say I am something that I am not. I am not a faggot. If I were I would not be afraid or ashamed to say it. But it seems that is what everyone wants to hear. Should I say – Okay, I'm a faggot – Would that make everybody happy?"

The ghosts that follow Emile are real. In spite of all he was and is, the final words of a dead person make for a strong indictment, unfair becomes fair and flippant name-calling becomes conviction.

For Emile Griffith, love was always a many splendored thing ... inside the ring, outside, it was the essence of what he was about. And what he gave was returned. He became the elder statesman of the sport, its beloved patriarch, adored by fans of five continents. In the twilight years of his great career, every time he entered the ring, he came out a winner, regardless of the decision.

Emile went to South Africa as a heroic sports idol, lost a close decision in a small fight, won a huge decision in a major fight, and left as a living legend. He almost left before any fight took place. The apartheid-oriented policies of this country never took into consideration that love, loyalty and honor dictated policies of its own.

When Emile arrived in Johannesburg, he learned that according to South African by-laws when a black is fighting a black, white is out – out of the stands and out of the corners. It seemed the only chance Gil Clancy had of working with his man was if he was willing to try an Al Jolson or Eddie Cantor vaudeville routine. Clancy was not a guy for make-up.

For Griffith, it was strictly a no contest – and he meant "No Contest."

"No Clahncy, no Griffith," he announced. *"Clahncy has been in my corner throughout my career. If they don't let him in, I won't fight."*

There were some weak attempts at saving face, some stammering and double-talk but a scorned government was brought to its knees by a black fighter standing up for his white trainer-manager to the cheers and plaudits of the people and the international press.

"Emile doesn't have a political bone in his body," Clancy explained. "He believes in what is right and he stands up for it all the way."

On August 9th, 1975, Emile Griffith climbed into the ring in Johannesburg and went ten rounds with a kid named Elijah "Tap Tap" Makhathini while the crowd and the press section roared for and cheered for Emile throughout the bout. When the final bell sounded and the decision was awarded to Makhatini, the crowd and the reporters all stood and continued applauding ... for Griffith. ... They were joined by the opponent, Makhatini.

Emile Griffith did not know how to age, so he didn't. In his mid and late 30's, while most of his contemporaries were trying a vitamin supplement known as Geritol, called watching the Lawrence Welk Show an exciting way to spend an evening and shopped for comfy slacks with elastic waistbands, Emile Griffith continued climbing up those four steps into the ring to test the meanest, toughest and best young fighters around. It wasn't that he won more often than he lost, but until his finale, no opponent, regardless of ability or ranking, had an easy night's work.

An unbelievable performance would be followed by a disappointing upset, then back to another exhilarating victory. Pushing forty, he beat some of the top contenders and rising stars of the sport. In Philadelphia he beat their native son, Bennie Briscoe; he went to Montreal and licked Donato Paduano. There was Maryland's young, native son, Leo 'Kid' Saenz, streaking towards a title shot with a 22-1 record. Emile fought him in front of all his friends, neighbors and fans in the Capital Centre in Landover. They loved Leo and tried very hard not to like Griffith. After he gave their hero an education he'd rather have done without, beating him soundly while tattooing him with every punch in the book, they couldn't help liking Emile. Not when this old warhorse took the time and had the graciousness to visit the lumped up loser in his dressing room and make him feel like a million bucks by shouting out, "Where's that tiger? I want to shake his hand. Leo, you are some good fighter. I enjoyed it."

"Me too," said Saenz.

"That's great," answered the victor. "We both enjoyed it. I hope we do it again soon."

"Not too soon," said Leo, with a sick laugh.

Then there were the other nights, like the night he lost a 12-rounder to Tony Licata in Boston, the night he dropped a hotly disputed decision for the light-middleweight title in Berlin, Germany to Eckhard Dagge, or the night he fought his 24th main event at Madison Square Garden (27 fights overall), breaking Tony Canzoneri's record of 23. It was against future middleweight champ Vito Antuofermo and youth would not be denied. In the dressing room after the fight Clancy didn't dispute the decision but said that Emile never got mad at Antuofermo - there was nothing to trigger him off, no punches that hurt him and Emile believed he was winning.

Emile himself spoke matter-of-factly to the press, holding an ice pack to his face, and stating that Antuofermo "never hurt me ... he tried to bully me." When his mother, Emelda, couldn't handle the setback as well as her son and entered the dressing room decked out in a lavender suit and large black hat, crying uncontrollably and caressing him, like a good son he turned and handed her his ice bag. "Here, you need this more than I do."

Emile swallowed the disappointment and simply moved into a higher gear. Two years later, the "washed up" fighter was scoring back to back knockouts over Dino Del Cid in four rounds in Cartegena, Colombia and Frank Reiche, in the tenth round in Hamburg, Germany.

But wherever he fought, he was revered by the crowds. At the tail end of his career, still on the road: *"Emile Griffith lost a controversial upset decision to French middleweight champion Joel Bonnetaz in Perequeux, France, one fan leaped into the ring and carried the 39-year-old former world welterweight and middleweight champion for a lap of honor to the crowd's wild applause."*

AP & UPI (4-16-1977)

Celebrating a 39th birthday is often traumatic – Jack Benny's symbolic milestone of youth's final frontier – but for Emile Griffith it was dramatic. They threw a party for him at Madison Square Garden with a big birthday cake and all the trimmings and told him he could make a wish. It was a silent wish but everyone knew what it was.

On the eve of his 39th birthday Emile Griffith fought his 28th fight at Madison Square Garden against a tough Irishman, Christy Elliott.

> *"Emile Griffith evoked occasional memories of greatness with a strong finish Wednesday night when he triumphantly celebrated his return to New York's Madison Square Garden on the eve of his 39th birthday by hammering out a 10-round majority decision over a bloody Christy Elliott.*
>
> *Griffith stole the spotlight in the boxing tripleheader, which drew 10,930 fans and a gate of $103,457. ...*
>
> *"Fight your best round, this may be your last round in Madison Square Garden," Clancy told Griffith, who was fighting in the famous New York arena for the 28th time in his 19-year career and first time in two years."*
>
> *- Herald Wire Services 2-4-77*

And, so, Emile Griffith fought his best round and made the wish that everyone knew he had made come true.

Emile always believed in himself. It was a belief that Gil Clancy instilled in him and a belief that Gil strongly shared. Sometimes believing distorts reality and mitigates logic. Gil Clancy refused to have his judgment compromised by devotion.

It was July 30, 1977 and they were in Monte Carlo, the Kingdom of Chance, where people go to defy the odds and probability. For Emile Griffith, who was fighting Alan Minter, the European Middleweight champ, it was a night when Probability and Destiny merged. There was no roll of the dice, no chance or hope of Luck intervening. That was not Emile's style. Heart and Determination were. And that he had in abundance, but the sands of the hour-glass had run out.

Gil Clancy watched as the fighter who had changed the course of both of their lives and who he cherished as one would a son fought a gallant but losing battle. He threw punches, but took more, he was knocked down, but got up and fought back and in a final effort, knowing he was well behind, captured the final two rounds. He lost as only a champion can lose and Gil knew it was time.

A couple days after returning to the states Emile was sitting in Gil's living room. The Clancys had this tradition of watching the sun set with a dry Martini. It was Gil's and Nancy's Happy Hour. Their martinis were very dry but it was not a happy hour. Emile was more nervous than before a fight and ran his hand across his head looking for hair that was no longer there. An untouched cup of tea sat on the coffee table before him.

"Emile," it sounded as though Gil had swallowed an olive, but he hadn't. "It's over. You're retiring."

"No, no. One more fight, Clahncy," Emile reached his hand out to him and it was more of a plea than a request. "Just not against one of those tall lefties."

"Emile, that's it. You've done it all. There's nothing more to prove." He walked over and placed his hand on Emile's shoulder. The fighter took a deep breath, got up and walked over to where the telephone was. He dialed and placed the receiver to his ear.

"Hi, Mommie, I'm here at Clahncy's house and I am not going to be fighting again. Clahncy said it was time for me to retire. ... Okay, I'll come over later." He hung up the phone. Gil and Nancy looked at him.

"She said if Mr. Clahncy said it, then that is it. I am retired."

Nancy pulled out a kleenex and there was a tear coming from Gil's eye – and it was not from a cinder.

CHAPTER NINETEEN

I would say it was not an easy time. It seemed that everything I loved in life was not with me anymore. The one thing I loved to do more than anything else – boxing – no more. The people I needed and loved the most - Matthew, even though he brought trouble whenever he was around, I missed him. Sadie and I spoke but I knew we lived two different lives in two different places. It was okay. We would always be friends. It was sort of like my family, Mommie and my brothers and sisters. I knew I had their love and I loved them, but it was a different kind of love. And there were my friends from the Times Square clubs. We had great times but it wasn't enough. I needed real love – another Matthew.

1979-Secaucus, New Jersey Youth Detention Facility

Belty's grin showed only where the two front teeth used to be. It didn't show why they were missing. "Hey, Luis, my man, you oughta have one-a them needlepoint shits to hang on the wall. You know, one what says 'Home, Sweet Home'. Welcome back! Man, your food ain't even got cold yet!" He laughed hard because he thought he was being very funny.

Luis Rodrigo didn't share that thought so he didn't laugh. He dropped the bedsheets, blanket and pillow that had been handed to him by the Supply Officer, next to the rolled up mattress on the bedspring that didn't spring. He had finished serving three months for breaking and entering less than three weeks ago. This time he was in for six months. He told the judge that there was a mistake made somewhere; he swiped half the amount that he did last time. How could they make him serve twice the time? He felt a month-and-a-half would be fair.

The judge congratulated him on his arithmetic but explained that was not the way things worked. There are many ways to deal with disappointment. Luis's way was to flop out on his bunk and very carefully study every spot, crack and blemish on the ceiling, staying in touch with the world around him with an occasional sigh. It was not unreasonable to assume that some sort of quiz on ceiling topography with a grand prize for the highest score was in the offing.

Although this behavior was not in keeping with the spirit of the institution, it was definitely preferable to many of the other methods of dealing with disappointment by his fellow inmates. A sigh was Luis's defense against life's harsh blows. And, usually, anger or an aggressive attitude, two sighs. Luis Rodrigo accepted the fact that there was no one to blame for his situation but himself. He was a kid who went with the flow and sometimes the current took him to places he never really wanted to be at.

That didn't mean that Luis never lost his temper or wouldn't stand up and fight for himself or for what he thought was right, even if it spelled trouble for him. There was the time he found himself sitting on an orange crate in the equipment room playing poker for cigarettes which was the traditional currency of the facility.

As this was poker and not solitaire, there were a few more players involved, each with his own crate. Among them was this kid Samoa. The closest he ever came to the island he was named after was when he walked out of the movie "South Pacific" which he thought was going to be about Iwo Jima or Guadalcanal with John Wayne running onto the beach from an LST firing fourteen machine guns. Instead he hears somebody singing about shampooing and washing a guy out of her hair. He was called Samoa because he had great yearnings. Whatever was within reach of any of the five senses, food or anything, he would grunt, "Hey, I want some mo'."

Now there were certain universal, indisputably accepted facts of life that were simply beyond question or discussion. One was that Luis knew he lived in a world where jacks always had to step aside for ladies.

Everyone knew that. It was just the way things were supposed to be. So, when Samoa starts gathering in the pot after laying out two jacks, Luis goes, "Hold on!" and points to his two queens that were every bit as visible as Samoa's two jacks.

It was then that Luis learned that if Samoa would have been in Sir Walter Raleigh's place, not only would he have had a very dry cape but England would have had a queen who could not cross the street. It was not so much that Luis Rodrigo was a student of history nor was he a knight on a chivalrous mission. He was a kid who wanted his cigarettes.

There were those who thought that Luis should be commended for upholding the honor of three queens- two pasteboards and one Elizabeth. Mr. Mullaney, the director of the Secaucus Youth Home was not one of those. Instead, he felt that Luis had to receive a punishment. Although the punishment he chose was not a harsh one – he wanted Luis to apologize for rearranging the map of Samoa – Luis refused. So, the punishment was escalated to "confined to quarters". To Luis Rodrigo, being confined to quarters was like Brer Rabbit being thrown in a briar patch.

So, there he was, lying on his bunk and sighing when the new correction officer walked in ready with what Luis was sure was going to be a lecture. "New" meant he wasn't there during Luis' previous stint but being lectured by one of the staff was not new to Luis. Whether it was a social worker, psychologist, warden or one of the officers, he was accustomed to being advised, scolded, warned or admonished, all the while shaking his head up and down. When it came to listening, Luis was like a sponge. He sopped it all up, bloating with the wisdom imparted to him and as soon as the door closed behind the lecturer – whoosh! – he de-bloated, let it all flow back out, like it was never in him.

"Have a Hershey bar," the officer said, holding out the offering and smiling. "Isn't this place fun?"

Luis sat up. This was different, so far, but this guy had to be coming in from left field. No matter, Luis had no intention of being disrespectful, at least, not until he finished his Hershey bar. "Fun? You gotta be kidding me, man, or you just putting me on?"

"You seem to think it's fun. You keep coming back like it's a resort."

Luis lay back down realizing there was no such thing as a free candy bar. It was going to be a lecture after all. "I keep getting invitations for free room and board. You know, I got a winning personality."

"Okay, personality counts. Every little plus helps, because you sure got an awful lot of minuses." The Guard says.

Luis saw that the smile never faded which made what he said sound much more friendly than it would have come across otherwise. "How come you're camping out in this place like it's home-sweet-home? You're not a bad kid. You're not a troublemaker, no attitude, no chip on your shoulder ... sometimes you even show a little respect."

Luis yawned. "Okay, what's next? You're gonna play "Hearts and Flowers" maybe?"

"You want to be a smart-ass, go ahead. But don't think you're impressing anyone. I know the road you're going down, Luis – every fork and every turn. I've been down it."

"Oh, yeah. So I guess you're gonna draw me a map, huh?"

"No map. Just trying to point you in the right direction."

"How come I'm so lucky I get this one-on-one treatment?"

"You better believe you are lucky. Maybe it's because I look at you and I see a little bit of myself a long time ago. First, get your butt out of this room. Being locked up in here doesn't do anything for you. Hang out with the right people, take some classes and learn something useful. Work with the system, not against it. You got a good head, Luis. Use it." He was repeating what he had heard nearly thirty years earlier when he first entered a place called Mandal.

Luis sat up again. He stared at the smiling black face in front of him and tried to figure out whether this guy was mouthing a textbook speech or really cared. He looked at the ID tag over the breast pocket of his jacket. "Emile Griffith"

"You think this is the first speech or lecture I ever heard? You know what gets me? All this fancy, high-sounding talk don't mean nothing because until you do your time on the inside of a lockup like this, how can you tell me what's good or bad to do? You have any idea what it's like being in a place like this?" Luis stared at him, but the officer didn't stare back. His eyes seemed to be looking or searching for something in the distance. Then Luis Rodrigo noticed, for the first time the smile was gone from the face of Emile Griffith.

***

Solitude and Silence were Emile's enemies. He had to be part of a world where noise, music and merrymaking prevailed. There were times when, caught in the throes of depression, self-pity or recrimination, he would retreat to one of his Times Square "sanctuaries" where all he looked for was the reassurance of a gentle embrace or an encouraging word of support.

But there were other times when he yearned for a world of loud, blaring music, laughter and a boisterous setting that squashed all but gaiety and hilarity. It was artificial, but it was so good. Jack Miller's bar in Jersey City became Emile's safe haven and second home across the Hudson. From the moment he happened to walk into the place in 1978 when he was training fighter's in a local gym it became part of his landscape. It was here that Jack Miller, his wife Alice and his sons Butch and Chris became an extension of his family. It was here that Emile was bartender, bouncer, chug-a-lugger, Chippendale-style dancer and all-around entertainer. It was here that Emile Griffith was able to let his hair down and feel completely at peace. With a wig, a pair of fake-diamond studded "granny" glasses, and a high-pitched, falsetto voice, Emile once again had the crowds roaring. It may have been Jack Miller's Pub but it was Emile Griffith's home. Behind the bar his five championship belts were displayed to announce that fact.

"Retirement" never had the right ring for Emile. At first he was apprehensive, being someone who had never really thought of the future before and who now found his future upon him. Then came the depression, when he realized he was no longer in the limelight and uncertain of what was expected of him. From there, exhilaration. Now Emile Griffith was as free as a bird, able to do anything he chose. But he was also a realist. He didn't fantasize frolicking on some exotic beach, sipping nectar from a fruit gourd. Coney Island with a can of Coke would be fine.

Even such a basic, down to earth lifestyle required replenishing the cash supply he kept stuffed in his pocket. It was always a phone call and, "All right, Howard, I need some more money" and the money would be forthcoming. One day, Emile decided that a grown man of forty should not be receiving an allowance so he decided to see what his small fortune amounted to. If he were blind he would have seen it just as well because there was nothing to see. Actually, there were things to see. There was the new $13,000 kitchen in the family's $50,000 corner house in Hollis. There was his mother's magnificent wardrobe, which was outdone and outglistened only by Emile's, there was his shiny Lincoln Continental with the dollar's worth of gas he kept putting into the tank. And then there were the countless little gifts and goodies to friends, relatives, acquaintances, all those who reached that soft spot in Emile's heart – and they were legion. So, Emile Griffith counted his blessings; there was not much else.

When Emile learned that the money doled out to him was strictly that, a dole, without a flinch he faced up to harsh reality. Neither was there a smile. The faucet that had been wide open had nothing more to spew. His bank account was drained. Whatever he asked for was coming from the pockets of his managers and surrogate fathers, Howie Albert and Gil Clancy.

There was an offer on the table for him to fight the just-turned-pro, former Olympic gold medal winner, Sugar Ray Leonard. He pleaded with Gil and Howie to accept it. Gil Clancy knew that you could not make yesterday become today. There would be no comebacks for his devoted charge.

Emile Griffith did not have to prepare a resume'. New Jersey State Senator Chris Jackman was a long-time fan and loyal friend of Emile. When he heard that his favorite fighter was looking for a job he sat down with Emile and had a long talk with him. After ruling out comebacks as a fighter, movie theater usher or a hat designer and examining all available options, Emile Griffith began his new career as a correction officer. It was a position where compassion, caring and concern were deemed to be good qualities. But there can be too much of a good thing.

***

It wasn't that Luis Rodrigo did not like receiving special attention. He couldn't understand why. Neither could he understand why someone who said he was a champion prizefighter would be working as a prison guard instead of living like a millionaire with chauffeurs, butlers and maids at his beck and call.

There also were things that Emile didn't understand. He couldn't understand why a kid like Luis was able to run wild instead of being watched over lovingly and appreciated. He couldn't understand why a correctional facility or jail didn't realize that what a kid like Luis needed was special care and attention, not punishment. What he did understand was that he could not turn away. Luis, almost eerily, looked like and reminded him so much of Matthew that Emile felt as if everything that was happening was preordained. So he continued bringing Luis little gifts, from candy to comic books, and Luis ate the candy and skimmed through the comic books, not caring or wondering why he was receiving such special treatment. Not until Movie Night.

Mr. Mullaney, the director of the facility, asked Emile to bring in some of the highlight fight films of his career to be shown before the Our Gang feature. Alfalfa, Spanky and Buckwheat wound up taking the night off. It was an all-Emile Griffith show. Seeing is believing. Until that night it was, "Oh, yeah, sure. He wuz a champ. So wuz my Aunt Tillie."

Now, forget Our Gang. Every kid in the place was on line to get Emile's autograph and feel his bicep or ask him about this fight or that one. Every kid except Luis. He watched as Belty, after waiting his turn, stood before Emile and realizing he had no paper, held out his bare forearm and said, "Sign it here, Champ – and write 'To Belty'."

Emile smiled at him. "Soap and water is going to take it right off, Belty."

"Ah, you don't gotta worry. I don't wash much."

Just before lights out Emile walked over to Luis, who was finishing brushing his teeth and asked him, "How come you didn't come over to me like the rest of the kids after the films? I thought maybe you were rooting for the other guy, but I made sure only to bring fights that I won."

"You told me the truth," Luis acted almost betrayed. "You really were a champ."

"You're making it sound like that makes me a bad person."

"I coulda sworn you were kidding around."

"An honest cop! Who woulda believed?" Luis thought. He now accepted Emile's gifts and friendship without suspicion. He wasn't playing any games. He was just a nice guy. Luis began looking forward to seeing this famous person, this celebrity who was now like a hero to everyone in the lock-up.

And that's why Emile Griffith would have been better off working in a pet store or a nursery school. He cared and was filled with compassion but he wasn't a disciplinarian. As tough as he was in the ring, that's how soft he was out of it.

Luis Rodrigo had three brothers, one sister, a mother who cared but didn't have time to show just how much and there was no father. To Emile, it was like finding a dual incarnation - his and Matthew's. He wanted to help Luis, to take care of him and raise him – in his image.

When Luis' six months were up there was no celebration. Luis was sad and Emile was sadder.

"*Yes, I was sad,*" Emile recalls, "*but at the same time I was excited. I felt like, well, I guess I felt like I had found someone who I really cared about.*"

A short while after Luis was released, Emile quit his post at the detention center. He felt he had a much more important job to fulfill.

CHAPTER TWENTY

There are many ways to manifest shock. Maria Rodrigo, Luis' mother, could have fallen over backwards on her kitchen chair or she could have fainted. Instead she just sat with her mouth hanging open, unable to speak. In fact, she was not certain that she was able to hear – at least what she thought Luis had said to her.

"What do you mean, somebody wants to adopt you? I'm your mother and you have a family."

Luis explained to his mother that he loved her and his brothers and sister and that they would always remain his family but he explained that he and Emile had this strong feeling for each other. He felt that the care and attention he got from Emile was very important to him. For the first time he knew what it was to have a father.

At first, Luis' mother was a little suspicious and very reluctant. Much of this apprehension was caused when Luis' friend Belty, who was never her favorite person to begin with, came over to visit one day shortly after getting out of the detention center. When she told him that Luis wanted to move in with Emile and be adopted by him, Belty leaned forward and whispered, not exactly confidentially, in fact it was louder than he normally spoke, "Jeez, I gotta tell ya because I feel it's my duty as a friend. The guy is a queer. He's a homo! Listen, I'm walkin' past the officers' locker room one day and the door is open. I give a look – accidentally, not intentionally – and what do I see? There's Mr. Griffith in girl's panties."

Luis had told her that Belty came to him with the same story and he confronted Emile who laughed and showed him that he wore what were called low-line men's briefs. Maria listened to her son's explanation. She wanted to believe him because she was afraid not to. Knowing Belty made believing that much easier. It was difficult for her to do, but she asked Luis if Emile ever did anything "funny" with him. Luis assured her nothing like that had ever happened. Again, she wanted to believe, but there was not going to be any quick yes or no. She had a lot of thinking to do.

There were other considerations. Mrs. Rodrigo realized that wanting to do and doing didn't always ride the same rail. She understood care and attention were necessities in raising Luis, but as hard as she tried, her ability to provide them was limited because she also had learned that they came in a package with time, and time was the one commodity that Maria Rodrigo never had enough of.

None of Emile Griffith's fights in the ring were tougher than the conflict faced by Maria Rodrigo.. It was a battle which filled one with pain, an internal struggle waged in her mind, her heart and her gut.

It's not an easy call for a mother to let someone else raise her son, but the more she saw of Emile, the more she realized how genuine his affection for Luis was. Also, as she saw how appealing and charming his smile was she began melting. As for Belty's claim that Emile was "a queer," "a homo," she dismissed it as just some more hot air coming out of Belty. Still, it was too big a call for her to make on her own, so she brought in a social worker. The social worker brought in another social worker – a supervisor. Then four kids, Luis' brothers and sister, sat down with Emile. He talked, he smiled, and he laughed. Six year old Lazarus, the baby of the family clinched the deal. Drop-jawed and speechless at seeing Emile's collection of belts, trophies, plaques, magazine covers with his picture and newspaper clippings, he replaced Emile's shadow with himself. When he tried following Emile, who was answering Nature's call, into the bathroom, Maria Rodrigo finally intervened.

"What is with you, Lazarus. Let Emile be."

Not fully understanding what was happening, Lazarus made a difficult choice. "It's okay, momma. You can trade Luis for Emile."

"There ain't no trade, baby. Emile wants to take care of your brother and be part of the family."

"You mean we get to keep both of them," he shrieked and jumped into Emile's arms. Then, turning towards his brother, "I knew that's what it was. I wasn't really going to sell you."

The decision was made.

In 1979, Emile Griffith, who needed a son to take care of, became the legal guardian of Luis Rodrigo, who needed a father to take care of him.

Dr. Ralph Bohm, a psychiatrist and a physician licensed by the New York State Athletic Commission, has known Emile Griffith for many years. He concurs that often, a young person who is deserted by a father who he has loved and idolized, searches ceaselessly to replace that love. So, it's understandable that for a young kid, sitting in front of a house in Charlotte Amalie, tossing a baseball in the air, hoping, to the point of praying to see the figure of the father who left him without even a goodbye walking down from the distant mountains, that search never ends.

Luis Rodrigo was not quite sure what to expect when he left to move in with the former king of the boxing world. If it was a castle surrounded by a moat – well, the Hudson River was pretty large as moats go, and the apartment on Glenwood Avenue in Jersey City at least had steam heat and running water, which is more than a lot of royalty-occupied castles of yore had. As far as servants to be at their beck and call and bring things at their command, all they had to do was say "Fetch" and a Doberman named Caesar, would deliver anything from a bone to a bedroom slipper. For Luis, life had become an adventure, and he looked hopefully towards the future while his new father stared backwards at the past.

Emile was left with two memories, one vivid and gratifying, the other wistful. The first was his ring career, the latter, his money – both memories, both history.

Towards the end of Emile's career, Gil Clancy refused to take his full share of the purses. In fact, for the last ten years of his career, Clancy worked without any written contract. Shortly after Griffith's retirement, Clancy was appointed matchmaker at Madison Square Garden. On his desk was a small plaque –

"To my Dad, Gil
The Best Trainer in the World
Your Son, Emile Griffith"

Since leaving the Secaucus Detention Center, Emile realized that he was very fortunate to prefer peanut butter to caviar and looked for as many downhill routes as he could find when driving so he could coast and conserve gas. He and Luis formed a duet and found themselves whistling and singing what became Emile's favorite melody, the Nedick's jingle, "What'll I do, Mr. Quick? – Here's what you do, Little Nick …" and Mr. Quick, whistled and sung by Emile, goes on to tell Little Nick about the fifteen cent breakfast special, which became their morning staple. Many mornings they shared the glass of juice, donut and cup of coffee.

One of the silver linings to their cloud was that they never had to worry about wasting precious time by going to the bank to make deposits. Another, as Luis pointed out to Emile, was that without a regular day job they could sleep late and spend the rest of the day doing whatever they wanted. Luis couldn't figure out why that did not seem to excite Emile. After all, he was not unemployed. He still had the weekend job as a bouncer at a local night spot, but the money he earned from that, however, was usually spent before the sun rose on Monday morning. One hundred and fifty pound bouncers are about as rare as sumo wrestlers on Weight Watchers. People who did not know who he was had some very exciting learning experiences. There were occasions when he provided better impromptu entertainment than any floor show.

O'Hara's Tavern in Jersey City had a good mix of office workers, stevedores and college kids from St. Peter's as clientele so Emile Griffith did not expect do be overworked when Kelly O'Hara hired him as a bouncer. He learned quickly that just as you cannot tell a book by its cover, you cannot tell a bar by its drinkers' occupations. Emile was walking around the floor, listening to the jukebox and smiling at the customers when, suddenly, he could no longer hear the jukebox too clearly. There was this guy who was the fullback of the St. Peter's football team shouting in a very menacing way at the girl sitting alongside him. Emile walked towards their table, hoping the situation would defuse before he got there. He wouldn't have minded if it were a quarterback. They were of manageable size. As he approached the table, the girl sprang to her feet and through choking sobs, shouted at her date that it was her wish that he visit a place other than heaven. With that, she headed for the ladies room. This made Emile feel very good, but not for long. Without signals being called, the fullback crashed through the throng on the dance floor, and sprinted in pursuit of his ex-girlfriend to the ladies room.

It became obvious to Emile that he was not going to hear the jukebox for quite a while. "You can't go in there," a chorus of young girls was shouting at the out-of-control fullback.

He went in there.

"Uh-oh!" was all Emile could think as he raced in after him, ignoring another chorus of "You can't ..."

This being Emile's first visit to a ladies room, he wondered if there was always so much bedlam. He also realized that he was not really needed as a wild, screaming pack of women were whacking away at the fullback with towels, pocketbooks and rolls of toilet paper as he had the cringing young lady backed up against a wash basin, shouting at her in a rage.

"Back off!" Emile ordered, stepping beside the girl in an effort to calm her.

"Who the Hell do you think you are?" the fullback snapped.

"Right now I guess I'm the ladies room attendant," Emile answered, "but pretty soon I may become your worst nightmare."

The snarling fullback stared down at Emile and pointing his finger in his face, growled, "You be smart and get your fucken ass outta here and get your nose out of my business while you have the chance."

"You're the college boy. You be smart. And start by getting your fat finger out of my face!"

"I'm warning you for the last time! Get off my case before I shove you down the toilet bowl and flush you away like a piece of shit!" which he emphasized by poking his finger within an inch of Emile's face.

Emile gave up on hearing the jukebox for a while as there was this loud scream that almost lifted the roof right off O'Hara's Tavern as

Emile's teeth clamped down on the offensive finger. With arms flailing like a wounded bird, sounding like an off-key soprano stuck on one note and looking like the Hunchback of Notre Dame following the jailer to the gallows, the now very docile, pained fullback, with his fat finger impaled on Emile's teeth, followed Emile out of the ladies room, through the club to the parking lot as the entire crowd laughed and applauded Emile Griffith, former welterweight and middleweight champion and current bouncer extraordinaire.

Later that night, Kelly O'Hara, hearing differing versions of the incident, asked Emile, "What were you doing in the Ladies Room?"

Emile thought for a moment. "Just chewing the fat."

Emile did not look down upon the profession of 'bouncer,' but seeing no great opportunity for advancement – where does one bounce to? – when Jackie Mason, the rabbi-turned-comedian, offered him a role in a musical comedy romp called "Sex-A-Poppin'", envisioning emulating all the Robinson's he knew, Bill 'Bojangles' and Sugar Ray, Emile jumped at it. Making it seem even more likely that this was an intervention of fate was the fact that the show was booked for Sunnyside Garden, the historic old fight club soon to be a Wendy's Hamburgers.

"I went out and bought myself a new pair of tap-dancing shoes," Emile recalls with a smile, "and practiced all my songs and routines. And what do you think? It was probably the quickest KO in Sunnyside Garden history!"

He spent a lot of his free time dropping in at his old Times Square haunts and also, his "incubator" – the Solar Gym, where he had learned his trade. He'd help out with many of the young fighters and it quickly became apparent that Emile had not just been a good student; he had the ability to pass on what was taught to him and fine tune a fighter. Recognizing Emile's ability and enthusiasm as a teacher, Clancy was impressed. With his and Howie Albert's help and assistance, Emile returned to the boxing world as a trainer. He worked with such name fighters as Wilfredo Benitez, Rodrigo Valdez, Bonecrusher Smith, Simon Brown, Doug DeWitt, Matt Farrago, Pedro Soto, Mitch Green and former featherweight champion Juan LaPorte, who to this day remains Griffith's close friend.

"Emile was always strictly a professional," Farrago recalls. "It was so unfair to him that some of his fighters, including me, had to have some kind of seed of suspicion deep in our minds because we heard that Emile Griffith was gay. Here he was, a great champion and a great trainer and that's the only way we should have seen him. It hurts me to say that it even crossed my mind when I had to share a trailer with him to sleep in while training for a fight. Another time I remember was when he gave me a massage after a workout and I started thinking. But his strong fingers just worked on my back muscles and I was ashamed that I even permitted any thoughts to enter my mind. Like I said, Emile was a great fighter and a terrific trainer and that's how I will always think of him and it's the only way he should be thought of."

Luis Rodrigo could not tell the unusual from the usual. True, he didn't share Emile's life in his heyday years, but coming in late to a bacchanalian feast, you very often have to settle for the leftovers. Luis gladly settled and he had no regrets. He even got a second mother, Emelda, thrown in the deal.

But along with all the pot-sweeteners, Luis remembers that they had quite a few bad-tasting experiences also. They were sharing an apartment on Highland Avenue in Jersey City with one of Emile's friends from the gay scene in Hell's Kitchen, Eddie Hernandez. It was convenient as the place was close to the gym where Emile was training a few fighters and having Eddie, who was an easy guy to get along with, share the rent was a big help. Luis walked in one evening to find Emile sitting at the kitchen table, his shoulders hunched and his hands covering his face. Next to him on the table was a crumpled note. It was from Luis' second-youngest brother Angel. Of all his family, Angel, who was about seventeen at the time, seemed to be having the most trouble understanding why Luis had left to live with someone else. He felt deserted, abandoned by his older brother.

Angel had traveled from the family's apartment in Jersey City to visit Luis but when he found no one at home he addressed a note to him and slipped it under the door. Emile, the first one to return to the apartment that evening opened the door, picked up the note, read it and slumped into the chair, alternating between sobs and snorts of anger.

Luis took the note, smoothed it out, read it and stared down at Emile. He leaned over to hug him but Emile pulled away, still trembling – whether in anger or agony, Luis wasn't sure. Angel's scrawling handwriting screamed out at him from the lined paper, asking "Why are you living with these faggots instead of being with your family?"

Luis had answers, lots of them. "He's a kid. He says things without thinking." "He doesn't mean it. He gets upset, he says stupid things." "When a kid is hurt he strikes out and tries to hurt someone else. He really loves you."

None of it mattered or sank in. Emile was in too much pain to listen to reason. Someone else's hurt didn't count. Luis forced his arms around Emile and hugged him. He felt Emile's arms tighten around him in return and as they held each other they cried softly. That's when Luis realized that he would have to protect and take care of Emile just as Emile was expected to protect and take care of him.

Angel's actions, though, were like a mosquito bite compared to the wasp stings of Emile's brother Franklin. His disapproval of Emile's friends and lifestyle was unshakable. But Emile says their differences or rivalry goes beyond that. "It could have been some sort of jealousy," Emile laughs, remembering their disputes went back to their childhood in St. Thomas. He was too young to search for reasons then, but he remembers his mother always felt there was something special about her first-born. He says that his Emelda had told him that before she gave birth to him, they had taken x-rays of Emile as a fetus and she told him that he was curled up in a boxing pose.

He recalls that some of his childhood scraps with Franklin got a little messy. There was the time that they got into a real brawl over something so unimportant that he can't even remember what it was all about.

What he does remember was that their island paradise home did not have the latest in plumbing facilities. When they had to relieve themselves, they would do so in a bucket and then empty that into a larger bucket or container outside that was called the "shit box."

Emile said, "I don't want to laugh because it wasn't funny, but I was so mad, I wrestled Franklin out of the house and dumped him right into that shit box. Wheeh!"

As Emile filled Luis in with many of the details of his life it made their bond even stronger. Luis felt as though he were sharing in the family history – his family. And gradually, he learned of Emile's battles and his trials during his career. He absorbed everything as he listened to Emile and read all the articles that Emelda had saved from newspapers and magazines. There was only one fight that Emile never discussed or brought up. If asked about it, he didn't call it a fight; it was 'the accident.' However, there were times at night, with the lights off, when Luis would occasionally be awakened by Emile's soft sleep talk or his crying out. That's when he learned that in his mind Emile Griffith was still battling Benny 'Kid' Paret.

It was only those who were with him at such times – Luis, Matthew and Sadie, who shared those unguarded painful moments. His lament was not only for Benny 'Kid' Paret, but more so for his widow Lucia and son, Benny, Jr. Although Mercedes didn't know Emile at the time of his fateful fight with Paret, she saw and felt the lingering hurt.

"I think part of him died after the Benny Paret fight. He didn't like to talk about it, but he did touch on it. And you can see that he was, and is, still hurting over it. I believe that going into the ring after that he was cautious. It just seemed to me that it was a lasting imprint with him. Actions speak louder than words and just the way, if you mentioned the name, he would like cringe."

Mercedes was not the only one who wasn't able to draw Emile out and talk about his feelings regarding Benny Paret. No one could. Not even Clancy, Howie Albert or Emelda. Those who knew him respected his privacy and pain. He had the ability to compartmentalize this slice of his life and store it in some secret place, locked away from his consciousness. Whether a self-imposed denial or a mental block, it served as his defense mechanism.

That's why Luis was so shocked when one evening Emile wondered aloud, without anything leading up to it, "I hope Benny's wife and kids are okay." He leaned over and hugged Luis. "She never would talk to me but I understand. His boy Benny, Jr. is about your age. I saw him a couple of times but I think they moved back to Florida." Then, as quickly as he opened up, he closed down.

CHAPTER TWENTY-ONE

Emile had never been a comparison shopper but the number zero for living expenses was too attractive to pass up. After making a decision to leave the Highland Avenue apartment in Jersey City when the rent became too steep, Emile explained to Luis that they would have to separate for a while, each moving back with his own family. What Emile didn't realize was that he now was Luis' "own family." When he thought back to the hurt and abandonment he had felt when his father had left him, and he was better able to understand the feelings that clouded Luis' smile. He tried easing Luis' feelings of abandonment by visiting and talking to his boy as often as he could. But Luis seemed to crawl up inside himself and Emile, as hard as he tried, found it almost impossible to reach him. Emile was afraid that he would lose Luis, and it was this fear that made him realize how much he needed him in his life. At the same time, he began to understand how much he meant to Luis. He made a silent promise that he would never do to his boy what his father had done to him.

It took several months before Emile was able to arrange for Luis to move back to Hollis and be part of the Griffith family. The house was crowded but they were together. Meanwhile, Emile didn't waste any time hitting the top rung as a trainer but he learned that unlike being a fighter whose destiny is determined mainly by his two fists, a trainer's destiny is often shaped by the whims, fancies and manipulations of others.

When Gregorio Benitez, the father of the young Puerto Rican super-star, Wilfredo Benitez, was unable to properly discipline or condition his son, Emile Griffith was brought in as head trainer and moved Benitez to the welterweight championship in a stirring victory over Carlos Palomino. The thank you he received was a pink slip as Gregorio Benitez restored himself as manager-trainer of his son, who two fights later lost his title to Sugar Ray Leonard.

Emile tasted similar treatment earlier when he took over the training of Rodrigo Valdez, who was to fight for the Middleweight title against Hugo Corro in Buenos Aires. When Emile arrived at the training facility in Argentina, he found out that he was the trainer in name only, that a friend of Valdez was the actual trainer. It turned out that these disappointments were minor league when he got the phone call from Maria Rodrigo.

Perhaps it was that Luis felt tossed aside, unwanted and rejected, maybe it was his way of thumbing his nose at everyone, maybe it was hanging out with the wrong crowd – it didn't matter. Bottom line, he had screwed up. He had been sentenced to six months at the Hudson County Jail for impersonating an officer. While he and Emile were living apart, Luis was found carrying Emile's old ID as a correction officer. He could have pleaded that since Emile was his legal guardian, no punishable crime or offense had been committed, but instead, he accepted full responsibility for his actions. Emile blamed himself.

So, two guys toed the line. One inside the lock-up, doing his work assignments without grumbling, catching his hour or so of fresh air and exercise and looking forward to getting back with the one person he wanted to be with – his "father."

The other, putting in a full day every day, working with kids and young men, teaching them a trade at which he was a master, a champion. And this so that he could raise a young man who reminded him of himself and the son he yearned for.

When Luis got out, it was the fall of 1983 and the price of the Nedick's breakfast special had gone up. They didn't care. They drove to Hollis for Emelda's special, pancakes and sausages. There the price never changed.

Actually, as long as there was cash in his pockets, price never mattered to Emile. And right now his pockets were bulging. He had a string of good fighters and he was making them better.

"When it came to living good, Emile knew how to do that, too," Luis said. "We'd go from one party to another, the next night we'd go bar-hopping. Emile would hire a limousine for the night and we'd travel around in style. Anybody who was his friend and needed a loan, Emile was there. When he first started taking me to bars I was shocked at first. There were men who were women, women who were men but Emile let everyone know as soon as we walked in that I was his son and he was very careful to watch over me. If anyone got out of line with me in any way, whether at a bar, at a party – and we went to plenty parties – Emile would be there with fire in his eyes.

That's how it was for Emile. Partying almost every night but in the morning he was back at the gym working with his fighters."

Emile Griffith was gaining a reputation as one of the better trainers in the sport, which made a lot of people very happy. Among the happiest was his family – until Junior made some drastic changes. He had honed James "Bonecrusher" Smith into a finely tuned fighting machine in preparation for his bout against Mike Tyson, and the Bonecrusher did what few others were able to at that time. He went the distance with boxing's most devastating heavyweight. Emile took home $90,000 as his trainer's fee. Emelda, who was accustomed to having Emile turn over all his paychecks to her, was ecstatic as she thought of how this bonanza would enhance the appearance of their home as well as her wardrobe. When Emile told her he was not turning the money over to her, but was putting it in a joint account for him and Luis, Emelda couldn't understand his behavior.

She asked him how and why he was doing such a thing. Emile stretched a point a bit by telling her that he had legally adopted Luis now, and he wanted to provide a decent life for both of them.

Emelda knew that Emile eventually intended to adopt Luis but he had made no mention of doing it at this time. She looked him in the eye. "Can I see the papers?"

"I don't have to show you anything."

Emile Griffith had made his Declaration of Independence. The fireworks that followed were not in celebration.

Although it became obvious after a while that the adoption had never taken place, Emelda, whose strong maternal instinct immediately endeared Luis to her and had her treat him as a member of the family, accepted the fact that Emile had the right to do with his money as he pleased. She just hoped that the money was being used for the right reasons. She also hoped that with Emile's next paycheck, things would go back to normal – naturally, Mommie's pocket book being "normal."

Simon Brown was a top priority project for Griffith. He liked him both as a fighter and a person. He worked with him diligently, molding him in his image. In 1989 Brown defeated Luis Santana for the IBF Welterweight title. Then, on the night of March 18th, 1991 Emile watched with pride and a tremendous sense of satisfaction as his protégé, Simon Brown defeated WBC Welterweight Champion Maurice Blocker in a unification title bout in Las Vegas, Nevada. When Referee Mills Lane stopped the fight in the 10th round, awarding the fight and the undisputed championship to Brown on a TKO, Emile could barely contain his joy. Another title – and another good-sized paycheck.

***

"I felt sort of caught in the middle," Luis sighs as he thinks back. "This was Emile's biggest payday since the Bonecrusher fight and Emelda didn't think it was going to happen again. Anyhow, she was hoping it wouldn't. So when Emile didn't give her any of the Simon Brown money, she was really disappointed. She started telling him about all the repairs needed around the house and that a house don't fix itself. And Emile just shouted back, 'Tell your other children to chip in some money.'"

"Emelda always made me feel like part of the family. That's why I call her 'Mommie.' But I knew to keep my nose out of family affairs. Sometimes I couldn't help myself, though. When Franklin comes stormin' into the house screamin' and yelling at Emile for not turning any money over to their mother, I stood there just shaking at first. He was standing up for his mother and I could understand that. But when he starts scorching Emile by shouting, "Go on, you faggot! Go downstairs to your man," Emile had to hold me back.

"I couldn't stand hearing him talk to Emile that way, but Emile calmed me down and told me to just ignore him. It was like he thought Franklin wasn't all wrong. I don't think he felt guilty about the money – maybe he did, I don't know, but he did feel bad. That was Emile. The next day he would be back to work as a trainer and bringing money back to his mother."

There was one more check that Mommie didn't get, but this was different. Later that year, Simon Brown was fighting Buddy McGirt with the title on the line. Emile, who was a handshake kind of guy, was supposed to receive a $25,000 trainer's fee.

When McGirt won a twelve round decision and the title, Emile took it as hard as if he were the one in the ring. After the fight, Emile received two things; a check in the amount of $5,000 and a pink slip from Brown's management.

"This was the worst." Luis closes his eyes, as though trying to blot it out of his memory. "He cried. He really cried. It hurt me so bad to watch it. He just wasn't used to being treated like this. Emile was the one who didn't even want to make the fight. Not at that time. He said McGirt was too big. So, it's not just that they don't listen to him. They blame him for the loss and the biggest insult is, they give him $5,000 instead of the $25,000 he was supposed to get. And that became nothing because he took that check, ripped it in half and threw it to the floor."

It took Emile a couple days before going back to his boys in the gym. The hurt was there and it stayed, but that's what champions are all about. With all the heavy duty stuff he was going through, Emile never neglected or short-changed his fighters.

***

"When I saw our boy Emile work, I kvelled," Howie Albert beamed. "Gil is Irish so he couldn't kvell, but he was so goddam proud – the two of us." He stopped and blew his nose. "This kid who Gil used to have to send out search parties to find and drag into the ring ..."

Howie watched as Emile pounded the ring apron, shouting instructions to one of his protégés, Matt Farrago, an undefeated middleweight who Emile wanted to keep undefeated. When the lesson didn't sink in the first time, Emile banged the canvas again and shouted, heaving a wet towel at Matt. The lesson sank in.

Emile had been to the top. He was heading back. That's what he was thinking as he packed his bags for his trip to Australia with Juan LaPorte.

CHAPTER TWENTY-TWO

July 1992

He didn't see the first punch, but he felt the explosion inside his head, dazzling bursts of brilliant colors and stabbing jolts of lightning. Instinctively his hands came up, fists balled. Nobody knew a fight better than Emile Griffith but this was not his kind of fight. There was no bell. Only sounds of cursing, laughing and labored breathing. No introductions. Fists, boots, chains and wooden clubs didn't need any. There was no rope-enclosed, twenty-foot canvas-covered square but, instead, a dark alley cluttered with open, brimming garbage pails whose stink mixed with the smell of urine, puke and what-not. And there was no Mommie and Cousin Bernie leading his "crazies" in cheering him on.

His right fist crunched loudly into a face he never saw. It sounded like a balloon popping as the nose gave way - and so did Emile's thumb. The blows came from everywhere. There could have been six, there could have been ten. He covered his face as best he could and took the beating on the back of his head and his body. Then he was sliding on the sidewalk, scraping his knees and palms on the rough, slime-covered cement. The neon lights danced from their Ninth Avenue window and marquee displays, pirouetting wildly, creating a bedlam of visual madness that engulfed Emile and became his universe. Each kick digging into his side or back drew a gasp but never a cry or shout. Seconds became minutes, minutes seemed a lifetime. Somehow, he gathered himself together and sprang to his feet. His legs were unsteady and he could barely stand but he threw punches and felt a confounding joy as his fist found its mark. Then they were all upon him and he was pounded back to the ground and the pain of each kick in the small of his back drove him into a dark cocoon and he stayed there, almost at peace.

***

Three hours earlier they had walked to the taxi lineup outside the International Terminal at JFK. It was a hot, steamy July night – a big difference from the crisp wintry air they had just left behind in Sydney, Australia. It's always more fun coming home a winner, but like Emile pointed out to former featherweight champion Juan LaPorte, it was a mixed bag sort of a loss.

Okay, you never throw up your hands and go "Hooray" when you lose, but when you're a featherweight who's bulked up to fight a natural junior welterweight and lose a close decision in his hometown and become the first fighter to go the distance with this guy, it's nothing to cry over either. As it turns out, this Kostya Tszyu goes on to become the junior welterweight champ.

Since Emile had taken over as LaPorte's trainer they had become close friends. It was his job to take care of Juan in the ring, a job he took seriously and did very well, but LaPorte, although much younger, looked out for Emile outside the ropes.

It was late and Emile asked Juan if he wanted to sleep over at his Hollis home which was about fifteen minutes from the airport. If he had it to do all over again, Juan LaPorte would definitely have said yes. But he said no. He waited for his friend and trainer to get in a cab and told him to go straight home. Emile smiled and the cab pulled away. Then Juan got into his cab and headed for his home in Brooklyn.

Emile leaned forward. "Eighth Avenue and 41st Street, please."

***

Luis Rodrigo jumped from his bed as the loud crash jolted him from his sleep. He reached under his bed for the Louisville Slugger he kept there. Luis was not a ballplayer.

"Who in the world is making such a racket this time of the night?"

"I'll check, Mommie." He couldn't restrain the break in his voice as he tried reassuring his adoptive grandmother. "You just stay here." Luis hoped Emelda Griffith, her body still fighting sleep, would ignore his request. He bounded down the stairs and felt a sense of comfort as he heard her footsteps behind him. Raising the bat above his head, he opened the door to the basement.

"Jesus Christ!"

Emile was sprawled on the stairway, his right arm wrapped around the banister, the top of which was broken off in his left hand. His clothes were filthy, blood-caked and torn and he looked like a rag doll that someone had discarded on the cellar steps. As Luis hurried to his side, the scream, "Junior! What happened to my boy?" pierced the air.

Freeing Emile's right arm and getting his left arm around his shoulders to support him, he saw that besides smudges of dirt and grease, Emile's face was not marked. Luis half-carried and half-dragged him up the stairs where Emelda was standing, hands clasped as though in prayer, her eyes now wide awake. Emile's face strained into a weak smile as he saw his mother.

"I fell, Mommie, I fell."

The only sound in the hospital room was the low hum of the kidney machine. Emile slept in drug-induced peace with Emelda sitting at his bedside holding his hand and Luis standing, staring out the window. Gil Clancy and Howard Albert, his managers throughout his ring career and now as much his family as any of his blood relatives, stood in the corridor speaking softly with Juan LaPorte, who had just gotten off the elevator.

"It's touch and go right now," Howie explained. "He has kidney damage and an infection that spread to his spine. What the hell happened? What was he doing at a Gay bar?"

"I don't know," LaPorte answered. "I get two cabs at the airport and tell Emile to go straight home and he says okay."

But home to Emile was bright lights and partying people. Emile Griffith liked people, all people, so he believed that everyone liked him. Sadly, that's not the way it was. It's not that he hadn't learned it before but he had just shrugged it off. This time the lesson came with a strong exclamation point.

Luis and Emelda had carried Emile to the bathroom where they undressed him and found a pouch with $800 in his underwear, the balance of his trainer's purse for the fight. They bathed him and put him to bed. It took them two days to realize how sick Emile was.

When Juan LaPorte got the call from a hysterical Emelda, he rushed right over. As soon as he saw how seriously ill his friend was, he had Luis call for an ambulance and they brought Emile to Queens General Hospital. Fortunately, Dr. Charles Gellman, a former fighter who went on to become a hospital administrator and angel to boxers in need of medical attention, heard about the seriousness of Emile's condition. Dr. Gellman brought in a consultant who found Emile near death, suffering kidney damage and a spinal infection. They transferred Emile to Elmhurst Hospital and once again, he was in a fight, this time for his life.

Emile Griffith didn't know who had slipped him the mickey but he was sure that's what happened. *"I know how I feel when I drink too much. That's not how it was. Someone bought me a drink and put it in front of me. In less than a minute, I feel my head's floating away, everything is blurry and I can hardly stand. That's when I headed for the door to get some fresh air and that's when it happened."*

They didn't get Emile's money but they may not have been looking for it. And they may not have known who their target was. A gay bar and a happy guy who sure looked like he belonged there. But Emile belonged to everyone. For Emile Griffith there was no boundary between communities, Gay or Straight. He loved the world and everyone who spun around on it.

The tubes ran from above the bed, from the side of the bed and from the pole next to the bed. Into him and out of him, they fed him, drained him, kept him alive.

CHAPTER TWENTY-THREE

1992 - Elmhurst Hospital

They told Gil Clancy that this decision might go against his fighter, but Gil knew his man. He knew the big heart that never quit and he knew how to get him to rise to the challenge. He sat at the side of the bed and moved his hand carefully through the maze of tubes to reach Emile's hand and clasped it between both of his. The cornerman was at work and he told his fighter what he had to do. This time there were no instructions, no commands or strategies, just a plea. He told him how a champion comes through with that big finish and that he was a champion. It was the last round of his biggest fight and he had to pull it out.

It was the dynamics between cornerman and fighter, father and son, a dark-skinned kid from a tropical paradise and a hard-bitten Irishman from Rockaway. One more time Emile Griffith gathered it together and responded to the imploring of Gil Clancy.

He went home and it took more than seven months for him to heal. The scar remains. His physical pain was mostly gone but there was a different pain – it was the pain suffered by others, but he could not help sharing it. This pain was not the result of the blows that landed, but rather that they were thrown at all - and their intent. Emile knew that what happened was not for money. He came away with all his money and is certain that no hands had groped to search for any.

There were some things that he would forget, some people whose faces wouldn't come together with a name. There were times he even mixed up Luis with Juan LaPorte, calling each by the other's name. He went back to work as a trainer but often things were hazy. Sometimes he'd forget about appointments. Remembering which train and which bus takes you to where was confusing but he had to handle it because he could no longer drive a car.

Always in demand to attend celebrity charity events and boxing fundraisers, Emile Griffith never turned down a good cause. But he was no longer able to go alone because he would sometimes become disoriented in a hotel and awakening at night, would wander off, searching for home.

But the basic Emile - the good nature, sensitivity and compassion - was never altered.

They honored Emile at Madison Square Garden and on July 1, 1993 Congressman Ron DeLugo honored him on the floor of the House of Representatives.

> *"Mr. Speaker, Madison Square Garden in New York City recently honored a great American athlete and Virgin Islands native son, Emile Griffith.*
>
> *During the 1960's and 1970's Emile Griffith was the six-time world welter and middleweight champion and after he retired from the ring he continued to dedicate his life to boxing by training others in the skills he practiced so well.*
>
> *Griffith won the welterweight title in 1961 from Benny "Kid" Paret, defended it aginst Indian Gaspar Ortega, but lost it to Paret in a rematch. In their third bout, Griffith battled to come back from a knockdown when in the 12th round he pounded his opponent into the ropes. Paret lapsed into a coma and 10 days later died.*
>
> *Though a champion fighter, Emile Griffith is a sensitive man and the death left him ready to quit boxing. He recently told the*

Associated Press, 'I wasn't the same person. I would have quit but I didn't know how to do anything else but fight.'

Griffith went on to win the junior middleweight and middleweight crowns. In 1965 and 1966, he won both the welterweight and middleweight championships. Boxing historian Bert Randolph Sugar said, 'Through th 1960's the best fighter pound-for-pound every year was Emile Griffith.' His ex-manager Gil Clancy said, 'He had every punch in the book, there was nothing he couldn't do in the ring.'

Emile Griffith's last fight in the Garden was in 1974, where he had more main card bouts than any other boxer, and he completed his career in the ring 3 years later. He went on to train other boxers including Juan LaPorte and Bonecrusher Smith.

Last year, Emile Griffith almost died from kidney damage after he was mugged and beaten on a Manhattan street. He spent months in the hospital recovering and still suffers pain in his back. He also was left with enormous hospital bills.

It has been 16 years since Emile Griffith stepped into the ring, yet today he remains one of the most popular fighters figures in boxing. He was a champion of the sport and remains a champion of the spirit. Emile Griffith is highly respected by the people of his native Virgin Islands where a ballpark is named in his honor. That Madison Square Garden chose to honor him shows the enormous esteem in which he is held.

Mr. Speaker, Emile Griffith deserves the recognition and thanks of this body for his unselfish contributions to boxing and sports and for the genuine sense of compassion for others and fairness for all that he exhibited both inside and outside the ring."

It was almost thirty years ago that he was honored by the House of Commons in Great Britain. Quite a two-bagger for a kid from the beaches and back alleys of Saint Thomas who left high school to become a movie usher in the Bronx. Reflecting on the honors, Emile smiles, "I guess I should be glad they don't know about all the fruit I swiped in Charlotte Amalie."

"When Emile came home," Luis recalls, "I made a promise. He took such good care of me, now I was going to take care of him."

It was a promise Luis worked very hard to keep, never shirking his duties as a loving caretaker. But there was a problem. "As bad as I wanted to stand behind Emile and be there for him, I was becoming more of a burden than a help."

Luis had been experimenting with drugs long before he met Emile. Marijuana and 'ludes were his subs for aspirin. Emile pleaded with him to break away but his young ward pleaded just as strongly that he couldn't, that the drugs kept him going on an even keel and that he was in complete control.

Luis didn't have to hide his habit because Emile, rather than have him do it behind his back, wanted everything to be in the open. They both tried, but some battles simply cannot be won. In time, Luis graduated to poppers and cocaine. He was no longer using drugs, they were now using him.

Taking charge was something Emile Griffith had been doing all his life. It was nearly three years since Emile had come home from the hospital after the mugging. He was once again strong. He had to be. He couldn't sit back and watch his boy come apart at the seams. Luis was losing his fight. Emile was not going to let that happen.

"Look at yourself," he badgered him. Then, grabbing Luis by the shoulders, he shook him and somewhere between shouting and crying, "Get off all that shit! What do you need it for?"

"To forget!" Luis shouted back. "That's what I need it for – to make me forget, to make me think of other things."

Emile eased his grip but did not let go of Luis who, in a cracking voice, described how all of his life he felt buried in shame, never telling anyone, not even his mother, how, at the age of eleven he had been molested and sodomized. He had been abused by someone he trusted, by a young man who was related to one of his mother's friends. "He taught boxing and martial arts at a local gym and would invite me up for free lessons. One day he gets me alone in the locker room and he forces me to be like a 'girl.' Then when he finished with me he laughed and said I was the best ever. I wanted to kill him and I guess that's when I started doing things to prove I was a tough guy, not no girl. And the shit I take, it helps. You understand? It helps!" His voice was breaking completely now and the words were garbled and distorted but Emile heard and understood each and every one.

Still holding Luis by the shoulders, he relaxed his grip and drew the boy to him in a strong embrace and with tears streaming down his face, he sobbed, "You're not alone in the world, son. You're not the only one."

"I'm not a baby. You don't have to bullshit me," Luis blurted, trying to pull away.

"*Now listen to me! What I'm telling you is so. And just like you, I never told it to anyone else before. So my hurt goes back a lot longer than yours. I was maybe a year younger than you when some creep back in St. Thomas who said he was my uncle did the same thing to me. The same thing, you understand? And I was every bit as ashamed — I felt destroyed for a while. I just wanted to run away from everything and everyone. That's just before I wound up at Mandal.*"

They looked into each other's eyes and Luis recalls that as the moment when an unbreakable bond was forged between them. "It wasn't that I didn't love Emile before. But now we had this shared experience of pain and shame that drew us so close ... we had each other to lean on and we were able to understand each other like no one else could. Emile didn't need the crutch to lean on like I did, but I promised him I would kick it. Now I had him. I didn't need any crutch."

With Emelda running the household and watching over Emile like a baby, Luis was merely the backup. . He continued cooking Emile's meals and helping out in any way that he could around the house, but as hard as he tried, he was not able to kick the habit.

"Luis, you got to seek help, boy. You're trying. I know you're trying, but you need professional help," Emelda would plead with him when they were alone. She may have had some diff erences of opinion with Emile about money going to Luis that was earmarked for her, but she never let it interfere with her treating Luis as one of her own.

Luis knew that she was right but couldn't summon up the courage or strength to commit himself.

Besides being Emelda's helper, there wasn't much more that Luis could handle. There were days that Emile would come home from the gym and find Luis sprawled out on his bed the same way he had left him in the morning.

His role as backup, as well as everything else, changed very suddenly. Emelda, who had been on dialysis for many years, slipped into a coma. She hung on and fought for a week. On June 15, 1997, Emelda Griffi th, as strong a matriarch as any family has ever known, died of acute kidney failure.

At the age of 59, a person is not thought of as a motherless child, but in Emile's case, he was just that. Lost without the comforting warmth and protective embrace of "Mommie", he just wandered aimlessly, unable to shed the tears that fl owed so easily for far less painful occurrences. Again, the fi ghter masked the pain of the blow.

Emelda's death was a profound shock to Luis. He wasn't a fi ghter, there was no hiding his pain. It was her passing that served as the trigger for him to act. He went into a drug rehab facility just after Emelda's death, going to an upstate facility for a year, then spending a second year closer to home, in Far Rockaway.

"I worried about Emile being on his own but I knew I would be no help to him unless I got clean."

Luis had good cause to worry about Emile. It was apparent that the accumulated blows of 112 fi ghts, a savage mugging in the alley of a Gay bar, abetted perhaps by the normal aging process now had him battling a form of dementia. Emile was always in there to win but this was one fight where the best you could hope for was a draw.

He was unable to travel to visit Luis so it was only when Luis got weekend passes during his second year of rehab and he would travel from Far Rockaway that they were able to see each other. He would stay with the six-time world champion in the basement room that Emile was relegated to in the house that he had bought for his family nearly forty years earlier.

When Luis "graduated" from the drug rehabilitation program in 1999 he moved into a small studio apartment in Hempstead with a friend, Jayson Phillips, and got a job as an electronics technician. It had already been spelled out to him by Franklin that he was unwelcome at the Hollis home, so he limited his time there to weekend visits with Emile, pretty much the same schedule as when he was quartered in Far Rockaway.

The home that Emile bought to house the family that he brought over from St. Thomas was put in his mother's name as his show of affection and devotion to her and his siblings. It was appreciated by all ... at first. But as time went on, though the glamour and luster of their brother may not have diminished, what he had done and who he was became taken more for granted.

Being moved around like a chess piece over the years, whether as a king or a pawn, never bothered Emile. When his brothers and sisters decided to sell the house, they voted that each sibling would receive an equal share. Although Emile originally purchased the house for $50,000, it was decided that repayment of that should be waived. Emile did not argue the point. They were his family and Emile agreed.

They also formed a family management team to run the house and collect rent while waiting for the sale to be consummated. A special session of the "board" was called when Emile, subsisting solely on a monthly disability check, fell behind.

"Emile was so upset that he called me to tell me he was running to the bank to cash his disability check," Luis remembers. "That got me very upset, the way they were treating Emile, who always did everything he could for them. So I went over to the house and spoke to Franklin who defended what was done by saying everything had to be done businesslike. I saw Emile was upset and that's when he said, 'Can I move in with you?' And I said, 'Sure you can. You know I love you, Emile.'

Jayson was great about it. Our apartment was small but we just threw a mattress on the floor and we were one big, happy family."

219

Entering his 65th year, Emile Griffith's awareness was not shut down. Rather, it functioned like a motor that had to be primed before sputtering and eventually shifting into gear. He also had this ability to harvest his many wonderful memories which, somehow he was able to convert to great expectations.

Emile fooled a lot of people. Many who remembered the singing, dancing bon vivant of years past were now counting him out.

But no one ever counted "Ten!" over Emile Griffith. He was too tough, too resilient and too courageous. That hadn't changed and it was not restricted to a small area within the ropes. It was always good advice for a fighter that when you're hurt, take a knee and gather yourself together, then come back and show everyone what you're made of.

Throughout his career, that's what Emile Griffith did. He always came back like a true champion and that's why he was idolized by the entire boxing world. That special trait – that ability has carried over to Emile's current battle. He may forget a few things and a few people but he never resents, regrets or holds a grudge. When the full implication of what happened with the house sank in, there was a momentary flash of resentment that quickly defused and turned into some sort of satisfaction at feeling that if that's what his family wanted, maybe it's for the best.

The size of his world shrank but he would never forget his family, among whom he included Gil Clancy and Howie Albert, a few friends who he saw on a regular basis and an occasional visit to his special world on the fringe of Times Square. He would still stop whatever he was doing or wherever he was going to give advice to a youngster or smile at or tickle a baby.

And he doesn't forget a March night back in 1962.

Emile woke up with a start. Luis knew immediately. It happened often enough that he was used to it. It was almost forty years to the day and Benny Paret was still haunting him. This time Emile wouldn't go back to bed.

"He asked me for his championship belts," Luis said. "He cherished those belts. Jack Miller, who had kept the belts on display in his bar when Emile was there, had offered to buy the five belts Emile had left but Emile wouldn't even consider it. Now he said he wanted to get rid of the 'death belt' – that's what he called the championship belt from that fight. In his mind getting rid of the belt was like getting rid of Benny Paret's ghost. So we sold the belt. He kept trying everything he could to free himself of Benny's ghost."

Emile Griffith had no way of knowing then that something was coming into his life that finally would free him.

CHAPTER TWENTY-FOUR

It was the early fall of 2002 when Gil Clancy called to tell me that he had just met with a film producer who was interested in making a documentary based on Emile Griffith's life and that he, Dan Klores, wanted to get together with me.

Our first meeting was at an Italian restaurant on Seventh Avenue, around the corner from Carnegie Hall. Dan, who heads a very prestigious public relations firm, impressed me with his enthusiasm and energy level. His idea was to focus on the Griffith-Paret fight and its effect on Emile's life.

I had already gathered together enough research material to short-cut his route and he spoke of working a book/movie package. The idea excited me, especially as Dan truly seemed to have Emile's best interests at heart.

When the project was explained to Emile, excitement was blended with apprehension at first. He knew what facets of his life would draw the most interest but Dan assured him it would be his story told his way. When Luis told him how much he would be paid, there was no longer any apprehension!

Dan Klores did not let grass grow under his feet. His associate producer, Jake Bandman, spent several days at my home office with a film crew, scanning my archival material and when we began on site filming, most of the present day interviews of Emile, Luis and Christine were shot in my home. Libby Geist, associate producer of Dan's Shoot The Moon production company, called me whenever a magazine or newspaper article was needed to substantiate a certain fact or to supply a photograph necessary for the documentary. Dan developed an "in house" media network but he did not sit in an office and delegate. He personally involved himself in ferreting out the difficult to find items or check the veracity of undocumented information. If there was an out-of-country or distant interview to be done, he would fly with his film crew to wherever they had to be and he handled all the interviews.

As smoothly as the project was going, what really brought it to another dimension began with an invitation I received from Hank Kaplan, regarded by the boxing world as its foremost historian and archivist. Hank, who lives in Miami, told me that he was in contact with Benny 'Kid' Paret's family and asked if I would like to meet Benny, Jr. He knew the answer before I gave it to him.

Fourteen hundred miles to the south the same feelings of excitement and apprehension that were felt by Emile Griffith in New York, were being experienced by a young man living in Miami.

Forty-one years after the event, Benny "Kid" Paret's widow, Lucia Paret, was still too emotionally fragile to discuss Benny's fight with Griffith, but Benny, Jr. wanted to learn as much about his father as possible.

We met in a fast food chicken restaurant in South Miami. Benny, Jr., at forty-three, looked fifteen years younger. Handsome and olive-complexioned, he was gracious and smiled easily. I brought along some magazine articles and photos of his father, which he pored over and studied hungrily. When I came to some very graphic shots of the final moments of the fight, I held them back, not wanting to upset Benny. He saw and reached out for them but I explained that I thought it would be better if he didn't see them. He said, "No, that's all right. I know everything that happened. I can handle it."

I placed a copy of Ring Magazine on the table with a photo of Benny 'Kid' Paret slumping to the canvas, eyes already closed. Next to it was a picture of the unconscious fighter on a stretcher. Benny, Jr. gave a quick look, then shuddered and shoved the magazine away. He couldn't handle it. At the end of our visit he said he would really like to meet "Mr. Griffith." Now I wasn't sure it was such a good idea.

Eight months later, November 8, 2003, Emile Griffith is walking north on the east side of Central Park near 79th Street. Dan Klores had brought Benny, Jr. and his mother, Lucia, to New York. Sadie, who had last seen Emile two years ago when he stayed with her and Christine in St. Thomas, felt it would be very good for Emile and Benny, Jr. to meet each other. "If Emile and Paret's son would meet it would be a healing process for Emile, not only for Emile, but for the son, and Emile wouldn't have to go to his grave regretting what happened."

As Emile neared 79th Street, a young man was approaching slowly from the north. Emile and Benny were told that they would be meeting each other but nothing was planned or rehearsed. It was strictly a spontaneous, impromptu meeting. A few yards south of 79th Street Benny Paret, Jr. and Emile Griffith stopped and faced each other.

It was as though there was a connecting rod from one's eyes to the others that locked them in place and kept them apart at the same time. Emile stared at the young man. His lips trembled and his arms began reaching out, almost spastically, like in an old one-reeler, frame by frame.

Benny took another step. "Yes," as though answering the unspoken question from Emile, "I am Benny Paret, the son, and I want you to know, I understand. I have no hard feelings."

Emile stepped forward quickly, wrapping his arms around Benny. Benny Paret leaned, grabbed hold of Emile and the two men stood embracing each other for a long moment, tears trickling down both their cheeks. *Dreams. They can appear at any time. The crowd in the Garden was standing and cheering on March 24th, 1962 as Emile Griffith and Benny 'Kid' Paret embraced in the center of the ring after a hard-fought battle.*

It took Emile Griffith forty-one years to be able to say "I'm sorry."

It was over.

CHAPTER TWENTY-FIVE

After The Show Was Over ...

Emile Griffith walked out of the Beekman Theater and turned quickly to look for Luis as he found himself walled in by the crush of people reaching for him and shouting his name. The premiere showing of RING OF FIRE had just ended and so had a major portion of his life. He sensed it. His memory and mental abilities had slipped to the point where he had to rely mainly on his feelings and habits. They were strong feelings and good habits. He smiled as he worked his way through the crowd of well-wishers but looked slightly confused as he whispered to Luis, "Well, I guess the whole world knows now."

Emile was right. Once again the whole world knew. Over the past twenty-five, thirty years, the controversial image of Emile Griffith had faded to near-obscurity and what remained was a great, legendary boxing champion who smiled for the cameras, signed autographs and was revered strictly for his past accomplishments in the ring.

Now the door was open, giving Emile the opportunity to free himself by facing down the demons of his past, demons that much of the contemporary world would first know to exist.

There didn't seem to be any show of regret or disappointment. Perhaps there was even a slight sign of relief. It was as though someone held up a mirror for all to see a reflection of Emile's life that he had never shared before and they applauded. They applauded for a prizefighter whose lifestyle seemed contrary and unacceptable to the machismo associated with that profession. They applauded a person who was subjected to covert ridicule and locker room jokes but rose above it by actions and deeds, earning respect, admiration and even adulation. And that person was he – Emile Griffith!

There was a time when you didn't have to guess what Emile was thinking. He was very good at expressing himself with style and flair. In recent years it had become a soul-search, looking into his eyes, interpreting a facial expression, or just guessing his body language. But there was no question as to what Emile's thoughts were now. There was a new sparkle to him, an exuberance and vitality that recaptured much of his old spirit. In his sixty-seventh year Emile Griffith saw the beginning of a new life, one where he no longer had to live in shadows and half truths. He was flushed by the sense of a new freedom. and when Luis told him that he was asked if Emile would consider working and speaking with gay support groups and young kids who were growing up under the same cloud that he had, his answer was an immediate and enthusiastic "yes." He could once again be a fighter, this time for a cause.

The very day after the RING OF FIRE premiere, in an interview with Bob Herbert of the New York Times, Emile Griffith stated that he was not gay but "after all these years, he wanted to tell the truth. He'd had relations, he said, with men and women. He no longer wanted to hide."

Actually, Emile Griffith never did hide. He always entered "his world" through the front door. That door was open to anyone. It's just that Emile perceived a larger world than most of us. His boundaries extended much further. And there were far fewer restrictions. Where others were able to like and appreciate, he was able to love. Where others felt sadness, he was able to cry. For those who expressed happiness with a smile or a laugh, how could they relate to the euphoria, the unrestrained joy of a singing, dancing and cavorting Emile Griffith?

Even after coming out and stating that he had both male and female partners, Emile still could not get himself to say that he was gay. Maybe it was a matter of definition. Perhaps in his mind, love was much more expansive than being restricted to "man" or "woman". A product of the 50's and 60's, discretion and secrecy became instinctive, especially for a professional athlete. A gay athlete would be an ex-athlete. The gay male carried the stereotype of the ridiculed, effeminate fop and Emile himself associated the word "gay" with an extremely effeminate male. That is probably why Emile would not call himself gay. It simply did not fit his personal definition or stereotype. Being called gay or asked about his sexuality did not seem to upset Emile. In fact, he showed great interest in any links or ties to his old haunts and friends who might resurface. Then it all changed.

It was September 12, 2004 when Emile and Luis received a call from an acquaintance telling them that he had come across an article on an internet website written by someone who claimed that he had been a close friend of Emile's, having known him from the historic Stonewall Tavern, the landmark bar in Greenwich Village where, in June 1969, the gay community rebelled against the police in a virtual 3-day war and Gay Power was born.

The drum-beating and hype for the upcoming release of RING OF FIRE had begun and Emile Griffith's name was once again in the news. It was important to separate the legitimate from the headline chasers.

Struggling with his memory and curiosity, Emile agreed to search out this person, Williamson J. Henderson. After a couple of missed calls and messages left, contact was made and they spoke first by phone. When Emile acknowledged remembering him, a meeting was set up for the following night in downtown Manhattan.

We met at a coffee shop on West 23rd Street. Henderson, president of the Stonewall Veterans Association, was a Peter Pan-like senior citizen who was whiter-than-white right up to the top of his floppy mop of scraggly hair. He greeted Emile in a way that you would expect from someone who had just met a long lost friend. First a handshake, then a friendly "Remember the good times" nudge. He looked at him approvingly. Emile looked at Henderson as he would a character from Disneyland, wide-eyed and not quite sure.

Of the good times that Henderson tried to have Emile recall, only one vivid recollection surfaced. Emile smiled as he remembered visiting Henderson's mother in Long Beach and then going out for ice cream. When the evening came to an end, Williamson J. Henderson, somewhat contrary to his website allusions, said that Emile never really hung out at Stonewall. "He didn't feel comfortable there. They were too gay for him. I never considered Emile to be gay. He just felt comfortable with some gay people."

I wasn't sure of Henderson's reason for saying that. It came across as an obvious and sudden change of tune. It could have been for the same reason that Emile wouldn't call himself gay. Could Henderson also link being gay with being effeminate, as enlightened as I presumed he was as president of a gay activist organization? Or perhaps he felt that he was beginning to lose Emile and was trying to placate him.

Emile pushed his unfinished bowl of cappelini aside and started getting up. Henderson looked at him, took a last bite of his cheeseburger and we left. We drove towards the Midtown Tunnel and stopped to drop off Williamson J. Henderson at Park Avenue and 36th Street. As he prepared to get out Henderson politely said goodbye, then winked at Emile, "You do remember the good times, don't you?" He opened the door and stepped into the street.

"I remember the ice cream by your mother's house." Emile closed the door.

***

Sadly, Emile's memory loss has made it unfair to subject him to interviews without a guardian by his side as he can easily be steered into making "newsworthy statements." There are many journalists who are sensitive and understanding of Emile's situation and they will make him feel comfortable and ease him into a relaxed posture. Under such conditions, his ability to respond to questions is maximized. Some interviewers have a confrontational approach, usually for audience appeal, that immediately intimidates Emile and his response is either to comply with words that are virtually put in his mouth or to get agitated and aggressive.

When asked about the RING OF FIRE documentary now, Emile often responds that he hasn't seen it. "What movie?"

Luis will remind him and jar his memory. But he remembers the essence of it and there is the sense that it has made a change in his life and has given him new purpose. However, much of Emile Griffith's thoughts, feelings and decision-making process are spawned in the minds of those he is dependent upon. Emile no longer originates ideas and plans but he will still be genuinely enthusiastic when an idea hits that certain chord and appeals to him. When Luis told him that he was asked if Emile would consider working and speaking with gay support groups and young kids who were growing up under the same cloud that he had, his answer was an immediate and enthusiastic "yes." He could once again be a fighter, this time for a cause.

Luis has a tough job. With love and devotion, he has accepted the role of Emile's decision-maker and caretaker; he handles all the calls requesting Emile's presence or offers of any kind. Business deals to autograph requests all come to Luis. He tries to make all the decisions, sometimes even those requiring professional help because he doesn't want to spend their money. He has learned it can be a penny-wise-pound-foolish approach.

As far as taking care of Emile, Luis watches over him like a mother hen. He measures out his various pills and medications, making sure that everything is taken on schedule. He lays out his clothes for him and makes certain all his daily needs are taken care of and calls him from work several times a day to check that he is alright.

Seven-and-a-half months after his meeting with Williamson J. Henderson, then-President of the Stonewall Veterans Association, and two weeks after the New York premiere of RING OF FIRE at the Beekman Theater a shocking announcement was made.

Emile Griffith was elected vice-president of the Stonewall Veterans Association.

Boxer elected VP of Stonewall Veterans Association
2005-05-01

Pictured is 6-time world boxing champion Emile Griffith, who holds one of boxings' unbreakable records. He has fought more title fight rounds (339) than any other world champion in history. Griffith was elected Vice President of the Stonewall Veterans Association (SVA) at the GLBT Community Center in Greenwich Village.
- Photo by Doug Meszler

I was ready to say "Congratulations!" I thought for a while and decided to say "Good luck!"

In April 2006 the Stonewall Veterans' Association distributed a flyer announcing that a meeting was scheduled for April 29, 2006 with the main attraction being **"GAY BOXING CHAMP EMILE A GRIFFITH."** It went on to state that the "special guest speaker is the legendary Middle-weight Boxing Champion Emile A. Griffith, Jr., who is also quietly Gay!"

When Emile saw the flyer he studied it for a long moment, then, with a questioning smile, asked, *"That's me, the Gay boxing champ?"* He seemed to dwell upon it for a while and less than five minutes later he was grousing, "Why are they calling me Gay?"

"Because you're the vice-president of the Stonewall Veterans Association," Luis answered him, "and you already said you were gay. You said it in your movie, you said it to the newspapers, and, anyhow, it was never a secret from a lot of your friends and people who know you."

"Okay, but why do they have to make such a big deal about it? Why do they have to advertise it and make me sound like a freak?"

It's like blocking a right cross! Here comes the punch and Emile Griffith is doing the thing that comes most naturally. He's protecting himself. As memory fades, so does Emile's self-assurance. That's when vulnerability sets in and reflex takes over. He reverts back to the days when incidents and experiences convinced him that discretion was the wisest path to take. Originally it was purposeful and intentional for Emile to compartmentalize his dual lives. It soon became instinctive. He wasn't protective just of himself, but of his circle of friends also.

Lobo transcended "friend" – by a lot. He and Emile were a popular man and man twosome on the Times Square gay circuit, so it was only natural to assume that Emile would be very proud to see Lobo on the cover of a magazine. Maybe he would have been if the magazine were Life or Saturday Evening Post – maybe even Good Housekeeping. But when he journeys over to Gleason's and his buddy Calvin, who is the caretaker at the gym, hands him a glossy magazine that is something close to the gay man's equivalent of Playboy, and grins, "Looks like Lobo is big time now. No butts about it!"

Hurricane Carter may have punched harder, but not by much. Emile did not go down but it seemed as though he was taking a standing eight-count as he stared at a rear view of his Lobo, looking pretty much the same as he must have the day he was born – just a lot bigger and this time he wasn't even covered by a blanket.

As soon as he recovered his ability to speak, Emile called Lobo and asked why he would pose with his backside looking like a Hollywood starlet's smile with no teeth.

Lobo's answer was short and to the point. "Money."

Hopefully, Lobo made enough to at least balance the ledger as Emile Griffith drove around town stopping at every newsstand and magazine store in the city, buying up every copy of Lobo's cover shot that he could find.

The strength and will to step forward after reliving his life with the Ring of Fire documentary brought a new vitality and spirit to Emile's existence.

In his more lucid moments Emile speaks quite candidly about his gay lifestyle. He has already stepped forward and proudly declared, "Hey, World, this is who I am and this is what I'm about."

That is when he talks about being involved so that perhaps he will make a difference in the lives of some young people. That is the Emile Griffith who waves and smiles at the crowd from a blue Cadillac at the Gay Pride parade. Unfortunately, the lucid moments are more and more fleeting moments.

It's not completely different from his days as a prizefighter when he would bound into the ring eager to win the big fight. But somewhere along the way his concentration and purpose would fade. He used to have a Gil Clancy in his corner that would snap him out of it and recharge his battery. This was a different arena and he was there by himself.

Climbing into that arena and fighting as a symbol for a gay and lesbian community, working for something he believes in with all his heart, is Emile's idea, but the plans and decisions are not always made by him. Often they are made for him. Thoughts, desire, intent and passion are there but he simply cannot carry them out. Recognizing the impact of an Emile Griffith riding high upon the chariot saluting the throngs, other people set the stage and push the buttons. Some of the planning, plotting and scheming may be self-serving but much of it is to achieve a common goal that they and Emile are jointly striving for. And when he, without warning, reverses himself, proclaiming with a petulant snap, "I am not gay!" shortly after acknowledging that he is, it is more than fading thoughts and memory. After learning to shield himself in a defensive shell from early manhood, it is not easy to break out of that shell after so many years of conditioning himself. It's sort of *"I am what I am but I ain't."*

Emile knows that he has skirted convention. He knows that he does not conform to a lifestyle whose boundaries and confines are too limiting and unnatural for him to abide by. Emile Griffith has long ago liberated himself. Actually, he did nothing – it was all quite natural.

An aware Emile Griffith <u>does</u> want to visit with Gay organizations. He wants to shake hands, greet people and talk to them, perhaps, even as one Liberated person to another. He wants to help bolster their egos, build their confidence and instill in them a sense of pride. It is a courageous move for a legendary boxing great. But courage was one thing that Emile Griffith never lacked.

EPILOGUE

Emile Griffith legally adopted Luis Rodrigo, now Luis Griffith, on February 10, 2004. They live in a small apartment in a high rise building in Hempstead, New York, only a ten minute drive from his "father", Gil Clancy. His other "father", Howie Albert, lives in Secaucus, New Jersey. The bond of loyalty and devotion that still exists among the three of them is not really unusual. It is what fairy tales are all about.

Although Emile is physically comfortable and functions well when among friends and familiar surroundings, since the mugging incident of 1992 increasing memory loss has had a noticeable impact on his life. He is almost totally dependent upon Luis, who does his best to see that Emile's life runs a smooth course. His decisions and choices are not always easy ones.

In a truly touching aftermath of the making of RING OF FIRE, Luis and Benny Paret, Jr. wound up working side by side for Dan Klores' public relations firm, Dan Klores Communications. It was Dan Klores' personal off-screen sequel to his award-winning documentary film.

Emile still visits some of New York's boxing gyms where his presence is always greeted with a near-reverence. Although he no longer trains any fighters, he freely gives pointers and advice and will occasionally work a fighter's corner as a second. Obviously, to Emile Griffith, boxing strategy is reflexive rather than analytical.

Emile Griffith was a charter inductee into the International Boxing Hall of Fame in 1990 and was inducted into the World Boxing Hall of Fame in 1984.

Much of his time is devoted to appearing at boxing events and signings where, in his milieu, he is once again the star performer captivating the crowd. He is also on the Board of Directors of Ring 8, Veteran Boxers Association of New York, an organization dedicated to "Fighters Helping Fighters." Although, as a board member, he has a voice and vote in all matter, his role is more that of an honorary, exalted elder statesman and over the years the Ring 8 membership has paid for Emile's medical costs and made certain that he lives in relative comfort.

Emile's visits with Mercedes and Christine in St. Thomas have become much less frequent as he can no longer travel by himself but Christine visits her father every year. Family has always been important to Emile and he maintains close ties with his brothers and sisters, sharing holidays and family events with them. Gloria, the oldest of the sisters, died suddenly of a heart attack in July, 2007. His cousin, Bernard Forbes, who worked Emile's corner through his whole career, passed away in his early fifties.

There was a time that Emile Griffith was sitting at the top of the world and he thought that time would never end. Perhaps it shouldn't have, but it did. Perhaps Emile should have learned from the experiences of others. He may have, but learning the lesson and passing the test are not the same. There is no bitterness. Regrets? Some. But they are outweighed by his thankfulness for what he does have, especially his love for his life partner and son, Luis. *"Maybe it is only natural for people to think that a World Champion is a person of great wealth. I don't know how many times I have been asked if I live in a mansion or a magnificent home. The truth is, I do live in a magnificent home – a cozy apartment in Long Island. What makes it magnificent is that I have my son Luis to share it with me and I am close enough to many of the people who are important in my life."*

Actually, Emile lives in a cramped studio apartment with Luis and another roommate, Jayson Phillps, who assists Luis in looking after Emile. With Luis and Jayson working, Emile spends much of his time alone in the small apartment watching television. His favorite program is Judge Judy. One of Emile's pet reproaches to friend or stranger is, "Watch out or I'll call Judge Judy on you!"

Fortunately, there are people who look after the former champion while Luis is at work. A peripherally-involved boxing personality, Keith Stechman, and boxing referee Wayne Kelly have befriended Emile over the years and they each take him to local boxing gyms about three or four times a week where his presence is always welcome and on these occasions Emile Griffith is back home. They also accompany Emile to various boxing functions when Luis is unable to go.

As far as great wealth, Emile knows that he may have done things that others consider unwise. But he always did what he considered was right. Throughout his boxing career his priorities were his mother, his large family and anything left was for Emile. He believes that if the clock was somehow turned back and he was given a second chance, it would be different – but he wouldn't swear to it.

"I was a real showboat – I loved fast cars. Jewelry and flashy clothes filled my drawers and closets and the doorman at every night club was my personal friend. And I was a devil! I tangoed, cha-cha'd and twisted my way around the world.

Sure I was told all about saving for rainy days. Howie and Gil had me put money into mutual funds and probably would have sewn my pockets shut if I had let them. Maybe I thought that the faucet would never turn off, but it didn't matter. I bought a nice large corner house in Hollis, New York and gave it to my mother. It was home for her and all my brothers and sisters and I did my best to make certain that they all received good educations. Everyone in my family has had a decent life. So, when I am asked whether I am wealthy, I cannot wish for greater wealth. Do I want more? I never said I wasn't selfish."

Emile sits back and thinks. He has memories. Some fade, some remain strong. He remembers as a little boy, lugging the water barrel up the hill from Magen's Bay. Perhaps that's what life is all about. It's a tough climb, but you feel good when you reach the top.

237

IN RETROSPECT

Being with Emile was always a pleasure. Simply stated, he's a good person, gentle, caring, a joy to be around.

But working with Emile was another story. It was a saddening, depressing experience, watching his memory and mind continue to fade to the point where his reasoning faculties were short-circuited. It was as though he was locked in a time warp that extended five minutes into the past before stalling. The simplest of questions extending beyond that five minute zone would be met first with a stare, a swallow, then a stock answer that could apply to anything from the weather to current events on the world stage. "Oh, you know how it is," gets dusted off and used on a regular basis. I was working with a far more coherent and expressive subject in our early discussions and interviews than our more recent talks. But through it all, Emile has remained steadfast and unshakable in expressing his concern for those he cared for and accepting whatever hand has been dealt to him as the hand of his own choice. Fate and Lady Luck get neither credit nor blame.

It was the early fall of 2001, one of our first sit-down interviews for the book. He was much more able to reason and make his own decisions then. We were relaxing on the rear deck of my house watching the boats glide by when Emile, who always felt comfortable and at ease there, turned to me and half-said, half-sighed, "You know what I want? Just a nice little house for me and my boy to call our own that some day I can leave for him." It wasn't what I expected to hear from someone who once lived in a flamboyant pad overlooking the Hudson, had closets stocked with the latest in the world of outrageous male fashions, jewelry to drown in, a Lincoln Continental that outshone all the bright lights of Broadway and had been the sole benefactor of a family so large, it fell into the category of clan or tribe. It was a lifetime away.

There was a time when it seemed that Emile Griffith had it all. It was a good time, a time easy to get used to. It was a time he didn't want as a memory. He wanted it as a reality. Emile Griffith tried to build reality on this simple hypothesis. Jake LaMotta had one championship belt and sat on the throne for less than two years as opposed to his own collection of six belts during a seven year on-again, off-again reign. Therefore, according to Emile Griffith's Theory of Relativity, it was a fairly reasonable assumption that his story was six times greater than Jake's based on belts or at least three-and-a-half times for time on the throne? "Look what happened with Jake. A book and a movie. Shouldn't my story be bigger than his?" This was not said begrudgingly, especially as he viewed Jake's success as a yardstick for his own.

I tried explaining to Emile that great achievements and accomplishments are only one ingredient in catching the public's eye; that it took a certain amount of notoriety to flavor and spice a story and give it that special appeal.

"It may be a strange world, Emile, but "bad" sells better than "good". You were a choir boy. LaMotta wasn't and it had nothing to do with his singing voice." I smiled at him. "Now, maybe if you would go out and mug a nun ..."

Actually, you can be a boxing historian and know everything there is to know about a great prize fighter named Emile Griffith. At the same time you would know nothing about Emile Griffith because Emile Griffith is not a prize fighter. At least, not by definition, not by stereotypic classification and not even by choice. Emile Griffith is not a fighter but he just so happens to be one of the greatest fighting machines of our time.

Jake LaMotta was a fighter who people understood. He was what a fighter was supposed to be – rough, tough, asked no quarter and gave none. Hitting people was what he was best at. He did his thing inside the ring and outside. They may not have liked him but they loved him. He was their kind of fighter. He wouldn't stop to play with little babies and he didn't help old ladies cross the street. Jake was tough and when he bounded into the ring in his leopardskin robe, you knew he was tough.

It's not that people didn't understand Emile. What they didn't understand was Emile Griffith in a pair of satin boxing trunks, fists covered with wine-colored leather gloves, body glistening with a fine sheen of perspiration, poised to strike. He was like a Picasso; a magnificent work of art, but to so many, a portrait that made no sense.

Three weeks before the Lennox Lewis-Mike Tyson fight, Emile and I were invited to visit Lennox at his training camp in the Poconos. We parked outside the main building of the Caesar's Brookdale Resort and were walking through the lobby towards the path that led to the athletic facility where the ring was located. It wasn't until I reached the rear door of the lobby that I realized "we" weren't walking. I was. Just as I was getting ready to have him paged, not believing that anyone could get lost between the front and rear doors of a relatively small hotel lobby, I spotted him.

He was kneeling next to a couch where a red-in-the-face, runny-nosed towhead about ten or eleven years old was in the process of very methodically driving his exasperated father crazy. I recalled hearing a few high-decibel nerve shattering shouts of "I wanna go to the Game Room!" or some reasonable facsimile as we first entered the lobby but these sounds I tune out. Emile doesn't.

I walked over prepared to gently pry Emile away and continue to the training camp. Instead, I stopped and stood frozen like a statue. Like everyone else in that part of the lobby, all I could do was look and listen in awe. Emile was simply being Emile, doing what comes so naturally to him. He spoke firmly but yet with such tenderness and compassion that I realized it wasn't a lecture as much as a plea. *"Do you know how lucky you are to have a father who cares for you enough to take you to a place like this? Do you have any idea how many children would give anything to trade places with you? My Goodness, sonny, you look so smart ... much too smart not to appreciate what your dad is doing for you. So, how about a big smile and a big hug and a Thank You for Dad and enjoy the day together."*

It wasn't an appropriate time, place or occasion for cheering or handclapping but you knew that inside, that's what everyone in that lobby wanted to do as the little guy gave this sheepish look, then broke into a smile and hugged his father.

That's Emile Griffith – yesterday, today and tomorrow. There's no thinking process or reasoning involved. To Emile, it's as natural as eating and sleeping. It's the way he is. He's the guest who helps clear the dinner table. He's the gentleman who bows and kisses the hands of all the women present. He'll skip a banquet or cocktail party, opting to entertain the kids outside.

Emile Griffith is victimized by living in a world of diversity that strives for uniformity. It is perhaps one of the great hypocrisies of our civilization. He has been placed under a media microscope, studied, scrutinized and categorized for living a life that is natural and comfortable to him. It hasn't always been easy and it hasn't been without pain, but it is not a matter of choice. He is living his life the only way that he is able to live it.

Conversely, there is only one way to judge Emile Griffith and that is by not judging him at all. Rather, accept him as a great champion and understand that Emile Griffith the prizefighter had three major flaws – or virtues. He was too gentle. He was too giving and he was too sensitive. At least for the world where he was king.

There are some things that Emile doesn't understand and others that he understands only too well. Long after our talk about "bad" versus "good" we were in the middle of nowhere speaking of nothing when Emile looked at me and declared, "I could never mug a nun."

I already knew that. Unfortunately, notoriety comes packaged in many shapes and forms.

Emile Griffith's Record

85-24-2
(23 knockouts)
1 No Contest

1958

Jun 2	Joe Parham	New York, NY	W 4
Jun 23	Bobby Gibson	New York, NY	W 4
Jul 21	Martin Leaks	New York, NY	W 4
Oct 6	Art Cunningham	New York, NY	W 6
Nov 17	Sergio Rios	New York, NY	KO 3
Dec 15	Larry Jones	New York, NY	KO 5

1959

Jan 26	Gaylord Barnes	New York, NY	KO 5
Feb 9	Willie Johnson	New York, NY	KO 5
Feb 23	Barry Allison	New York, NY	KO 5
Mar 23	Bobby Shell	New York, NY	W 10
Apr 27	Mel Barker	New York, NY	W 10
May 25	Willie Stevenson	New York, NY	W 10
Aug 7	Kid Fichique	New York, NY	W 10
Oct 26	Randy Sandy	New York, NY	L 10
Nov 23	Ray Lancaster	New York, NY	KO 7

1960

Jan 8	Roberto Pena	New York, NY	W 10
Feb 12	Gaspar Ortega	New York, NY	W 10
Mar 11	Denny Moyer	New York, NY	W 10
Apr 26	Denny Moyer	Portland, Or	L 10

Jun 3	Jorge Fernandez	New York, NY	W 10
Jul 25	Jorge Fernandez	New York, NY	W 10
Aug 25	Florentino Fernandez	New York, NY	W 10
Oct 22	Willie Toweel	New York, NY	KO 8
Dec 17	Luis Rodriguez	New York, NY	W 10

1961

Apr 1	Benny "Kid" Paret	Miami Beach, Fl	KO 13

-Welterweight Championship of the World

Jun 3	Gaspar Ortega	Los Angeles, Ca	KO 12

-Welterweight Championship of the World

Jul 29	Yama Bahama	New York, NY	W 10
Sep 30	Benny "Kid" Paret	New York, NY	L 15

-Welterweight Championship of the World

Nov 4	Stanford Bulla	Hamilton, NY	KO 4
Dec 23	Isaac Logart	New York, NY	W 10

1962

Feb 3	Johnny Torres	St. Thomas, VI	W 10
Mar 24	Benny "Kid" Paret	New York, NY	KO 12

-Welterweight Championship of the World

Jul 13	Ralph Dupas	Las Vegas, Nv	W 15

-Welterweight Championship of the World

Aug 18	Denny Moyer	Tacoma, Wa	W 10
Oct 6	Don Fullmer	New York, NY	W 10
Oct 17	Teddy Wright	Vienna, Austria	W 15

-Griffith claimed the newly created Junior Middleweight
Championship following his win over Wright; He defended once 2/03/63),
then abandoned his claim

Dec 8	Jorge Fernandez	Las Vegas, Nv	KO 9

-Welterweight Championship of the World

1963

Feb 3	Christian Christensen	Copenhagen, Denmark	KO 9

-Junior Middleweight Championship of the World

Mar 21	Luis Rodriguez	Los Angeles, Ca	L 15

-Welterweight Championship of the World

Jun 8	Luis Rodriguez	New York, NY	W 15

-Welterweight Championship of the World

Aug 10	Holly Mims	Sarasota Springs, NY	W 10
Oct 5	Jose Gonzalez	San Juan, PR	W 10
Dec 20	Rubin "Hurricane" Carter	Pittsburgh, Pa	LK 1

1964

Feb 10	Ralph Dupas	Sydney, NSW, Australia	KO 3
Mar 11	Juan Duran	Rome, Italy	NC 7
Apr 14	Stan Harrington	Honolulu, Oahu, Hi	KO 4
Jun 12	Luis Rodriguez	Las Vegas, Nv	W 15

-Welterweight Championship of the World

Sep 22	Brian Curvis	London, England	W 15

-Welterweight Championship of the World

Dec 1	Dave Charnley	London, England	KO 9

1965

Jan 21	Manuel Gonzalez	Houston, Tx	L 10
Mar 30	Jose Stable	New York, NY	W 15

-Welterweight Championship of the World

Jun 14	Eddie Pace	Honolulu, Oahu, Hi	W 10
Aug 20	Don Fullmer	Salt Lake City, Ut	L 10
Sep 14	Gabe Terronez	Fresno, Ca	KO 4
Oct 4	Harry Scott	London, England	KO 7
Dec 10	Manuel Gonzalez	New York, NY	W 15

-Welterweight Championship of the World

1966

Feb 3	Johnny Brooks	Las Vegas, Nv	W 10
Apr 25	Dick Tiger	New York, NY	W 10

-Middleweight Championship of the World; Under New York Rules, Griffith automatically vacated the Welterweight Championship

Jul 13	Joey Archer	New York, NY	W 15

-Middleweight Championship of the World

Aug 1 -Griffith lost a lawsuit to retain the Welterweight Championship of the World

1967

Jan 23	Joey Archer	New York, NY	W 15

-Middleweight Championship of the World

Apr 17	Giovanni "Nino" Benvenuti	New York, NY	L 15

-Middleweight Championship of the World

Sep 29	Giovanni "Nino" Benvenuti	Flushing, NY	W 15

-Middleweight Championship of the World

Dec 15	Remo Golfarini	Rome, Italy	KO 6

1968

Mar 4	Giovanni "Nino" Benvenuti	New York, NY	L 15

-Middleweight Championship of the World

Jun 11	Andy Heilman	Oakland, Ca	W 12
Aug 6	"Gypsy" Joe Harris	Philadelphia, Pa	W 12
Oct 29	Stanley "Kitten"	Hayward Philadelphia, Pa	L 10

1969

Feb 3	Andy Heilman	New York, NY	W 10
May 12	Stanley "Kitten" Hayward	New York, NY	W 12
Jul 11	Dick DiVeronica	Syracuse, NY	KO 7
Aug 15	Art Hernandez	Sioux Falls, SD	W 10
Oct 18	Jose Napoles	Inglewood, Ca	L 15

-Welterweight Championship of the World

1970

Jan 28	Doyle Baird	Cleveland, Oh	W 10
Mar 11	Carlos Marks	New York, NY	W 12
Jun 4	Tom Bogs	Copenhagen, Denmark	W 10
Jul 15	Dick Tiger	New York, NY	W 10
Oct 17	Danny Perez	St. Thomas, VI	W 10
Nov 10	Nate Collins	San Francisco, Ca	W 10

1971

Mar 23	Rafael Gutierrez	San Francisco, Ca	W 10
Apr 10	Juan Ramos	St. Thomas, VI	KO 2
May 3	Ernie Lopez	Las Vegas, Nv	W 10
Jul 26	Nessim Cohen	New York, NY	W 10
Sep 25	Carlos Monzon	Buenos Aires, Argentina	LK 14

-Middleweight Championship of the World

Dec 10	Danny McAloon	New York, NY	W 10

1972

Jan 31	Armando Muniz	Anaheim, Ca	W 10
Feb 21	Jacques Kechichian	Paris, France	W 10
Mar 30	Ernie Lopez	Los Angeles, Ca	W 10
Sep 16	Joe DeNucci	Boston, Ma	W 10
Oct 11	Joe DeNucci	Boston, Ma	W 12
Dec 18	Jean-Claude Bouttier	Paris, France	LF 7

1973

Mar 12	Max Cohen	Paris, France	D 10
Jun 2	Carlos Monzon	Monte Carlo, Monaco	L 15

-Middleweight Championship of the World

Nov 2	Manny Gonzalez	Tampa, Fl	W 10
Nov 19	Tony Mundine	Paris, France	L 10

1974

Feb 5	Tony Licata	Boston, Ma	L 12

-NABF Middleweight Championship

May 25	Renato Garcia	Monte Carlo, Monaco	W 10
Oct 9	Bennie Briscoe	Philadelphia, Pa	W 10
Nov 22	Vito Antuofermo	New York, NY	L 10
Dec 10	Donato Paduano	Montreal, Que, Can	W 10

1975

May 31	Jose Duran	Cali, Columbia	L 10
Jul 23	Leo Saenz	Landover, Md	W 10

| Aug 9 | Elijah Makhatini | Johannesburg, Trans, SAfr | L 10 |
| Nov 7 | Jose Chirino | Albany, NY | W 10 |

1976

Feb 9	Loucif Hamani	Paris, France	L 10
Jun 26	Bennie Briscoe	Monte Carlo, Monaco	D 10
Sep 18	Eckhard Dagge	Berlin, Germany	L 15
	-WBC Junior Middleweight Championship of the World		
Oct 24	Dino Del Cid	Cartegena, Columbia	KO 4
Dec 4	Frank Reiche	Hamburg, Germany	KO 10

1977

Feb 2	Christy Elliott	New York, NY	W 10
Apr 15	Joel Bonnetaz	Periqueux, France	L 10
Jul 19	Mayfield Pennington	Louisville, Ky	L 10
Jul 30	Alan Minter	Monte Carlo, Monaco	L 10

A Tribute from Nino Benvenuti

Dear Emile,

It is my great pleasure to learn that there will be a book about your life.

It is easy to speak of you as a great champion and even easier from the human angle. I have had the great fortune to have you as an opponent of great valor and of a gallantry that one cannot often find in a sport. There is not a single day of my life that someone does not approach me to speak to me of you. Naturally, they recall our first match of April 17, 1967.

It was three in the morning in Italy and the RAI made a connection by radio with the MSG; that news venture broke the record for the number of listeners. Almost 20 million people remained standing near their radios. Among these were many young boys, who now are men who remember that night as an indelible memory.

There is often an emotional moment when these men remember their fathers who kept them awake to listen to the news chronicle that no longer exists!

They speak of me and of you in the same way. I want to confide a memory which will always be unforgettable for me. It is about the second match at Shea Stadium. That was the hardest match of my entire career. There was a moment, in my corner, when they wanted me to quit. I had a broken rib, a hand I couldn't use and blood in my mouth that was almost suffocating me. I was protecting my body because I was in so much pain that I had to take the blows to my face.

I had to squeeze my teeth. My aim was to stay on my feet with the end of the 15th round, which for me construed a victory. It's for this reason that I remember our second fight as the most important of my career. I was able to get in that ring those points of reference that have served in my life to help me to overcome such times which were equally difficult ... almost like that 15th round.

It's been beautiful having known you. You are an extraordinary person, so full of feeling, of honor. After the ring, we had so many occasions to get to know each other better. There were the times you came to Italy and the most wonderful memory was when you became the Godfather at my son Giuliano's confirmation.

I think of you with so much affection!

Unfortunately, the distance that separates us and the busyness of our lives don't permit us to have a closer connection. On March 4th, the anniversary of our third match, I would have loved to have seen you again. In Brescia, they had organized a celebration to commemorate that great battle; I would have embraced you with such pleasure. I hope that your ailment is not serious and that it doesn't create problems for you. I wish you every happiness in all you do.

I am waiting with great anticipation to read the book, where certainly there will be some small remembrance of our friendship.

Dear Emile, receive a strong embrace from your fraternal friend and the joy of keeping me in your thoughts as you are in mine.

About the Author

Author of the highly acclaimed biography/social history **BUMMY DAVIS VS MURDER, INC** and the comedic novel **THE TOMATO CAN, RON ROSS** has also contributed numerous boxing articles to various magazines, newspapers and internet websites. He was also a consultant and appeared in the feature length documentary **THE RING OF FIRE; THE STORY OF EMILE GRIFFITH.** A native New Yorker, Ron has been involved in almost every phase of the boxing world. He and his wife Susan divide their time between New York and Florida.

- George Kalinsky, official photographer for Madison Square Garden, author of Garden of Dreams: Madison Square Garden 125 Years, The New York Mets: A Photographic History, The New York Knicks: The Official 50th Anniversary Celebration

Printed in the United States
117908LV00001B/225/P

9 780979 994722